COO

ALSO BY JOHN LEO

HOW THE RUSSIANS
INVENTED BASEBALL

Two Steps

Ahead

of the

Thought

Police

John Leo

WITH A FOREWORD BY PETER JENNINGS

Simon & Schuster

NEW YORK LONDON TORONTO SYDNEY TOKYO SINGAPORE

SIMON & SCHUSTER
Rockefeller Center
1230 Avenue of the Americas
New York, New York 10020

SIMON & SCHUSTER and colophon
are registered trademarks
of Simon & Schuster Inc.

BOOK DESIGNED BY
BARBARA M. BACHMAN

MANUFACTURED IN THE UNITED STATES OF AMERICA

3 5 7 9 10 8 6 4

Library of Congress Cataloging in Publication Data
Leo, John.
Two steps ahead of the thought police / John Leo.
p.   cm.
1. Popular culture—United States.   2. United States—Social
conditions—1980–   3. United States—Politics and government—1993–
I. Title.
E169.04.L465   1994
973.928—dc20   94-8670
CIP

ISBN: 0-671-88698-3

CREDITS

The following essays originally appeared in *U.S. News and World Report* and appear by permission of *U.S. News and World Report*: Whitey to Whitey: Drop Dead; "Sir, You're a Murderer!"; Caffeine Made Me Do It; The White Maleness of *Jeopardy!*; The Man Who Occupied Teddy's Brain; Give Ozzie and Harriet a Break; The Subcommittee on Disabled Speech; Revenge of the Language-Stretchers; No-Fault Syntax; The F-Word Flows Like Ketchup; Manly Deeds, Sexist Words; Reporting Through Prisms; Our "Let's Pretend" Social Policy; Drowning in Rights; The Politics of Hate; An End to Welfare; Fire Hydrants and School Blockades; Why Graffiti Matters; The Itch to Censor; Throw Away the Key; A "Victim" Census for America; The Gingrich Who Stole Christmas; Bill

(cont. on p. 320)

FOR KRISTIN, KAREN,
AND ALEX

ACKNOWLEDGMENTS

Thanks to Mort Zuckerman, Roger Rosenblatt, Beverly Larson, Amanda Urban, Mike Ruby, Mimi McLoughlin, Chris Ma, Wray Herbert, John McMeel, and Jackie Leo.

CONTENTS

4 . "IF I COULD BE LIKE NEWT"
SOME OF OUR BEST FRIENDS ARE POLS

5 . "A CLOAK OF SILENCE AND DENIAL"
RACE, ETHNICITY, AND IMMIGRATION

6. "Protecting a Roomful of Fruit from Venereal Disease" Our Wayward Schools

7. "If It Feels Bad, Attack It" The Tyranny of the Hurt-Feelings Movement

8. "Just Another Marlboro Man from Outer Space" Our Zany Popular Culture

9 . "WHO KILLED FEMINISM?"
SEX, HARASSMENT, RAPE, AND IDEOLOGY

10 . "THIS ORGY OF NON-KILLING"
ABORTION, ETHICS AND LAW

11 . "IF YOU FEEL COMFORTABLE, YOU'RE PROBABLY OPPRESSING SOMEONE" DISPATCHES FROM THE CULTURAL WAR ZONE

FOREWORD BY PETER JENNINGS

DECEMBER 20, 1993

I first heard John Leo holding forth across a dinner table some years ago. I don't remember what the subject was but the temperature at the table was rising and Leo was thoroughly enjoying the sound of contentious minds rubbing vigorously against one another. After all, he had started it.

It is a rare occasion when what John has to say doesn't get his readers into high gear pretty quickly.

Often he get to fractious issues while other commentators are still wrestling over last week's news. He has something provocative to say about most everything that divides us and he never leaves us confused about what he thinks.

Whether he is dissecting political correctness, which he did long before most other people, or citing how the "I am a victim" tendency has run amok in the land, whether he's writing about family values (he really has them) or taking on courts he believes are legislating social behavior, John's page in *U.S. News* is one of the most invigorating anywhere. He even has a devoted following among those of us who think he's sometimes off base. And thank goodness for small favors: he has a sense of humor.

The highest compliment one journalist pays another is the admission that he or she has "borrowed an idea for further development." I have "borrowed" from John, more than once.

PART ONE

"ASK THE DUNDERHEADS"

An Introduction to Nineties Culture

WHITNEY TO WHITEY: DROP DEAD

When you pay your six dollars to see the big biennial art show at New York's Whitney Museum of American Art, the fellow at the cash register gives you a little attendance pin to wear. Mine said: "I can't imagine ever wanting to be white." In a flash, you know you have stumbled into yet another politically correct art show meant to frighten the white folks (and, of course, the male folks and the straight folks).

Agitprop art has been on the rise for several years. One museum after another has caved in to pressure and staged PC exhibitions that feature occasional dollops of actual art and great helpings of trendy propaganda about victimization, imperialism, patriarchy and the dreadful stigma of white skin. Now it's the Whitney's turn. "Whiteness is a signifier of power," the catalogue explains, and wearing the button lets whites "absolve themselves of some of the privileges of cultural imperialism."

Since wearing these buttons is supposed to be mandatory, the catalogue chortles a bit about how visitors "have little choice" about pinning on a slogan that's self-loathing when worn by whites, racist when worn by nonwhites. More racial togetherness, PC style.

The button gimmick is a clear signal that very low expectations for this show are the most reasonable ones to have. One exhibit consisted of jars full of pieces from jigsaw puzzles, each with the face of a nonwhite person pasted outside. Perhaps this was meant to show that the dominant culture fractures the lives of minorities.

Another exhibit featured about two hundred videotape movie boxes, each with a message in English or Spanish about how unfair Hollywood is to Latinos. One box, for the sci-fi movie *The Nest*, had this label: "Have you ever noticed that the villain is always a Puerto Rican?" (Actually, in *The Nest* the villains are all mutant cockroaches.)

By current Whitney standards, almost any angry sentiment seems to qualify as art, even a one-paragraph news clipping pinned to the wall behind plexiglass. Giant letters running across one room said: "In the rich man's house the only place to spit is in his face." A large section devoted to women's rage has a piece of plastic vomit on the floor, just like the ones sold in novelty stores, but much larger. A work by Sue Williams screams, "The art world can suck my proverbial———." (The catalogue tells us that this "wrenches painting away from its white male domain.")

One exhibit shows three grotesque casts of a larynx and tongue, presumably the remains of murdered women, accompanied by the sounds of women's laughs and cries. The larynx and tongue are made out of lipstick to represent "the silencing of women through the use of a specifically gendered material—lipstick."

Donald Moffet's "Oh, Baby: Sheet with a f———hole," consisting of a sheet with a hole in it, was missing when I attended. The guard said it had been damaged and removed for repair. Someone had touched the nearby "Chocolate Gnaw," a giant work in brown lard by Janine Antoni ("Antoni critiques a patriarchal community where eating is transgressive," said the catalogue), and then wiped his or her hands on Moffet's sheet, perhaps not realizing it was a work of art.

At most exhibitions, artists do not post signs explaining their work, but at PC shows they always do. The itch to harangue is just too strong. A curtain made up of floor-to-ceiling branding irons carries this helpful explanation: "We started to brand to think about how we'd been branded as people . . . as gendered subjects, as sexual subjects in culture." I get it.

When artists don't lecture us, the guides do. Two large paintings—of Hansel and Gretel and of Santa Claus with small children—are surrounded with smaller ominous pictures of danger and abuse. A guide said chirpily: "These story boards show that underneath 'normal' family life, a lot of sinister things are going on, a lot of child abuse and evil."

Speaking of those darned nuclear families, what should appear right near Hansel, Gretel and Santa? Nude and bland manikins of a hand-holding family—father, mother, young boy and baby girl, all exactly the same height—about four feet tall. These are eerie pieces, with some esthetic power. Was this a putdown of a dumb-looking white family? The guide said no. But she added brightly that this is one room in the show where male heterosexual Caucasians can pause and see representations of themselves on display. (Gee, thanks.)

In two numbing hours at this organized shambles, I learned that the world is neatly divided into good and bad. Good: women, nonwhites, homosexuals, transvestites, gang members, glory holes, people with AIDS, gays in the military. Bad: America, straight white males, family, religion, hierarchies, lipstick, liposuction, fatism and penises not attached to gay men.

It's hard to imagine the Whitney, once a great museum, coming back from a self-induced disaster of this magnitude. This is one more grim, whining, monocultural victim show, with all voices singing the same old song: "Hey, Hey, Ho, Ho, Western Culture's Gotta Go" (lyrics by Stanford University and Jesse Jackson). In a phrase used at all these shows, it's about replacing the center (mainstream America and its values) with the margin (the race-and-gender ideologues and their allies).

The Whitney catalogue makes this clear: "Marginality, in effect, becomes the norm while the center is increasingly undefinable and perhaps irrelevant." In other words, it's about a cultural war to destabilize and break the mainstream. The only question is why institutions of the center should join this crusade to do themselves in. Ask the dunderheads at the Whitney.

WATCHING ALL THE GIRLS GO BY

What happens if a newspaper publishes an article about blue-collar workers who like to sit by the sidewalk at lunchtime and watch the women go by?

Well, it depends. If the article comes out the conventional way, convicting the watchers of grave sexual harassment, no feathers will be ruffled. But if the article fails to point out that the men are all hopeless swine, an uproar will follow.

That happened at *The Washington Post*, where the style section made the horrendous mistake of doing this story backward—listening to the watchers and interviewing them, instead of just ringing up the National Organization for Women for a comment on how bad they are. As Mary Hadar, editor of the *Post* style section, said, the idea was to report "What could they be thinking?"

Very mild things, as it turned out, at least on Vermont Avenue and H Street in Washington, D.C., the day that *Post* reporter Phil McCombs showed up. As he tells it, the workers are a multiracial and mostly polite group of males who enjoy watching the passing parade. He mentioned some unspecified "graphic" comments the men made in private. One very crude and two mildly crude private comments are quoted. But in general, the men seem affable and almost staid.

The men are shown to be equal-opportunity watchers, admiring females regardless of age or race. There are no humiliating catcalls, smacking sounds or obscene suggestions. When they speak to the women, they seem to just say hello. One man says he thinks a "shallow whistle" is okay, if it's done with respect.

The men are protective of the woman who drives the concession truck every day. They keep a lookout for a stranger who has been following her around for two years. The married men talked a lot about their spouses. The unmarried ones talked about the search for a dream wife.

McCombs said he saw no women crossing the street to avoid the workers. The women's reactions ranged from ignoring the men to a wink, a smile or a hello.

So what was the uproar about? NOW, Nine-to-Five and the D.C. chapter of Men Against Rape were outraged and demonstrated on Vermont Avenue. They carried fliers charging that the *Post* piece "succeeded in romanticizing street harassment, and scapegoating working-class men and male construction workers." One distraught demonstrator said she felt very betrayed by the *Post*.

The demonstrators, and a few people in the *Post* newsroom, talked about these men as if they were working to make the world safe for the rapists of tomorrow. Rus Funk, a member of D.C. Men Against Rape, told me that "these attitudes objectifying women are the same attitudes that support rape."

This is a familiar rhetorical device in the highly ideological field of sexual harassment: associating small offenses or nonoffenses with serious harassment or rape. The *Post*'s ombudsman, Joann Byrd, went along with this kind of rhetoric. She quoted an unidentified *Post* editor as saying, "Can you imagine if the *Post* ran a similar piece on domestic violence" (thus putting woman-watching and woman-bashing in the same bracket).

In her column on the case, Byrd wrote somberly that McCombs's article "did not reflect contemporary sensibilities about sexual harassment." (Translation: the article did not reflect the current newsroom sensibility that harassment is everywhere, even in the normal male tendency to admire the appearance of passing females.) She writes as if the comments of construction workers are just too toxic to print in a raw state, unaccompanied by the correct newsroom perspective.

"If the people involved in Wednesday's story had been sensitive," she wrote, "substantive reporting would have appeared alongside the men's voices." But the whole idea of the piece, after a zillion newspaper articles on what pigs these guys are, was to finally let them speak in their own voices without all that "substantive reporting" pointing out the amazing horror of sidewalk watching.

There's a class problem too. The upper-middle-class folks at the *Post* deal with the blue-collar men as if they were a strange, mysterious tribe. ("What could they be thinking?") Sounding like Margaret Mead trying to figure out the Samoans, Joann Byrd thinks, "We need to know why some men still line up and visually or verbally rate the bodies of women walking past."

Maybe I can help here. The men line up because very few dining tables are put out on city sidewalks for lunchtime use. So construction workers tend to sit along curbs, steps or walls, thus forming what we anthropologists call a line.

Since they usually don't bring books or stock portfolios with them, they tend to look around while dining. And they tend to check women out, as anthropologist Helen Fisher said on Connie Chung's show, because they have been doing this for thousands of years or so, biology being what it is.

The *Post* ran a follow-up story on the demonstration on Vermont Street. The only person who seemed to make any sense was a laborer, who says he sits on the wall to eat his lunch and looks at everyone. "I have never heard anyone here make any rude comments to women," he told the *Post*. "I might say Hi or How ya doin', but I say that to men who pass too." He seemed baffled that this behavior would get him involved with anyone's political agenda. But what does he know about newsrooms?

"SIR, YOU'RE A MURDERER!"

Nobody rioted at the sixth international AIDS conference in San Franciso. This was a big blow to AIDS activist Larry Kramer, who had called for "massive disruption" and "a f——ing riot," so I phoned him to see how he was coping with the bad news.

"I knew nothing would happen; that's why I stayed home," said Kramer, who is the founder of Act-Up, the anti-AIDS group. With Kramer absent, Act-Up's biggest cheese in San Francisco, Peter Staley, was able to present himself as a moderate. Staley actually got himself invited to address the conference, even though Act-Up was carrying on as usual, tying up traffic here and there, baiting police and drowning out a harmless little talk by the secretary of health and human services.

"Ah, we play a little good cop and bad cop around here," said Kramer, the perennial bad cop. Kramer didn't seem to mind that I had referred to his group as a bunch of gangsters in this space a few months back. Act-Up began as Greenwich Village's answer to the Red Guards. It is cloning itself in other unsuspecting cities, so now you don't have to move to Manhattan or Washington to have your rights trampled and your church invaded. You can get it done right at home in places like Minneapolis and Oklahoma City.

Since Kramer is stressing what a sane and reasonable group Act-Up is, I remind him of what his people did to Stephen Joseph, the former New York City health commissioner. Joseph adjusted estimates of AIDS cases down a bit. So Act-Up tossed paint on his residence, occupied his office, harassed his family with phone calls, shouted down his public speeches and hounded him for weeks everywhere he went, even in restaurants. Another victim of Act-Up told me, "If you get on their wrong side, they're hellbent on silencing you. They're a youth cult, a bunch of spoiled, angry children with no understanding of politics or the mechanisms of American democracy."

But this is not Larry Kramer's view. "What do you want me to say? Joseph was a very hated man who cut off all dialogue with our community. We did it as a last resort." Kramer said that many of the people Act-Up used to attack are now allies. "Take Ellen Cooper of the FDA," he says. "We were calling her a murderer only last year. This year she gave us a lot of credit." Yes, but some of these murderers-turned-allies seem to be suffering from the Stockholm Syndrome. Nothing concentrates the mind of an AIDS researcher quite so strongly as the vision of a career threatened, an office occupied or a family harassed for weeks or months. Even Stephen Joseph has been saying nice things about his tormentors, like a newly released stewardess describing the many endearing qualities of her hijackers.

"Larry, have you guys invaded any churches lately?" I asked politely. This is a veiled reference to Act-Up's expedition into St. Patrick's Cathedral. Gays stormed the church, tossing condoms and screaming to interrupt Sunday mass. At least one of the maddened invaders stomped on a consecrated Communion wafer. At the time, I wondered what the gay reaction would be if some burly guys from the Knights of Columbus busted into an Act-Up meeting, slinging rosaries into people's faces and stomping on whatever the membership holds sacred, maybe an Avedon portrait of Larry Kramer.

"That was controversial in Act-Up," Kramer acknowledged. "Things got out of hand at the cathedral, but in retrospect, you guys gave us the power by complaining so much. You turned us into an army of menacing guerrillas."

Against all odds, Kramer and I are now getting along rather well. I suggested mildly that the newly moderate Act-Up might want to reconsider its long-term commitment to phone harassment. After my original column on Act-Up, I got hissing late-night calls for nine days. Most of them began with the word "sir" and ended with the phrase "you murderer," so I could tell in a flash it was Act-Up. "You guys can dish it out, you should take it too, or just disconnect the phone," Kramer said. This is basically my own view, though I would prefer to be hissed at during daylight hours. My wife hates it when I chat with my sputtering detractors at 3 a.m.

"John," Kramer said, "you could be the first conservative, right-wing columnist to be a hero and tell what's really going on. The National Institutes of Health wasted a billion and a half of the taxpayers' dollars on three stupid AIDS clinical trials, and while they were doing it, another seventeen thousand people died. NIH is a bureacratic nightmare, a swamp of incompetence." As a result of the sweetness and light in San Francisco, Act-Up will have more access to NIH committee meetings.

"Larry, does this mean you won't be screaming for violence anymore?" "No, there should have been violence in San Francisco," he said. A minute later he talked fondly about the Irgun, the anti-British terrorist group that helped found Israel and blew up a lot of innocent people along the way.

"I don't think the world needs a gay Irgun, Larry," I suggested mildly. "If you stopped invading churches and terrorizing doctors' families, you might find you have more allies than you think." "It's easy for you safe, straight guys to say that," he replied. "Just picture what it's like if just about every one of your friends is dead of AIDS." Pause. "There's a positive piece on me coming out in next week's *People*," he said. "It will balance out your column."

I tell him the column won't be that bad. For putting up with a hostile interviewer, he'll get his say. "I just want to be loved," he said. Good grief. What a comment from a philosopher of rioting who dreams of a gay terrorist movement. No cynicism here about tough-guy activists showing their human side. I just wished it expressed itself in more concern for other people's rights.

CAFFEINE MADE ME DO IT

In the dark ages, about twenty years ago, obscene phone callers were creeps who got their jollies by anonymously harassing women with heavy-breathing references to their private parts. Now, like Richard Berendzen, who resigned as president of American University over his unusual phone habits, they get to go on *Nightline* to explain that they are blameless victims of an uncontrollable impulse disorder. Berendzen even hauled along a docile psychiatrist who argued plaintively that Berendzen's little habit was a shadow attempt to repair a childhood problem. Not a dry eye in the house.

These uncontrollable forces have been piling up at a record rate. As columnist Charles Krauthammer points out, we have Pete Rose's disorder (pathological gambling, 312.31 in the *Diagnostic and Statistical Manual of American Psychiatry*), Marion Barry's disease (alcoholism, 303.90) and Berendzen's impulse (telephone scatologia, 302.90).

The dread disease of caffeinism (305.90, supine dependence on cola or coffee) has already been cited in a criminal case or two. We have inhalant abuse (305.90, dependency on aromatic hydrocarbons), and solemn listings for difficulties of ordinary life (arithmetic and reading problems). A few years ago, the psychiatrists came within an inch of inventing a disease called paraphilic rapism, which would have been used by defense attorneys for every rapist in captivity.

When Sol Wachtler, the chief judge of New York state's highest court, was arrested for extortion and threatening to kidnap the fourteen-year-old daughter of his ex-lover, many New Yorkers were under the impression that some crimes may have been committed.

Not so, according to John Money, a prominent sexologist and medical psychologist. In an op-ed piece in *New York Newsday,* Money wrote that Wachtler "was manifesting advanced symptoms of . . . Clerambault-Kandinsky Syndrome (CKS) . . . a devastating illness."

CKS is a disease that can be diagnosed from three hundred miles away (Money is professor emeritus at the Johns Hopkins University and Hospital in Baltimore). In fact, it is so easy to spot that the diagnoser need not even telephone the diagnosee or know much about him. All the diagnoser has to know is that the accused is blameless. In plain English, Money suggests that Wachtler was irresistibly lovesick, that is, suffering helplessly under "the spell" of erotomania.

Money is very hard on the FBI for failing to recognize that they had a spellbound CKS sufferer on their hands and not some kind of criminal. "The law-and-order treatment of people with CKS," Money wrote sternly, "is the equivalent of making it a crime to have epileptic spells."

He is no novice at converting dreadful behavior into dreadful disease. When Richard Berendzen was arrested for his obscene phone calls, Money thought that such cases were similar to epilepsy too. He is becoming a familiar traveler on a path that has become a highway: presenting an enlightened medical model of quirky and criminal behavior.

In retrospect, the 1980s seem to have ushered in a golden age of exoneration. When the decade began, the sociological excuse (society-made-me-do-it) was clearly petering out. But a half dozen disciplines combined to fill the alibi gap quite nicely. Law, psychiatry, neurology, nutrition, biology and pop psychology all helped explain why almost nobody can really be held accountable for harmful behavior anymore. We are becoming a nation of victims, and we are running out of victimizers.

Law plus nutrition gave us many variations of the Twinkie defense (sugar-made-him-kill). Law plus dubious psychiatry gives us the promising anabolic steroid defense. (A bodybuilder broke into six Maryland homes, set fire to three of them and stole cash and jewelry. A judge ruled him guilty but not criminally responsible because his frenzied use of anabolic steroids for weightlifting left him "suffering from organic personality syndrome." No jail time.)

Law plus the sociological excuse in disguise offers us the "homosexual panic" defense. (A man killed a homosexual who made a pass at him in San Francisco, then tried to argue in court that this violence was an involuntary triggering of sexual attitudes induced in him by his sheltered, small-town Texas upbringing. The judge wasn't having any of this, but some lawyers think that "panic" defenses will soon become common.)

Pop psychology joined the party by conjuring up new addictions, which have been used successfully to allay guilt and get offenders off the hook. In Los Angeles, a hacker named Kevin Mitnick copped a plea after being accused of breaking into a corporate computer system and stealing an expensive security program. Did the judge see Mitnick as one more computer nerd with no conscience? No, she saw him as the victim of an insidious space-age ailment called computer addiction, and sentenced him to a year's treatment for this "new and growing" impulse disorder. Bonnie and Clyde came along too soon. Nowadays they could settle for a year at the Betty Ford clinic as victims of compulsive bank-robbing addiction.

(Actor Chevy Chase says he's never going back to the Ford clinic because it's dedicated to the concept that "it's not your fault that you take dope or you drink, that it's something beyond your control." A smart man.)

As real addictions have been converted into diseases (alcoholism), bad habits have been upscaled and transformed into addictions (yesterday's hard-to-break smoking habit is today's nicotine addiction). In pop psychology, addiction theory started out as a catchy metaphor: in love and sex, some of us behave almost as if we were addicts. Pop-psych consumers loved the idea and took it quite literally. Now people freely talk of being in the grip of previously unknown addictions ranging from sex to jogging and chocolate eating. Actress Valerie Bertinelli says she is addicted to her husband.

The most popular addiction is to sex, and we now have earnest sex-addict support groups and Sexaholics Anonymous. The only problem with sexual addiction, as marriage counselor and sexual therapist Marty Klein says, is that it doesn't exist. No matter. It's popular anyway. Klein says: "Sex addicts are told they have nothing to feel guilty about." That's the whole point of being one.

In the nineties we are probably in for a heavy wave of biological determinism. As gene-mapping proceeds and the physiological correlates of behavior are discovered, we will hear even more arguments about irresistible forces. And so-called syndromes will be tailored to political constituencies. Post-Traumatic Stress Syndrome, which once applied narrowly to severe psychic aftershock, has splintered into many legally promising pseudo-ailments, including action addict syndrome, postabortion syndrome and oppression artifact disorder (delayed shock of oppressed peoples such as homosexuals and blacks). Will we eventually have an ailment for every constituent and every need?

The problem with all this is that you can't run a society, or cope with its problems, if people are not held accountable for what they do. We seem hellbent on depicting ourselves at the mercy of ever more irresistible forces. The way we are headed, the only generally acknowledged responsibility for our actions may be to explain them away on *Nightline*.

The Steve Howe case shows how an imaginative defense made a shambles of major league baseball's drug-control regulations. Howe, banned from baseball for life for a long series of cocaine violations, beat the rap in arbitration: the players' union successfully argued that he was a victim of "attention deficit hyperactivity disorder (ADHD)." The novelty here is that apparently no one had ever thought of using ADHD (a diagnosis usually referring to hyperactive children) to excuse drug behavior in a thirty-four-year-old. But it worked. Like gold lying around inside mountains, psychiatric syndromes and disorders are there to be mined.

In Milwaukee earlier this year, an imaginative defense lawyer cited "cultural psychosis" as the reason why one teenaged girl shot and killed another girl for her leather coat. (Society, in this case the violence of inner-city life, conditioned her into thinking that problems are resolved by gunfire.) This is a version of "the devil made me do it," not very far from Post-Traumatic Stress Syndrome, which shows signs of developing into an all-purpose excuse, covering almost every variety of ugly behavior undertaken in the wake of some other ugly behavior. The director of Chicago's Community Mental Health Council argues that the predatory aggression of city life can cause PTSS. This sounds as though it would make almost anyone arrested in a rough neighborhood eligible for a PTSS defense.

It should be said, however, that people at the top of society are far more likely to get away with psychologized and neurologized excuses than people in rough neighborhoods. John Money offered his epilepsy analogies, not after drive-by shootings, but in defense of a college president and a chief judge.

Money was hardly the first to smother the Wachtler case in dubious psychiatry. From the day of Wachtler's arrest (he was hustled off to a hospital with a psychiatric ward, not to jail), the newspapers have bristled with the terminology of psychological excuse—stress, sickness, aberration. "It must be attributable to some illness," said one former justice.

The psychologized vocabulary of moral evasion afflicts the whole society, but is it most corrosive when it lets the powerful off the hook. If a society is constantly being corrupted from the top, as ours is, it is crucial to our sense of justice that high-placed perpetrators be held accountable, and not disappear into the mists of psychology.

THE WHITE MALENESS OF *JEOPARDY!*

Catharine Stimpson of Rutgers is speaking, very softly, in Gramercy Suite B of the New York Hilton, and those of us at the edge of the overflow crowd can't hear. Stimpson, widely regarded as a reigning princess of political correctness, seems to be explaining that PC ("the alphabetical dyad") doesn't actually exist.

I get the bright idea to head for the convention session next door in Gramercy Suite A, where I can learn more about the nonexistence of PC by listening through the wall. Entering the room, I brush past a woman who is muttering about "white male linear thinking." Then, placing one of my white male ears firmly to the room divider, I hear Stimpson comparing political correctness to UFOs. Slowly, it dawns on me that in Gramercy A, a speaker in a green dress is saying something more interesting. She is attacking Alex Trebek's TV game show, complaining testily about the "white maleness of *Jeopardy!*"

Torn between the UFO explanation of PC and the whiteness of

Jeopardy!, I tune back in to Stimpson, who is now carrying on about the "fatheadedness" of the anti-PC people. Then the green-dress anti-*Jeopardy!* woman gives way to a black-shirt male who is answering an earnest question from the floor: is it OK, in college English classes, to teach music videos instead of literature? Black-shirt thinks it's just fine, though he says, derisively, that it might upset some "traditionalists," and the audience chuckles appreciatively at the putdown.

Welcome to the Modern Language Association's convention, the annual gong show of the academic world. This is where some eleven thousand college teachers of language and literature gather each year to hear papers on such topics as "Jane Austen and the Masturbating Three-Button Jacket," "Between the Body and the Flesh: Performing Lesbian Sadomasochism," "The Poetics of Ouija" and "Transvestite Biography."

Beneath this apparent freelance zaniness lies a consistent purpose. Once the preserve of tweedy and bookish professors, the thirty-two-thousand-member MLA has long since been taken over by the race-and-gender crowd. Now it is a hard-edged heavily politicized academic group that looks at western literature (when it looks at all) solely as the ideological expression of white male dominance. "Every year I say this convention can't get any worse," says a professor who's afraid to offer her name. "And every year they prove me wrong."

The air is thick with the incantatory words "hegemonic," "privileged" and "dominant," plus lots of near-words like "liberatory," "interdiscursive" and "heterotextuality." In one room, a lecturer from San Francisco State rails against "white supremacist patriarchal capitalism," adding that "capitalism must be destroyed in our time." In another, Sara Suleri of Yale mocks a donation to her university that would set up a chair in western civilization. "Western civilization?" she asks. "Why not a chair for colonialism, slavery, empire and poverty?" And Steven Wartofsky, of Loyola University in Chicago, talks of "a desire to *forget* history," which he predicts "will begin at next year's MLA . . . with the displacement of white male Eur-Americans' texts."

This is no place to talk about literature and many of the panels set up to deal glancingly with the subject are quickly converted to higher purposes. A scheduled discussion of E. L. Doctorow's novel *The Book of Daniel* turns out to be a long rant about the "McCarthyite" 1950s by a young professor who seems to know very little about the period. The general tone here is angry and confrontational, with intellectual opponents (none of whom seem to be on the premises) denounced as "the enemy." The presidential address, given by Houston Baker, Jr., a black professor from the University of Pennsylvania, is a vitriolic attack on white dominance as allegedly represented by fraternities on the Penn campus.

The vacationing ideologues here are suffering from a swarm of radical isms, but the central one, totally dead in the real world, is Marxism. It is a vulgar Marxism, adapted by British radicals, and it goes like this: whether we acknowledge it or not, everything we do or say works to support our ideological interests. Realizing that all creative writing is already political, the left works to reveal literature as the expression of an elite ruling class. So literary studies are properly a branch of left politics and nothing more.

It's hard to imagine that an entire profession is careening off the rails this way, but it is indeed happening. The good news is that a few people are willing to resist. One of them is Feroza Jussawalla of the University of Texas–El Paso. She passionately supports multicultural studies, but her paper bluntly complains about the heavy politicization of the field. "Teaching diversity or multiculturalism," she says, "has come dangerously close to indoctrination of a political point of view rather than teaching culture," and she says there's intimidation and censorship too for the politically incorrect. She calls for freedom from both the old "scholarly humanist elites" and the new "elitist hegemonic Marxists" who now ride herd on the MLA. It's a terrific paper, a small ray of light in the mineshaft of MLA dogmatisim.

THE MAN WHO OCCUPIED TEDDY'S BRAIN

Imagine my surprise when the phone rang and Joe McGinniss came on the line. "Hello, John," he blurted out. "You must be wondering about my new Teddy Kennedy book . . ."

Uncanny how he can get into other people's minds, I thought. Actually I had just finished reading *The Last Brother*. And I was wondering about it. Many people were. Doubts lingered in the air. Everywhere.

"Joe," I pointed out, "some people say your book is basically a cut-and-paste job written from clippings and William Manchester's book

The Death of a President. Other people say you shouldn't have made up a bunch of Teddy Kennedy thoughts and feelings and stuffed them into his brain. Teddy's nonfictional, Joe. He's not a character in a novel."

At this point, I paused. There was an awkward moment of silence. The fat was in the fire, he must have thought. Years from now, he would look back on this pause and wonder about its fateful connection to the Kennedy legend and the Kennedy secrets. Too many secrets. Too much legend. Too many pages. Too little editing.

But that was in the future. For the moment, he had to be thinking that nothing could be done except to keep talking. He could hardly have failed to realize that Teddy Kennedy might have said, "It's good to talk things over," though there was no evidence that he actually did.

Our conversation would continue. It would have to. There was nothing to do but go on.

With surprising readiness, McGinniss acknowledged that Teddy is nonfictional. But he insisted that his book was legit. "It's true that most biographers don't make up quotes and thoughts," he explained. "But I'm not just a biographer, I'm a ruminator. We ruminators go for inner truths that transcend journalism. Check my Author's Note."

I flipped to the back of his book. Sure enough, there was the Author's Note, right where nonruminating biographers usually put the sources, index, and footnotes. It said plainly that *The Last Brother* is "at least as much a 'rumination' as a biography."

What are the rules for writing ruminatively? I wondered. How do you know which thoughts to make up? Simple, Joe said. All you had to do was immerse yourself in the life and thought patterns of your subject. Then you get to infer thoughts at key moments. That was how he could present so many of Ted's innermost feelings, feelings that Ted may not even have known he had.

"So on page 231," I said, "I notice you have Teddy thinking that Jack's aides—Larry O'Brien, Pierre Salinger and others—were such hotshots that "it was as if they were not just of a different generation but of a more evolved species, possessing a brilliance and an utter nervelessness that he knew—however much he might try to pretend otherwise—would always be beyond him."

Joe nodded. Under the new rumination rules, I asked, can you actually have Teddy thinking that Pierre Salinger is a more evolved species? Is it really ethical to insert a thought like that into a living brain?

McGinniss shifted in his seat and glanced fleetingly at his watch. "That's the inference I get," he said with quiet confidence. "Of course, other immersion specialists may infer differently. Let them write their own books."

Something was bothering me and I wanted to put it politely. "Joe," I asked, "if you really have access to Teddy's brain, while you're rooting around inside there, why don't you haul out something brand new, instead of the same old stuff from clippings and books?"

I must have said this wrong, because McGinniss took it amiss. Somewhat tartly, he asked how many of my columns have been turned into major miniseries.

"Joe," I said, "let's talk about the semi-erased inferences. You suggest that Teddy could have thought of drowning himself, but erase it with 'not that there's any evidence that he considered this.' Same thing when you raise the question of whether J. Edgar Hoover ordered the killing of Martin Luther King, Jr., which you sort of take back with 'The answer is unclear.' "

I didn't bring up all the unerased inferences, that Rose Kennedy thought her dead daughter Kathleen deserved to die, that Joe Kennedy might have arranged for Sam Giancana and the mob to tip the West Virginia primary toward Jack.

McGinniss ran his fingers through his graying hair and scratched his left armpit thoughtfully. "Ruminators have to go where their informed imagination takes them," he said. "And by the way, how do you know when I'm scratching or looking at my watch? This is a phone conversation."

Joe was a bit testy now. He thought about getting a beer. Yes, he would really love a beer right now. Did this anxiety go back to a stormy relationship with his father? I couldn't possibly miss comprehending that. . .

"Leo, stop that," he shouted. "You have no way of knowing whether I want a beer or whether my sled was named 'Rosebud.' What kind of journalist are you anyway?" Yes, I thought sheepishly. I couldn't have failed to understand that he was right.

Author's Note: the author is not entirely sure whether the above conversation actually took place. No matter. He thinks it's true, and that's the important thing.

GIVE OZZIE AND HARRIET A BREAK

The term "family values" is not an invention of Dan Quayle, not a code phrase for racism, not a complaint that women should quit the workforce, not an unsophisticated yearning for the family of the 1950s. It is simply the current term for resistance to the long assault on the nuclear family that began in the 1960s.

It's important to know the history. The liberation movements of the sixties asserted the rights of individuals against the power of institutions, and the institution hit hardest was the family. Feminism, of necessity, arose as a reaction to the traditional family, and the other movements fed into its early antifamily mood: the New Left, sexual liberation and the me-first pop therapies that preached personal fulfillment over social obligation. On all sides, the family was loudly denounced as a nest of oppression and pathology. Flak was not aimed just at the rigid, father-as-dictator family but at the idea of family itself. A psychiatrist named David Cooper called the family "a secret suicide pact . . . an ideological conditioning device in any exploitative society."

This assault from the left bred its own reaction, which plugged into the wider trend toward social conservatism. By the time of Jimmy Carter's disastrous White House Conference on the American Family in 1980, both the profamily and prorights "liberalist" positions were set in stone. Liberationists got the meeting's title changed to the White House Conference on Families (plural), which in effect downgraded the intact family to one family form among many. One attendee said this verbal change was necessary to reflect "the impressive diversity" of the American family, an early use of the word "diversity" to mean "anything goes."

Two sociologists, Brigitte Berger and Peter Berger, zeroed in on the enormous significance of the insistence on "families" over "family": What appeared to be—in plain English—the disintegration of the American family was to be labeled something healthy and positive. In their book *The War Over the Family*, the Bergers wrote, "The empirical fact of diversity is here quietly translated into a norm of diversity . . . demography is translated into a new morality." The allegedly innocent semantic shift, they wrote, "gave governmental recognition to precisely the kind of moral relativism that has infuriated and mobilized large numbers of Americans."

The entire war over the family is implied in that word change. The war has been about the conditions under which children are raised and the conflict between self-fulfillment and sacrifice. One side says what everybody thought was obvious until the 1960s: that stably married parents are best, especially if those parents are willing to put children's interests ahead of their own personal fulfillment.

The other side, shaped by social movements born in hostility to the family, has emphasized freedom from family obligations and the alleged resilience of children in the face of instability at home. It has been chiefly interested in the family for pathologies it can address (domestic violence, incest) and for rights that can be asserted against it (a residue of the sixties view of family as inherently oppressive, and an increasingly narrow rights-based version of morality). Its honorable insistence that single mothers be treated with respect has been used as a wedge to normalize the no-father home. This justified the shortchanging of the young. (If the father who runs out on his kids is merely creating another acceptable family form, how is he any better or worse than the father who stays committed to his "double-parent family"?)

Data on the devastation of families have begun to turn the debate around. So has the soaring rate of births to unwed mothers: 27 percent in 1989, 19 percent for whites and 66 percent for blacks. The pattern is the same in Hollywood as in Harlem: American children are far more likely to grow up with only one parent than they were just a generation ago.

The Census Bureau says we now have 10 million single-parent households, nearly three times the number we had in 1970. Regardless of class or race, these children, as a group, are far more at risk than children who grow up with both parents.

A study of eighteen thousand students sponsored by the National Association of Elementary School Principals showed that children from one-parent families achieved less and got into more trouble than children from two-parent homes. The missing parent was such a heavy factor that youngsters from low-income two-parent families outperformed students from high-income single-parent homes.

There is a long literature on this, and though the data are not one-sided, the overwhelming bulk of studies point in one direction. The sociologist Amitai Etzioni says of the research: "The body of data leads to the inescapable conclusion that single-parenting is harmful to children." The National Commission on Children said so in words almost the same as those used by Quayle: "Rising rates of divorce, out-of-wedlock childbearing, and absent parents are not just manifestations of alternative lifestyles, they are patterns of adult behavior that increase children's risk of negative consequences." In addition to performing less well in school, these children have more psychological and behavioral problems and are very likely to become single parents themselves.

Nothing about this is mysterious or hard to figure out. As Chester Finn, former assistant secretary of education, says, "With rare exceptions, two-parent families are good for children, one-parent families are bad."

Any country serious about its future would move to confront this unfolding disaster, but in fact the opposite is occurring. The truth is that the elite in this country considers single parenthood a nonissue. In effect, that elite has decided not to look very hard at how children pay the price for the growing emphasis on individualism and personal fulfillment. We once exerted heavy pressure on couples to marry and stay together to avoid forcing children to pay this price. But now fulfillment is king. And the upper middle class is rich enough to afford breakups and planned single-parent homes. As a result, Christopher Jencks writes, in *Rethinking Social Policy,* that "elite support for the two-parent norm has eroded."

This is particularly true of the media elite, where Murphy Brown lives. The media culture tends to frame issues in terms of options, choices and lifestyle. This is a noncensorious culture in which it is considered tacky to emit any discouraging words about other people's choices and lifestyles. Indeed, part of the silence of the media on the damage to children comes from the fear of seeming to criticize or hurt the feelings of parents, usually women, who are raising (or who are forced to raise) children alone.

A by-product of this attitude is an ocean of feel-good journalism and programming intended to raise the self-esteem of single mothers. Part of the result is the detoxifying of people who put children through this intentionally. Sample headline from a major newspaper: "Who Needs A Man? Unmarried and Uninvolved, More Single Women Are Looking to Casual Acquaintances and Fertilty Clinics to Conceive Babies They Plan to Raise Alone." This helps promote the birth of at-risk babies.

It amounts to cheerleading for the unraveling of the social structure, a common affliction of those who labor in medialand.

But there are some promising signs of change. The Rockefeller commission emphatically called attention to the need for two-parent families, a breakthrough after so much propaganda on "alternative family forms." Black intellectuals have begun to relegitimize discussion of the connection between family form and social ills—forbidden by the left since the Moynihan Report of 1965. For instance, columnist William Raspberry says, "My guess is that the greatest increase in child poverty in America is a direct result of the increase in the proportion of mothers-only households." Some prominent feminists now talk about the subject without bristling hostility, emphasizing family over the old agenda of sexual politics. Polls have started to show shifts from stark individualism to concern for the family, responsibility and community. In short, a call for bolstering the family is beginning.

Yet in the media the old howitzers boom as if it were still the 1960s. The almost daily fusillade of "Ozzie and Harriet" jeering derides the goal of the intact family as a form of nostalgia. An op-ed piece said that the nuclear family is "fast becoming a relic of the Eisenhower era." *The New York Times* recently referred to the intact family as "the Republican ideal." (Do all Democrats idealize nonintact families?) A week later, it reported that the current "family values" campaign is based on "the warm appeal of the idealized 1950s family as embodied in 'Father Knows Best.' " This sort of tiresome sniping serves no function. It is the work of people who do not realize that the sixties are over, the family is in crisis and the discussion is moving on.

PART TWO

"LET'S GET BACK TO ENGLISH"

Language and Word Games People Play

THE SUBCOMMITTEE ON DISABLED SPEECH

Wishing to employ the correct modern term for disabled, the Philadelphia Federation of Teachers set up a "Committee for Members with Special Needs." It didn't work. A homeless person came by, announcing a special need for housing. Then it became the "Committee for Members Who Are Physically Challenged," but a frightened fifth-grade teacher showed up, thinking it was a support group for instructors intimidated by their unruly students. So now it is known as the "Committee for Disabled Members." "Everybody understands the words and nobody protested," said James Gallagher of the committee, satisfied at last.

The descent into accurate English as a last resort is ever more arduous. In the disability rights movement, one must grope through a fierce blizzard of euphemisms: the uniquely abled, the differently abled, the exceptional, the handi-capable, the inconvenienced, the developmentally disabled, handicappers, injury survivors and people with differing abilities. A recent bulletin from the movement lets us know that Porky Pig, formerly a stutterer, should be listed as speech-impaired, whereas Mr. Magoo is visually handicapped and Captain Hook is orthopedically impaired.

From the Pentagon to feelgood self-esteemers, everyone seems to be contributing mightily to the steady debasement of the Mother Tongue. Entrenched euphemisms include senior (old), differently sized (obese), meaningful downturn (recession), work stoppage (strike), quarantine (blockade), male sexual dysfunction (impotence), educational equity (quotas), undocumented workers (illegal aliens) and substance abusers (winos and junkies).

On the PC front, we have dominant culture (the mainstream), underrepresented groups (blacks, Indians and Latinos), survivor (victim, as in incest survivor), monocultural (white), Third World (nonwhite) and "racist!" ("I disagree with you on that"). Diversity means racial representation, as the office of "diversity manager" on so many campuses makes quite clear. (A group composed of St. Francis, Vivaldi, Falstaff, Jackie Onassis, Hitler and Mick Jagger would not be diverse, since all are monopigmented.) "Colored people," as in NAACP, is racist, but the backward construction "people of color" is progressive. Terms keep sliding: Indians became Native Americans or Amerinds, but since both terms include the dread name of a Eurocentric explorer, the preferred term is now indigenous peoples. "Oriental" has been declared a racist word, so all college departments of oriental studies that do not wish to be burned to the ground in the name of tolerance should rename themselves rather quickly.

PC-oriented newspapers, such as the *Los Angeles Times,* employ this remote campus tongue as if it were real English. The *Times,* which uses physically challenged without irony, once referred to a rap star's Eurocentric suit. This meant ordinary western clothes and not a suit that believes Europe to be the focal point of all world history.

Pentagonese has come up with a new euphemism for friendly fire, or shelling your own troops: incontinent ordnance, which sounds like something June Allyson warns us about in TV commericals. The definition of peace ("the temporary cessation of hostilities") does its bit to attrit, maul and collaterally damage the language.

Animal-rights activists insist that the word "pet" is demeaning and should be replaced by "animal companion." But that term is itself under fire because it implies that humans are somehow distinct from the rest of the animal world, an idea which reeks of speciesism. While a new and improved term is being dreamed up, pets can be called "friends" and "protectors." And animals are never "wild." They are "free-roaming" or "free."

Campuses are particularly vulnerable now to the spread of oddball feminese. Two of these terms—herstory and womyn (the latter circulated by the same segment of the population that spelled America "Amerika" during the 1970s)—actually made it into the new and outstandingly softheaded *Random House College Dictionary*. The distinguished Pittsburgh columnist, brother Peter Leo, says that if female history is "herstory," then a history of humanity should be his'n'herstory, and a man who contracts herpes should be listed as a hispes survivor. Word comes that a feminist professor now calls her seminar an "ovular." Let us hope that no one tells her the etymology of "testimony." Otherwise she might have womyn ovarifying in courts across Amerika.

Finally, as a public service, here is how a few familiar books and movies might be translated into modspeak:

Beauty and the Beast—A lookism survivor and a free-roaming fellow mammal.

War and Peace—Violence processing and the temporary cessation of hostilities.

Les Misérables—Persons with special needs.

Three Blind Mice—A triad of visually impaired, wall-dwelling protectors.

Old Yeller—Senior animal companion of color.

Snow White and the Seven Dwarfs—One of the monocultural oppressed womyn confronts the vertically challenged.

Men at Arms—The myn are at it again.

REVENGE OF THE LANGUAGE-STRETCHERS

Derek Humphry knows that words matter. A leading figure in the euthanasia movement, Humphry says his side lost at the polls in Washington state largely because it first lost the battle over language. The pro-euthanasia campaigners talked broadly about "aid in dying." But the media and public, Humphry says, "used the real words with relish"—suicide and euthanasia—and Initiative 119 went down.

In passing, Humphry pointed out the vagueness of "aid in dying." It can mean, he says, "anything from a physician's lethal injection all the way to holding hands with a dying patient and saying, 'I love you.' " Anyone who stretches a phrase to cover both killing and moral support is a serious player in the language games.

This is, in fact, a big trend in the fast-growing field of language manipulation. Specific terms give way to ever broader and more vaporous ones. "Blind" or "legally blind" was replaced by "visually impaired," which includes everyone who wears glasses. "Child abuse" now seems to cover almost anything a parent or parental figure can do wrong. "Substance abusers" (formerly addicts and drunks) now includes any person who overuses or misuses anything at all.

More often word stretching occurs for frankly polemical reasons. "Family" has been stretched to make nonfamilies eligible for various family benefits. The no-marriage, no-child, no-kinship "family" is well entrenched. Now the word is seriously used to refer to group renters, childless couples, and even single people living alone.

A New Jersey court ruled that group renters, male college students on renewable four-month leases, fit the definition of family. To circum-vent zoning restrictions, two groups of recovering alcoholics in Cherry Hill, New Jersey, insisted they were families too. A spokesman said, "Residents consider themselves a family and no other family in the country has to announce itself or explain itself." As in *Through the Looking Glass*, the word means what the speaker wants it to mean.

If groups of collegians and alcoholics constitute families, it is hard to see why an army barracks or a touring basketball team couldn't be considered "nontraditional families" as well. The state of California seemingly endorses the view that a family is what anybody thinks it is. For a ten-dollar filing fee, the state issues gold-seal certificates to all comers declaring that they are a family, even if they live alone or the rest of the family is made up of goldfish. The idea is to set the stage for individuals to reap family benefits offered under sixteen hundred different state laws.

Another popular form of stretching is to associate some low-level complaint with a higher-level one involving violence, thus presumably startling everyone into paying attention. A columnist complained re-cently about "intellectual genocide" in D.C. public schools, meaning that students aren't taught well and aren't learning basic skills. Betty Friedan regularly complains about the media's "symbolic annihilation of women" (she means there still aren't enough news stories by and about women). A Manhattan man, dying of AIDS, said his death should be seen as "a form of political assassination" (he means the government should have spent more fighting AIDS).

Act-Up, the radical group of AIDS activists, insists that there is no moral difference between negligent complicity in the AIDS crisis and the act of murder. Since its view of negligence is a broad one, its constantly shifting list of "murderers" has included Ronald Reagan, George Bush, former New York City mayor Ed Koch and Arthur Sulz-berger of *The New York Times*.

At Harvard Law School, a year after the stabbing murder of a law professor, a tasteless student parody of her work was widely denounced as "a second murder." That language made it into a screaming headline in a national women's magazine: "A Harvard Killing—Mary Joe Frug Was Murdered Twice."

"Censorship" has undergone verbal inflation too. In normal English, it means control of utterance by government. But in the past two or three years, it has been used to include artists who apply for NEA grants and don't get them ("economic censorship") as well as various boycotts and decisions by a few cable systems not to carry MTV.

These stretching exercises are often more than publicity-grabbing hyperbole. Sometimes they are conscious attempts to ratchet up a minor offense into a major one. Ogling a woman, once considered harmless or merely rude, is considered sexual harassment now, and is often mentioned in the same breath as rape. Notice how the University of Minnesota's definition of sexual harassment blurs all lines between a glance, lack of sensitivity, serious harassment and rape: "Sexual harassment can be as blatant as rape or as subtle as a look. Harassment . . . often consists of callous insensitivity to the experience of women."

The verbal work of folding the entire category of harassment into the category of rape goes on all the time. "Sexual harassment is a subtle rape," a psychologist named John Gottman told *The New York Times.* "Sexual harassment is a subset of rape with overtones of blackmail and extortion," columnist Carole Agus told her readers in *New York Newsday.*

The term "domestic violence," for instance, once referred to physical assaults in the home. Now it includes psychological abuse. Lenore Walker, a specialist in the field, defines wife battering to include bullying and manipulation ("making women do things they otherwise wouldn't . . . by eroding their self-esteem"). This mimics what happened when some definitions of date rape expanded to include what used to be known as seduction. For instance, Andrea Parrot, a rape expert at Cornell, says that "psychological coercion" is rape, which seems to include all the begging and wheedling that young men do for sex. The feminist writer Robin Morgan says that any sex not initiated and controlled by female desire is rape. This would presumably include a tired wife accommodating her husband's desires.

A similar blurring occurs in the hate crime field. Often it's not very clear whether we are talking about violence or nonviolence, crimes or noncriminal bias incidents, serious social offenses or minor and ambiguous run-ins. The National Institute Against Prejudice and Violence in Baltimore keeps feeding the media statistics on campus "ethnoviolence," but it defines violence to include slurs, graffiti and perceptions of slights. Even self-defined minor psychological injuries—simple cases of hurt feelings—count as violence.

Here are two ethnoviolent incidents listed in a brochure at MIT: (1) "In one of my courses in freshman year, the professor would rarely call on any black student and the few times he did he asked embarrassingly easy questions," and (2) "At times professors would ask me to drop a course when I didn't think it was appropriate. . . . I was outraged."

The effect of this tactic is to increase alarm about what's happening on campus, and to raise doubts about the aims and methods of statistic-keepers. "Hate crimes" in many instances include remarks and behaviors that aren't crimes, just as seduction isn't rape and asking easy questions in class isn't racial violence. Let's get back to English.

JOURNALESE, AN ENGLISHLIKE LANGUAGE

I am a recognized expert on journalese, the arcane lingo of reporters and pundits. To the delight of friends, I can do instant translations from journalese to English. For instance, "omnipresent" means insufferable, as in "the omnipresent Yoko Ono." "Freewheeling" means crooked, "high-minded" means unworldly, and "increasingly distracted" translates as senile. "Scandal-plagued" is journalese for guilty. The term is affixed to the names of veteran suspects who have somehow escaped indictment.

What did the *Washington Post* Style Section mean when it referred to a certain woman's "blushed, taut face"? Simple: too much makeup, too many facelifts. A congressman referred to as "a master of detail" is a drone. In politics, a "rising star" is a friendly low-level source whom the reporter envisions as an extremely useful gusher of tomorrow. "Racial unrest" is a race riot that the journalist failed to attend. "Well-respected" indicates a liberal who has just defected to a conservative cause: "Even the well-respected Senator Forbush supports the administration's compromise plan for moderate fire-bombing in Botswana."

The central function of journalese is to convey the reporter's actual opinion while avoiding the confining limits of bad taste and libel law. Suppose you are a fair-minded journalist and you wish to point out that

Senator Forbush is a clod. Do you type "Forbush, the well-known incompetent"? Not at all. You simply write that the poor fellow's reputation is "still dogged by doubts about his competence." Or if you feel he should be indicted, depict him as "haunted by allegations," which, as a responsible and thorough reporter, you are obliged to dig up and embellish.

One reporter wrote about "the lusty old city of Yonkers" during a crisis over housing integration there. This meant that the reporter thought of Yonkers as a crude unfashionable place, something of a backward frontier town accidentally plopped down next to New York City. He also mentioned, rather casually, the "Tudor-style Scarsdale home" of the Yonkers corporation counsel, thus establishing, in a brilliant three-word burst, that a key official who is trying to avoid integration lives in a fancy house outside the city limits.

Journalese users are genetically predisposed toward hyphenated constructions, the more meaningless the better: in-depth interviews, blue-ribbon panels, tree-lined streets. In the whole history of American journalism, fewer than twenty streets have failed to be identified as tree-lined.

Thus we learn about "ill-fated" airliners, "pre-dawn" raids, the "high-minded Bill Bradley and his much-maligned speaking style," "the controversial let-burn policy of fire-scarred Yellowstone Park," and the nation's leading victim of cosmetology, "mascara-dependent Ivana Trump." "Self-styled" indicates someone whom the reporter sees as grotesquely uppity, as in "self-styled hotel queen Leona Helmsley." "Self-appointed" modifies the word "critic" or the phrase "moralist Jimmy Swaggart." This usage is meant to underline the dangers of criticizing or moralizing on a freelance basis, without an official appointment by a recognized journalese-speaking authority.

Hyphens come so easily to adjective-minded journalists, that many can effortlessly pack six or seven into a single sentence: "In an opposition-defying pre-dawn escape from his turmoil-ridden island nation, long-embattled dictator Ferdinand Marcos fled into self-imposed exile on a tree-lined street in beautiful, not-yet-aware Honolulu."

The Middle East has contributed most of the classic hyphenated adjectives in journalese: oil-rich, much-troubled, war-torn, violence-plagued. But the current hyphen champion is "-driven." Here is *Women's Wear Daily* on the cutting edge: "Rather than being consumer-driven and product-driven, they have become cash-management-driven." Elsewhere, golf and baseball have been decribed as "ego-driven," magazines are "writer-driven" or "reader-driven," advertising is said to be "choice-driven" and one business after another is revealed to be "profit-driven" (and not "loss-driven," as we might have imagined).

One branch of journalese deals with the vexing question of covering a political leader who does not pay much attention to politics, a problem in the United States for years and recently a problem in other nations, too. A sophisticated journalist will point out that the politician "prefers to leave details to subordinates," "is detached from day-to-day decision-making," or "has a hands-off managerial style." Later he will be described as "disengaged," the familiar journalese word for "out to lunch." In Greece, when Andreas Papandreou was disengaged by romance, thus throwing the whole government into turmoil, reporters lurched in the general direction of truth by writing that "he is in regular telephone contact with his aides." Canny readers all understood that this meant "he is not in contact with his aides—he is in contact with his girlfriend."

The murderous compliment is one sure sign of a skilled journalese user. "She certainly looks younger," for example, indicates major facial surgery, just as "she looks marvelous for her age" means the writer wishes you to think of the woman in question as old.

"He is known to have a keen sense of humor" signals us that we are about to read a truly appalling joke. In a profile on keen-humored Steve Forbes, son of Malcolm Forbes (you are six inches from joke), he is cited as quipping hilariously that Elizabeth Taylor's birthday would not be a company holiday. (You have passed joke. End laughter.)

Like Eskimos who can distinguish among many different kinds of snow, skilled journalese-users can easily distinguish two kinds of silence: everyday run-of-the-mill silence and "stunned silence," a censorious form of quietude that reflects the reporter's own indignation. At the end of a major trial, there are two traditional modes of sobbing: "quietly" and "uncontrollably." The latter is the more overtly penitential rich-guy's style, and was shrewdly detected by reporters covering the conclusion of the Mike Milken trial.

The rise of feminism has reshaped much journalese. For instance, in reformed journalese, women no longer have any hair color. Even if the hair in question happens to be Kelly green with tangerine frosting, no male reporter will mention it in print. Similarly, all the traditional terms for bimbo, such as "one-time beauty queen," have fallen into vague disrepute. Now they can be found only in *People* magazine, which functions as a museum of prefeminist usage. It has referred to "would-be cheerleader Donna Rice," "sometime model Donna Rice" and Jessica Hahn, "who has been around the block." (No such rich vocabulary has emerged yet to indicate male bimbos. We are left with the sole term "womanizer," which roughly translates as "out-of-control male slut.")

Under current usage, the skilled journalese-user must append something upscale to the standard accusation of bimbosity: "Emerging from the Tidal Basin with Senator Forbush was the former exotic dancer Fifi LaRue, an acknowledged authority on municipal bond ratings."

Journalese is an omnipresent, well-respected, oft-hyphenated and need-driven language that slashes through the dull patina of mundane objectivity and lets readers know what you really think. Where would we be without it?

MY PARTNER, THE WAITRON

Quiz time. What's wrong with the following sentence: "My wife, the waitress, put the ketchup on the lazy Susan."

Many of you probably think this is just a normal, inoffensive English sentence. Not so. It contains three wholly objectionable examples of careless speech.

"Lazy Susan" is obviously offensive to women, particularly to women named Susan, and has therefore been changed to revolving tray, or relish tray. "My wife" is also a backward phrase implying that women are defined by men and subordinate to them. The correct term is now "my partner." "Waitress" is wrong too. What we need is a unisex word for people who wait on tables. The new *Random House Webster's Collegiate Dictionary* has suggested the term "waitron." Our last noun, "ketchup," does not seem to have offended any organized groups, and therefore is still okay. So the new formulation would be, "My partner, the waitron, put the ketchup on the revolving relish tray." Got it?

Let's try another one. See how many errors you can spot in this sentence: "Algernon is driving me crazy—he's acting so queerly these days, always beating the drums for that cause of his."

Again, the correct answer is three. "Crazy," like "idiot" and "moron," is a slur on the mentally impaired. "Queer" is off-limits because homosexual groups are sensitive about it. And "beating the drums" is a verbal tomahawk chop against Native Americans, subtly implying that Indians are primitive and warlike. A sensitive, modern person would avoid all these wounding references and simply say "I find Algernon a bit disturbing and unusual, always actively pursuing his cause." Much better, no?

We know that almost everything we say in English turns out to crush the feelings of somebody, somewhere. Even the feelings of nonhumans are at stake. For instance, we can't call our dogs and cats "pets" any more, because "pet" (like "wife") is a power word implying that we are somehow on a higher level than Fido or Blackie.

The basic equality between the two-legged and four-legged mammals in each domicile is properly expressed by the new term for pets: "animal companions." This also applies to our many, lovely no-legged companions such as goldfish and snakes. (By the way, the modern term for no-legged, or one-armed, or one-legged, is "limb-deficient." Interestingly, both Captain Ahab and Moby Dick were limb-deficient mammals, possibly a key to new interpretations of Melville's famous novel.)

Next test question. Check this sentence for flaws: "A huge number of freshmen, both white and nonwhite, including many older students, showed up for freshman orientation."

Four errors here. "Older students," those going back to school after time in the workforce, are now known by the nondemeaning term "nontraditional students." "Freshman" is, of course, sexist, since it includes the word "man." "Orientation" is wrong because it contains the word "orient," offensive to Asians as a Eurocentric "western" word for those who live in the "east" (orient). Nonwhites is a negative derived identity. The correct term is "people of color," "though some are partial to "world majorities." "Whites" is still okay, though some on campus are beginning to favor advanced terms like "monoculturalists" and "historically nonsubjugated peoples," or "the population not actively recruited" for college and the workforce.

So let's make the sentence: "Many students, some historically nonsubjugated, some nontraditional, some people of color, showed up for the introductory freshperson program." Now it's correct.

It is worth noting that there has been some resistance to the term "people of color," partly on grounds that it seems backward, like calling "First Avenue," "Avenue of First."

For instance *Spy* magazine says that if nonwhites are "people of color," then priests and ministers should be "people of collar"; angry folks should be "people of choler"; and those who live in Denver must be "people of Colorado." This is, of course, reactionary japery and must be censored by campus and off-campus authorities so that freer speech may continue to evolve.

Final test item. What's wrong here: "Dear, did you see that Jackie McCord is no longer unemployed—she's just been named postmaster of Sag Harbor!" Three mistakes again. "Unemployed" has been changed to "nonwaged." "Dear" is just as offensive as "my wife." In fact, the state of Pennsylvania has ruled that the words "dear," "sweetie," and "honey" may no longer be used by staff at long-term nursing homes in the state, since they are inherently degrading to clients.

The final mistake is calling Ms. McCord a postmaster, when the correct term is "postmistress." Though some of the new wordpersons are firm on this, in truth there are a few difficulties here. It would mean that famous male painters of the past would remain "old masters," while equally famous females would have to become "old mistresses." Similarly, a female member of the Teamsters union would be a teamstress, just as a male seamstress would logically become a seamster. This problem is being worked on. Perhaps we should learn from the change in the word "waitress," and merely replace "postmaster" and "postmistress" with "postron."

Remember, it's a living language, and like tough but loving parents, we must keep whacking it into shape, or it may never live up to our expectations.

NO-FAULT SYNTAX

"Obviously, some mistakes were made," said John Sununu, referring to his travel adventures as White House chief of staff. This is a wonderful nonapology, which seizes the blame and casts it firmly into outer space. Having achieved quotability, Sununu rested. But he could easily have gone on, paddling along in the passive voice ("Aisle seats were reserved and filled" or "Haircuts in Hawaii and stamp auctions on Samoa were flown toward") without actually associating himself with any of these mysterious and expensive travel decisions that people keep saying he was somehow involved in. Of course, Sununu could have been protecting the identity of some loyal assistant who misguidedly put the boss on all those planes and limos. It's possible that the aide sent him hurtling along to all those ski slopes and far-off dental appointments without bothering to inform him about it.

Probably not, though. More likely, Sununu was just making exceptional use of the traditional passive voice to fudge things as best he could. President Bush played right along, saying that Sununu had apologized to him, not for screwing up, or for ethically dubious behavior, but for any embarrassment that the travel controversy might have caused. The president said his heart aches for the Sununu family "because they've been through a lot . . . kind of what I refer to as a piling-on syndrome." Sununu and his family are passive here, either bystanders or victims. The active and therefore blamable forces are both abstractions: the travel controversy and the piling-on syndrome.

"Mistakes were made." That phrase showed up in the Justice Department report on Waco too. William Schneider, a political analyst for CNN, calls this usage "the past exonerative," a sharp phrase, quoted in William Safire's language column in the Sunday *New York Times Magazine*. Marion Barry, the embattled ex-mayor of Washington, is a hall-of-fame performer in wielding the past exonerative. When asked why he lied about being "chemically dependent," he replied, "That was the disease talking. I did not purposely do that to you. I was a victim." By combining the three languages of addiction, victimology and political evasion, Barry thus brilliantly positioned himself as the victim of his own mouth. This is the "Night of the Living Dead" defense: As in many a scary horror movie, an outside demon invades your body, pours in some gruesome chemicals that you yourself would never ingest and then, to cap it off, uses your very own voice to lie to the press!

Language indicating that one is merely the victim of one's own action is not new, just wildly popular. In the movie *Heartburn*, Jack Nicholson told his pregnant wife, Meryl Streep, that the crisis caused by his extramarital romance "is hard on me, too." Nice touch. Now the past exonerative and other slippery passive usages are rampant (or should that be, are being run rampantly?) throughout the press. The *Washington Post* reporter fired for plagiarism "had the misfortune to get caught at a moment when the press was focused on the issue of plagiarism" (*The New Republic*). Alcoholism "extracts a disproportionate toll" from minorities (*The New York Times*). Donald Kennedy, who resigned as president of Stanford after a funding scandal, "was caught up in a (post-Trump-age) purge" and "paid a high price for failing to meet strict standards" (various educators interviewed by the *Boston Globe*). Actually, he quit because under his leadership, Stanford used more than a million in federal research dollars to pay for flowers, antiques, receptions and yacht depreciation. In the modern manner, Kennedy, like Sununu, took no personal responsibility, generally positioning himself as a scapegoat.

The past exonerative can also be employed to exonerate people accused of success. Ali A. Mazrui, the Afrocentrist professor who dislikes the western world and all its works and pomps, writes that as a result of the Industrial Revolution, "economic preeminence was bestowed upon the countries of Europe and North America." Like Sununu's mistake-makers, Mazrui's capricious bestowers are unnamed, though it is clear that the bestowal had nothing to do with economic or cultural achievement. With any luck, it just as easily could have happened to Guam or Uganda.

These passive constructions work best if one favors a set of abstractions that can be blamed for pushing people around—society, the privileged, the dominant culture or just social expectations. Writing in the current issue of *Tikkun* magazine, critic Josh Ozersky notes that "like many a higher doctrine before it, 'political correctness' has a strong distaste for the active voice." So do more and more books of social criticism. Naomi Wolf's current book, *The Beauty Myth*, for example, is heavily written in the passive voice. This is because, at root, she is selling a conspiracy theory: men have created a devastating social juggernaut, the ideal of female beauty, that coerces all women to constantly waste their energies worrying about their appearances.

All writing courses tell students to stick to the active voice as much as possible, partly because the passive voice is the natural home of limp and evasive writing. It is also a terrific screen to conceal choices, responsibility and moral conflicts. Mr. Sununu, could you please recast that for us in the active voice?

THE F-WORD FLOWS LIKE KETCHUP

While some of us have joked about the unmentionable T word ("taxes") and the L word ("liberal"), it turns out that the original F word is growing more mentionable every day. In fact, It seems further along on an improbable march toward respectability than, say, the Mayflower Madam or Richard Nixon.

That is a pity. Until recently, when it began popping up on bumper stickers and the T-shirts of dewy-eyed children defended by American Civil Liberties Union lawyers, the F word was the most taboo word in American English, partly because every society needs such a word (it gives us something to mutter under the breath after hammering a thumb), partly because it combines sex and aggression in a primitive, male way. Since one of the jobs any society has is breaking the link between sex and aggression, it makes sense that the word upholding that link is taboo.

Yet the word is all around us now, like air pollution. Consider some of the major perpetrators, assembled here in no particular order.

Turn on the World Series and there is Dodger manager Tommy Lasorda, who must have mouthed thirty such words in front of the dugout cameras before the series was over. Lasorda once used the F word 144 times in a pep talk to his players, who counted them to pass the time. He is a successful, sixtyish executive who may need about half a million F words to get him through an average year. Among players, one standout is the Mets' Lenny Dykstra, who felt the need to share the F word with us 160 times in his autobiography, *Nails*.

Then there is playwright David Mamet, whose *Glengarry Glen Ross* set an F-word record for a Pulitzer Prize play—ninety-three—and had theatergoers with any sensibilities feeling as though they were incompetent pitchers being worked over by an imflamed Dodger manager. Perhaps indicative of a trickle-down effect in the theater, drama critic Robert Brustein of Harvard's Loeb Theater is good for two or three F words per review these days.

F-bashing of movie audiences is an industrywide sport. Like teenagers with ketchup, moviemakers can't seem to resist pouring it over every available script. A telling example is *Adventures in Babysitting*: Average age of the four lead characters, about 13; number of F words in film, about 13. Despite stiff competition, the all-time F-word champ in Tinseltown is the Al Pacino remake of *Scarface,* which is one long F-word assault, with rare timeouts for chain-sawing or perforating a mobster or two. "Why do you have to say 'f——' all the time?" asks Mrs. Scarface, the only compelling question raised by the dreadful Oliver Stone script. As usual, reliance on the F word and near-total lack of inspiration seem to go hand in hand.

In the F-word-drenched field of stand-up comedy, we have the greatly talented but clearly out-of-control Eddie Murphy, with 214 F words in one taped performance. At least the word is used correctly: Murphy, the owner of a major attitude problem, really means to combine sex and aggression in a primitive, male mode.

Among recording artists, the titleholder in use of F words is not the Sex Pistols or Frankie Goes to Hollywood but Richard Nixon, for the Watergate tapes.

If the F word had a press agent, we would be hearing more about the big breakthrough at *The New Yorker.* We persist in thinking of *The New Yorker* as a raging hotbed of decorum and taste. But these days, the monocled Eustace Tilley cocks an eyebrow, stares down his aristocrat's nose and says, "[bleep]." A short story by Robert Stone in the magazine featured one "f——," one "f——er," three "f——ings" and four "f——in's," plus assorted references to anatomical parts and waste products, both human and equine.

Sad to say, *The New Yorker* appears here to be a victim of fashion, a breathless dowager slipping into her first punk miniskirt. Eustace, we ask you: is this necessary?

Some of this is the writer-editor game, with the writer trying to push back the boundaries of taste and the editor attempting to stand fast. ("They keep trying to sneak the word —— past me," Executive Editor Ben Bradlee says of his *Washington Post* staff.) The writer is in a no-lose situation: either the word gets into print, establishing yet another dubious landmark for human freedom, or it doesn't, in which case the editor is revealed once again to be a stodgy, parental naysayer.

There are other reasons for the spread of the F word, of course-increasing sexual frankness, particularly in the vocabulary needed to discuss the AIDS crisis, and the Vietnam experience, which, like World War II, injected more barracks language into normal civilian discourse.

But the F word is making two big leaps here—from private to public and from oral to written. A word with a very limited, semirespectable function as a civility breaker and safety valve is making itself at home nearly everywhere. You no longer have to stand next to Lenny Dykstra to catch his F words; they are available in packages of 160 at B. Dalton's.

Robert Gottlieb, former editor of *The New Yorker*, once said the F word is just a part of our language in the post-Vietnam era and will appear in his magazine as "a very modest sprinkling" when there is no good way to avoid it. Gottlieb said the magazine had "no policy at all" on the F word and that he had "never given it a moment's thought." That is just the problem: When you get to be the editor of *The New Yorker*, you're supposed to spend a minute thinking about standards. Maybe even two.

MANLY DEEDS, SEXIST WORDS

Preoccupied with pressing personal matters, most of us are totally un-aware that the state of Maryland is undergoing a profound motto crisis.

The problem is that the state motto, "Fatti maschii, parole femine," is sexist. It's an archaic Italian phrase from the crest of the Calverts, Maryland's founding family, and it translates as "Manly deeds, womanly words."

Gregory Stiverson, the assistant state archivist, tried gamely to put the best face on things. He said the Calverts were just making the point that "it's better to do things than to sit there mouthing off." Maybe so, but the motto says men act, while women sit around and yammer.

That may have been fine in 1648, but nowadays it's controversial. For a month or more, the state legislature squirmed and scratched its collective head about what to do.

It should have consulted my esteemed brother, Peter Leo, the *Pittsburgh Post-Gazette* columnist and all-round expert on these matters. He recommends a unisex version: "All of us, men and women alike, do a lot of stuff and then talk about it."

On the other hand, my esteemed spouse, Jacqueline Leo, the hard-charging executive, says Maryland should definitely keep its motto no matter what anyone thinks, but translate it as "Men take out the garbage; women tell them to do it."

My own version is an even more inspiring one: "Women and men—two great genders! Talk and action—two great things!" This can fairly be called both rousing and inclusive, though it does in fact leave scant room for unforeseen new genders doing unforeseen great things. Still, it is better than "Maryland—sexist since 1648; wanna make something of it?"

Writing in *The Washington Post*, Neil Genzlinger says the mindset that produced "Fatti maschii, parole femine" might just as well have come up with "Forza brutale, gambe stupende" ("Brute force, great legs"). Come to think of it, that could be the motto of the Tailhook Association, placed directly under the official seal (two crotch-grabbers poised on a field of empty beer bottles).

The *Post* had the wit to run a contest for a new Maryland motto. The winner was "Maryland: wait, we can explain . . ." Other entries included "Maryland: home of its residents" and "Maryland: it looks better in the dark."

That last entry reminds me of an unkind remark made about New Jersey by author Josh Greenfeld. Driving up the Jersey Turnpike at night past all the fiery refineries, Greenfeld remarked that "New Jersey looks like the back of an old radio." (Possible state slogan: "Come to Jersey—live in an old radio.")

In the late 1970s, Jersey came up with a promotional slogan, "New Jersey's Got It!" As a proud native of the Garden State, I naturally felt that this slogan was about as creative as we Jerseyites can expect to get. But I still thought it could be improved. How about, "New Jersey's got it! But relax, it's not communicable." Or perhaps: "New Jersey—where Jimmy Hoffa is buried." (Variation: "Come to Jersey—you'll never leave. Hoffa didn't.")

Last year Philadelphia held a contest for an official city slogan. The winner put everyone to sleep: "Welcome to Philadelphia—enjoy our past and experience our future." (And try to ignore our present.) In the *Philadelphia Inquirer*, staff writer Dan Meyers suggested a catchier slogan: "Welcome to Philadelphia—hey, that's my car!"

Actually, some of the real state mottoes are almost as weird as that. Connecticut's is "He who transplanted still sustains," New Mexico's is "It grows as it goes," and Michigan's is "If you seek a pleasant peninsula, look around you." (Jersey version: "You want big-time oil refinery living?—You got it!")

The state of Washington uses an Indian term as its motto—"Al-Ki" ("By and by"). Apparently the early settlers called Seattle "New York Al-Ki," meaning that the tiny community would one day be a great city. Since "By and by" seems to mean later, eventually, or we'll get around to it, this logically should be the motto of Washington, D.C., not Washington the state. Just imagine thousands of alert capital bureacrats doing their level best every day to live up to the motto "By and by."

In Maryland, the Italian consul in Baltimore offered legislators a way out. If "interpreted logically," he said, and "in the perspective of twentieth-century language," the motto could be translated as "Delicate words, resolute action." In plain English, the wise consul semed to be saying, why don't you solve the problem by mistranslating the text? Good idea.

So right now it looks as though Maryland might settle for the English version "Strong deeds, gentle words." Then again, maybe it should be "Strong words, mild action." Whatever. The moral is, "If you seek a pleasant mistranslation, look around you. By and by, after 345 years, you'll get it."

REPORTING THROUGH PRISMS

Jeffrey Schmalz of *The New York Times* died in late 1993 of a brain infection caused by AIDS. I was sorry to read about it. Schmalz was a good reporter. By all accounts he was a good man as well. But there was a problem with his reportage. He was turning out highly emotional coverage of the disease that was killing both him and the movement he identified with—gay rights.

None of this was dishonest. He was totally open about what he was doing, and wrote about the conflict. In his stories, as in his life, Schmalz the reporter wrestled with Schmalz the advocate. Usually the reporter won, but not always. A year ago, he wrote that after twenty years of by-the-book impersonal reporting, "Now I see the world through the prism of AIDS."

Through that prism, people with AIDS seemed quite different from other terminally ill patients. They seemed like larger-than-life martyr-heroes. Schmalz's emotions poured into his writing: sometimes anger, sometimes affection or a strong surge of empathy. His interviews occasionally ended with hugs (Mary Fisher, an AIDS sufferer who addressed the Republican convention) or the desire to hug ("I wanted to hold him," Schmalz wrote after his interview with Bob Hattoy, the activist with AIDS who addressed the Democratic convention).

Schmalz was no propagandist, but he clearly had a point of view and he sometimes ignored news that embarrassed mainstream gays. He wrote about lesbians and gays in military uniform at last spring's Gay March on Washington, but not about the more bizarre contingents of demonstrators. (None of the March's weirdness made it into the *Times*, though it was all over C-Span.)

Sometimes the Schmalz prism turned into a hall of mirrors. In interviewing Randy Shilts, a prominent gay reporter, dying of AIDS, who was "a journalist, not an advocate," Schmalz certainly seemed to be writing about himself through Schilts. "Straight people should be giving awards to those of us with AIDS who go on being productive members of society," Shilts said in the interview. But the Shilts quote could also be read as a Schmalz comment about himself.

Okay, so Schmalz was a courageous man and a good reporter, under great stress, who was allowed to violate just about every rule of conventional reporting. Why worry about it now? Because we don't know yet whether his reportage was an exception or a harbinger of things to come. A lot of people think it was just an understandable exception. When your best-known gay reporter says he is dying and specifically asks to cover AIDS in his last days, it's hard to say no. This is particularly true if you have an old track record for making life miserable for gay staffers.

Still, what Schmalz was allowed to do at the *Times* was a huge departure from the norms of journalism, and it's fair to wonder what comes next. Sydney Schanberg, a *New York Newsday* columnist and Schmalz's former boss at the *Times*, writes that Schmalz "was able to push back the boundaries at the nation's most important newspaper" and that his "tightrope act" of being "an affirming AIDS beacon but not an activist . . . was his gift to future reporters, those who want to extend journalism's limits."

Pushing back boundaries? Extending journalism's limits? Personally,

I don't want reporters to be affirming beacons for any ailment or any cause. I want them to park their prisms at the door, and just tap out the news as objectively as possible. Even under a death sentence, such as Schmalz's, I think it's wrong for reporters to bring their allegiances and travails into their stories. And if you think it was a good idea for Schmalz to do this, try imagining similar reportage colored by other diseases or other allegiances. Opinion belongs in op-ed pieces and columns.

A few years ago, all this would have been totally obvious to anyone in the business. But now it's not. And the reason is that the same pressures against objectivity and detachment that hit the universities a decade or so ago are beginning to hit the newsroom now. Then we heard that college curriculums were really politicized expressions of the dominant culture. Now we are starting to hear that the rules of journalism were set by and for white males, or straight white males, and that "excluded" voices and perspectives must be added. Schmalz seemed to buy a bit of this. He once wrote that blacks writing about blacks and women writing about women represented "the cutting edge of journalism." But it could only be the cutting edge by departing from traditional standards and inserting the reporter into the story.

Dorothy Gilliam, *Washington Post* columnist and current president of the National Association of Black Journalists, wrote a few years ago that "Part of the mold that needs to be broken is the illusion that journalism is a quasi-science. It isn't. Journalism is a subjective, value-driven exercise. There is neither one truth nor one way to frame reality." This is the multi-truth vision of what the news should be. If it means that newsrooms should be as varied as possible so the collective news judgment of the staff is broader and surer, then fine. But if it means that the reporter's perspective determines a "truth," or that news should be filtered through tribal prisms, then journalism is in trouble.

HUGO LASHES NEWSROOM

What can you say about a hurricane named Hugo? If you are a storm-tossed reporter, just about anything you like. But it is best to remember that in journalistic lingo it is obligatory that storms be viewed as persons.

"A hurricane has a mind of its own," a weather forecaster told *The Washington Post.* Just so. But its mind is small, and unresolved childhood problems are apparently large. This is why people like Hugo go around ravaging, slamming, threatening and unleashing wrath and fury before regretfully coming to their senses, "whimpering out in rainfall over southern Canada."

Hugo may be our most therapized hurricane so far. Perhaps overexposed to Geraldo Rivera, *Time* magazine saw Satanist influences, comparing Hugo to "a holiday cruise ship from hell" and pointing knowingly to its "devilishly timed onslaught on Charleston." This was in the cover story. A sidebar explicitly rejected the Geraldian analysis, beginning with the sharp theological rebuke, "It was an act of God." *Newsweek,* on the other hand, hinted at the influence of a bellicose military parent. Its cover story, "Hugo Is a Killer," pointed out analogies to three American conflicts: the Civil War ("a pounding reminiscent of the Confederate bombardment of 1861"), the Indian wars ("It was the wild west and the Indians") and World War II ("towns like Christianstaad looked like miniature Hiroshimas").

In headlines, the *New York Daily News* favored the traditional S&M explanation for hurricanes: "Hugo Lashed Puerto Rico" and "Puerto Rico Is Racked." But in the text, the tabloid broke new ground by viewing Hugo as an aspiring actor. Mark Prendergast, reporting from Room 416 in the San Juan Howard Johnson, wrote that his balcony "became an impromptu gallery for Nature's Show of Shows." He was particularly impressed when the hurricane's "ferocious eye, casting a passing, sidelong glance, staged an awesome performance." Hugo may have been in a musical. Another news reporter, Michael McGovern, pointed out that the storm passed through Folly Beach, where Gershwin wrote *Porgy and Bess,* whereas Prendergast was reminded of *Les Miserables* (the Hugo connection).

The truth, however, is darker than the newsweeklies and the *News* would have you believe. Hugo was no ordinary, beered-up rowdy or overblown actor. He was a rapist. A Massachusetts television reporter said Hugo "stripped and violated." Juan Gonzalez of the *Daily News* accused Hugo of raping a rain forest. The *Boston Globe* quoted someone as saying, "Those islands were caught naked, and Hugo was just able to have its way." And Dan Rather himself used the word "rape" to describe Hugo's behavior.

This is a very serious charge against Hugo, but we can be sure that his many friends will rally around when he is extradited, whimpering, from Canada. He may be eligible for the Twinkie defense, or perhaps the American Psychoanalytic Association will find him the blameless victim of an affliction known as "paraphilic rapism," a suggested defense of rape. *Time* magazine may have laid the groundwork for the Flip Wilson defense—the devil made him do it.

Personally, I think Charleston is to blame. She obviously led him on. She knew Hugo's reputation, but she stayed to meet him anyway, bedecked with all those flimsy, see-through cottages. What else did she expect?

WOODY AND YOGI EXPLAIN IT ALL

"The heart wants what it wants," Woody Allen told Walter Isaacson of *Time* magazine. This shows that even under pressure, with scandalous charges breaking around him, Woody can still think up catchy axioms. He's been doing it at least since "Ninety percent of life is just showing up," and "When you do comedy, you are not sitting at the grownups' table."

Given the circumstances, his new saying is somewhat short on humor. But it's just as clearly the work of an intellectual. It is an updating of Blaise Pascal's "The heart has its reasons which reason knows nothing of," the only difference being that Pascal didn't write his famous line to defend an affair with his longtime lover's adopted daughter.

Woody's new aphorism is based on identity, a fancy way of saying that the second half just repeats the first half, thus producing some instant alleged wisdom. Suppose you complain to your butcher that the pork chop he is trying to sell you has several troubling green and black spots on one side. He might well reply, "It is what it is, lady."

Pre-Woody examples of this type of quotation would include "A rose is a rose is a rose" (Gertrude Stein), "What matters is what matters" (William Bennett), "There's finished and there's finished" (Mario Puzo), "A jerk is a jerk" (many authors), "You can observe a lot by watching" and "It ain't over till it's over" (both by Yogi Berra) and the most famous of all, "When you're hot, you're hot; when you're not, you're not" (Flip Wilson).

Possibly all these lines flitted through Woody's mind as the *Time* interview wound down, with thoughts of Flip and Yogi jostling with those of Pascal, William and Dan Quayle, who once observed, "Teachers are the main people who teach our children."

Thinking up memorable aphorisms is harder than it seems. Who can forget "If you've seen one slum, you've seen them all" (Spiro Agnew). Eugene McCarthy created two brilliant sayings, one on congressional reform ("If you purify the pond, the water lilies die"), one on presidential campaigning ("Never say anything that anybody might remember").

Senator Bill Bradley recently said, "Get an elbow, give an elbow." This is an ex-jock's version of "An eye for an eye." Had he been a hockey player, instead of a hoopster, he might have simply said, "A tooth for a tooth," or perhaps "A bent nose for a bent nose." Runner-up to Senator Bill for most solemn aphorism of the year, and the clear winner for pith, is William Bennett's "Hanging works." (He is obviously correct—look at the low recidivism rate among the hanged.)

Political aphorisms probably should be placed on the endangered list. In four years, President Bush came up with only one notable one, delivered to news-starved reporters during the seasick summit at Malta: "If you're looking for a surprise, the surprise is that there's no surprise."

Michael Kinsley is a steady source of good aphorisms. "Conservatives are always looking for converts, whereas liberals are always looking for heretics," he wrote. I would remove the "whereas" and stick in a semicolon, but this is picky. The best revised and reversed campaign slogan came from Mark Shields. He was writing about Eleanor Holmes Norton, who was running for the job of nonvoting representative from the Distict of Columbia, even though she had not paid her taxes for eight straight years. "Representation Without Taxation" should be the slogan, Shields said smartly. This is no aphorism, merely the political wisecrack of the year.

The wounded remains of those who gallantly try for aphorisms can only give us pause. Here, for example, is an attempt by Mark Kleiman, a lecturer at Harvard's Kennedy School of Government, to aphorize over the perils of drug legalization: "In a singing contest, never award the prize to the second soprano until you've heard her sing, even if the first soprano was awful."

A manful effort, but it lacks minimum daily requirements. People rarely walk around quoting twenty-five-word maxims with two conditional clauses, particularly when the imagery evokes the classic "It's not over till the fat lady sings (eight words, one clause, just one soprano). Here is Norman Mailer, writing in *New Woman* magazine: "Novels are like wives—you can't talk about them. But movies are different—they are like mistresses and you can brag a bit." Or how about Werner Ehrhard, partially eclipsed inventor of Est: "It's fun to be yourself; the self is fun to the self." (Werner, go to your room; take M. Scott Peck, M.D., with you.)

Years of aphoristic analysis reveal surefire construction methods, for example the familiar *a* is to *b* as *c* is to *d* ("Treating heroin addiction with methadone is like treating scotch addiction with bourbon"— Thomas Szasz) and the relativistic but evocative *a* is *a* to you, but *b* to me ("One man's ceiling is another man's floor"—Paul Simon).

If this is no help, try knocking off an existing aphorism: "When you're hot, you're hot, and when you're not, everyone's watching." The most knocked-off seem to be "Patriotism is the last refuge of the scoundrel" and "Religion is the opiate of the masses." Recent contenders here include Barbara Ehrenreich ("Work is the secret hedonism of the middle class") and Jefferson Morley ("Moderation is the opiate of the centrists").

Morley's bold defense of moderation recalls Gene McCarthy's antimoderation aphorism: "Most accidents happen in the middle of the road," as well as my own judicious tailoring of "Let it all hang out": "We might perhaps consider letting half of it hang out."

Woody Allen, of course, had no time to sit around buffing and polishing aphorisms. He had to come up with one right away, preferably one that made him look good. There was no external agitator to blame things on, so he pointed the finger toward an internal one: the heart. This is not the male organ normally cited to explain affairs such as this, but it was a shrewd choice. The heart, after all, enjoys a good reputation in America, and has its own holiday, Valentine's Day. So it's in good shape to take the fall. "The heart" wanted something, and dragged Woody along, kicking and screaming, fully against his will. There was nothing he could do—he was clearly a passive victim of erratic heart action. As Flip Wilson said, in a less polished version of the same idea, "The devil made me do it." Woody, welcome to *Bartlett's*.

PART THREE

"HOW DOES THE BATHER KNOW WHEN TO SCREAM?"

Community, Rights, and Family

OUR "LET'S PRETEND" SOCIAL POLICY

Marshall McLuhan used to ask: "If the temperature of the bath water rises one degree every ten minutes, how will the bather know when to scream?"

The point of this quasi-aphorism—that people have a tendency to adjust to a gathering disaster instead of confronting or escaping it—is also the point of a brilliant bit of social criticism in the winter 1993 issue of *The American Scholar*.

The article, by Senator Daniel Patrick Moynihan of New York, has a jawbreaking academic title, "Defining Deviancy Down," but its point is very simple: America is undergoing a profound social crisis, and the nation has more or less decided to pretend that it isn't happening.

Moynihan doesn't use the word "pretend." He uses the psychological word "denial," and the sociological word "normalizing," but it amounts to the same thing. By "normalizing," he means that some excruciatingly hot bath water is now accepted as a normal, everyday feature of American life. Once defined as normal, it needn't be confronted, or even much commented on.

Crime is the most obvious example. Inner-city kids are routinely gunned down by stray bullets while walking to school or sitting in their apartments. Sounds of gunfire are not unusual in schools and upscale neighborhoods. A New York judge, Edwin Torres, says that "the slaughter of the innocent marches unabated: subway riders, bodega owners, cab drivers, babies; in laundromats, at cash machines, on elevators, in hallways." In a letter to Moynihan he talked of "the numbness, this near narcoleptic state" of the public that no longer expects anything better. People have simply adjusted to it as a new reality. As Moynihan says, "The crime level has been normalized."

Moynihan talks about welfare, a problem he has studied for almost thirty years. According to a projection for children born in the year 1980, he says, 22.2 percent of white children and 82.9 percent of black children will be dependent on welfare before reaching age eighteen. These are stunning numbers. In a nation that cared about its future, a real marshaling of resources would be under way. But as Moynihan says, "There is little evidence that these facts are regarded as a calamity in municipal government." Or in state or federal government either.

Like crime and welfare, the broader social crisis has been normalized as well. The crisis can be easily sketched in by the astonishing statistics on teen pregnancy, family breakup, teen suicide, street violence, murders by children, the burgeoning jail population, sexual disease, child sex abuse, drug use, gun incidents in schools and so forth. Taken together, these statistics show a vast social disaster unfolding.

How has the nation come to accept all this so stoically? Moynihan argues that society can handle only so much deviant behavior before it overloads and begins to accept the behavior as normal. An example would be the current attempt to legalize drugs because drug abuse is so widespread and jails are full. This is roughly what happened under deinstitutionalization, when mental patients were dumped on city streets, redefined as functional or "homeless," and became part of the normal landscape.

But there are other redefinitions that do not follow overload, but often precede and help produce it. Observe the redefining that occurs when "illegitimate birth" becomes "out-of-wedlock birth" and then "single parenting." Or when family breakdown is verbally refurbished and emerges as "alternative family structure."

The redefinition of the fatherless or broken family as an optional, worthy family form has been a fateful step in allowing the social crisis to loom as large as it is. A casual attitude toward family breakup and single parenting is an important article of faith among the intelligentsia, "the chattering classes" in the press and academe. In fact, it has hardened into an ideology that dismisses the two-parent norm as Ozzie-and-Harriet nostalgia.

This is a rather important dereliction on the part of the intellectual class. So far no amount of real-world evidence has shaken this faith that family structure doesn't matter, and that single parenting is somehow just as good as two-parent childrearing. The evidence is in and it is incontrovertible: children raised in single-parent homes, as a group, pay a devastating price economically, psychologically and emotionally for the absence of the missing parent, typically the father. Fatherlessness and family breakup stand out in research as key variables in most statistics measuring the social crisis.

One family expert, David Blankenhorn of the Institute for American Values, says that the social science data on the impact of single parenting is so clear, but so unacceptable to the intelligentsia, "that it's the equivalent of having to argue over and over that the world is round. If it were just a matter of evidence, we wouldn't be having this debate. It would be over."

When evidence is clear, and bright people won't accept it, we are in the presence of psychological denial. The sad truth is that America's social crisis won't be solved, or even addressed, until there's enough outrage to cut through the denial and pretense that keep it going.

DROWNING IN RIGHTS

Consider the deranged homeless man on the corner, screaming at passersby. He may be in rough shape, but he is bristling with rights. He has the right to welfare and the right to medical treatment. If he is too confused to want his broken leg set, he has the right to no treatment and, presumably, the right to a permanent limp. He has a right to loiter: The antivagrancy laws are mostly gone. In New York City he has the "right to shelter." He also has the "right to no shelter," which the city can override only to keep him from freezing to death. He pretty much has the right to live (and to shriek and defecate) wherever he wants. And derangement is not sufficient cause to bring him back to the asylum for the care he obviously needs. He may be dangerous, but if he hasn't proved it yet by physically harming himself or others, he has a right to remain crazy on the streets. Call it "the right to permanent public madness" or "the right to die unhelped."

The problem here is not lack of compassion, but the quiet lunacy of a rights-based approach to the problem of homelessness and mental illness. In New York, the court-imposed "right to shelter"—the city must now come up with a free bed for anybody who requests one—has forced a beleaguered and nearly bankrupt city to pay staggering costs. It is drawing more people into the program (just as the "right to welfare" did), and it siphons away millions of dollars that might have been better spent on a more direct approach to curb homelessness. The city has always had shelters, but note that nobody voted to make a free night's lodging a "right." Rights rhetoric, plus one judge, imposed it.

Our politics are being distorted by this language of rights. Mary Ann

Glendon, professor of law at Harvard, calls it "rights talk," and her book with that title argues that "discourse about rights has become the principal language that we use in public settings to discuss weighty issues of right and wrong, but time and again it proves inadequate." In rights talk, every need and desire and cause tends to emerge as a right: animal rights, smokers' rights, prisoner rights, consumer rights, victim rights, housing rights, the right to drug treatment, the right to clean air and guns and privacy, the right to die. The abortion controversy keeps conjuring up unsuspected new rights, most recently "the right to know" (the sex of a fetus) and "the right not to be born" (abortion in cases of seriously deformed fetuses).

In her earlier book, *Abortion and Divorce in Western Law*, Glendon showed that America is the only nation in the world that views abortion, legally and popularly, as a clash of rights: the right to choose versus the right to life. In most European nations, the fetus has no automatic right to be born. The issue depends on circumstances. And a pregnant woman has no absolute right to abort. In some societies, counseling is mandatory and good reasons are required before sacrificing the life of a fetus. The compromise that eludes America seems impossible because of the national (and judicial) addiction to the rhetoric of rights talk.

Why do so many people talk this way? Well, it's a very useful language for those demanding services. Defining and protecting rights is important in any political culture, but this culture has reached the point where the obsession with individual rights is making it hard for us to think socially, let alone restore the balance between individual and community rights, between personal rights and personal obligations. Rights-talk has become so overwhelming that it distorts, coopts or obliterates issues that are clearly social. ("Animal rights," for instance, is an example of an obligation decked out as a right: sea slugs and cockroaches don't have "rights," but humans have a responsibility to treat the animal world and the environment with more care and respect.)

As Glendon argues, rights talk polarizes debate; it tends to suppress moral discussion and consensus building. Once an agenda is introduced as a "right," sensible discussion and moderate positions tend to disappear.

Rights are trump cards. After all, if you have a right to something, that right or entitlement cannot be compromised away by the give and take of politics. It soars above brokered consensus politics, usually by demands upon courts and bureaucrats. Our judicialized politics, in which the Supreme Court, and not our paralyzed Congress, is the real legislative tribunal, both reflects and encourages rights talk. Rights talk constantly pleads for an end run around democratic politics, government without the messiness of gaining the consent of the governed.

Glendon thinks that as a language, "the American rights dialect" has begun to invade private discussions—that families, clubs and town meetings are aping the public take-no-prisoners rhetoric of unyielding interest groups. And the notion of a common good is constantly eroded. Glendon writes: "Our overblown rights rhetoric and our vision of the rights-bearer as an autonomous individual channel our thoughts away from what we have in common and focus them on what separates us." It also keeps our politics tightly focused on grievance and oppression: if an agenda is presented as a set of rights that the majority refuses to endorse, then it follows that the majortiy must be bigots bent on domination. Rights talk thus becomes the official tongue of overheated, self-absorbed, no-compromise, fragmented intergroup politics. The language and its lexicographers and rhetoricians have a lot to answer for.

THE POLITICS OF HATE

Hate-crime laws are not very controversial, but they should be. Take the Bias-Related Crime Act up before the city council of the District of Columbia. If the act passes, criminals who attack anyone because of race, creed, ethnicity or sexual orientation would face one and one-half times the current maximum punishment.

The general idea behind this bill, and all the others like it, is that special protection is due to blacks, Jews, homosexuals, Hispanics, Asians and others who are often attacked for being what they are, unlike, say, middle-aged white Protestants in country clubs.

That sounds fine, but there is an obvious problem. The legislation in effect divides America into two classes: those whose skulls can be cracked with a criminal penalty of, let us say, six months in jail, and those whose skulls are better protected by government and thus warrant nine months in jail if cracked. You could, of course, look at it the other way round: the District of Columbia is thinking of offering hatemongers a one-third discount on their sentences if they attack a generic white-bread American instead of a minority group member.

This is an odd business, but let us be fair. You don't qualify for those three extra months in the jug just by smashing a Hare Krishna over the head with his tambourine. You have to indicate contempt for the cult itself. Most of the time it comes down to any anti-Krishna epithets hurled during the crime. This gets courts into a maelstrom—calibrating the actual hate content of insults when adrenaline flows. If a white mugs a black and delivers a slur in the process, is it a "hate crime" or an ordinary mugging with a gratuitous slur attached? Why should courts be in the business of judging these misty matters? If the skulls of all Americans are equally valuable (that is, if this is a democracy), why not just give everyone nine months for cracking any cranium at all?

When there is strong resistance to such laws, their backers adopt a backup position: they push for hate-crime statistics laws. Politicians love to vote against hate, so these bills tend to pass easily. Congress passed a national one. It requires the Justice Department to break down and list all crimes by "manifest prejudice based on certain group characteristics," a vague and infinitely expandable standard.

What's wrong with compiling hate statistics? On the face of it, not much. Hate is a bad thing. Publicizing and deploring it is a good thing. But this is an expensive bill in terms of scutwork and dubiously spent man-hours. The rationale for it (better deployment of law enforcement personnel, the discovery of unsuspected hate problems) is massively unconvincing. Then why is it being pushed so hard? The real answer, I think, is that more and more aggrieved groups want to magnify their victim status. This is one of the little intergroup truths nobody talks about: the more victimized you seem, the more political leverage you have. If the stats showed, for example, that in the wake of the Rushdie affair, anti-Moslem crime in America seemed to be approaching the level of anti-Jewish crime, it would amount to a strong case for far greater public attention. Moslem status in America would be greatly enhanced. Doors would open. Wisecracks about the ayatollah would begin to sound like hurtful religious and ethnic slurs. Press coverage of the Middle East would be scrutinized more carefully for anti-Moslem bias. Access to educational materials used in schools' tolerance programs would increase. Moslem sidekicks would turn up in sitcoms. The Democratic party would put a Moslem on every committee.

But you cannot win the victimization olympics without lots of plain hard work. Moslem leaders would have to mount a major campaign stressing the victim role and urging believers to report any offense, however slight or ambiguous. More important, they would have to convince Moslems to feel more victimized than they currently do. Otherwise they lose. Homosexuals understand this process clearly. This is why gay activists have made "gay-bashing" a major promotional and organizational issue for years. It is an explicit decision to opt for horror stories, anger and the victim's role. As the gay writers Marshall Kirk and Hunter Madsen say in their book *After the Ball,* "Gays must . . . be portrayed as victims of violence and humiliation . . . and countless other miseries."

Real victims should complain. The problem is that we have evolved a broad politics of group victimology in which slights and crimes get all tangled up with the social goals of the complaining group. One by-product is elliptical and dishonest debate. In the House debate on the statistics bill, Representative George Gekas, a Pennsylvania Republican, wondered why homosexuals should be one of the victim categories, and not, say, the elderly, the disabled, abused children, bus passengers and slain policemen. Gerry Studds, a Massachusetts Democrat, rose to respond. "Gay-bashing" is the most frequent form of hate crime, he said. Besides, "there is no centuries-old tradition of hatred against bus passengers, policemen, the handicapped and the young."

This was not just an exchange between a gay congressman and a congressman unsympathetic to gays. It was also a classic exercise in comparative victimology: Studds made too vast a victim claim for his own group, in the process brushing off quite similar claims on behalf of the old, the disabled and abused children. Gekas tried to deny homosexuals high victim status because he knows, as the gays know, that sustained victimology can lead to political gains and more social approval.

There is no way to overstress how this spread of victimology poisons our politics. It perversely breeds competition for Most Favored Victim status. It pushes angry people into leadership positions and undermines optimism and balance. It has balkanized and enfeebled the national Democratic party. Isn't it time to stop?

MORE STIGMA, PLEASE

Behind the Murphy Brown flap is the old issue of stigma, society's attempt to remain unapologetically appalled by certain behavior. This is not an era in which many people are eager to come out in favor of stigma. But there are a few exceptions. Ed Koch, while still mayor of New York City, said we should probably try to revive the stigma against unwed mothers. (To protect himself, he should have suggested a brand-new stigma against absent and oblivious unwed fathers.)

This is strikingly similar to some recent commentary on the decline of the family, white and black. For example, sociologist William Julius Wilson has argued fiercely that the disintegration of the inner-city black family has been mostly due to economics, but now he is willing to talk the language of stigma: "The decline in marriage among inner-city blacks is not simply a function of the proportion of jobless men. . . . It is reasonable to consider the effects of weaker social strictures against out-of-wedlock births."

Though the word stigma has a righteous, almost medieval, ring to the modern ear, attempts to stigmatize are all around us. Both of our national political parties, for example, are in the process of reattaching the old stigma of being on welfare. That traditional faint stigma once served to motivate people to get off the dole as quickly as possible. It faded in the sixties as welfare came to be seen as a "right" or as society's poor response to structural economic problems.

An example of a recently concluded stigma contest is smoking. The battle is over, and the antismokers have won. The burning and inhaling of dead plant matter will continue, but it is now a defiant, rearguard activity, best undertaken in a spirit of sheepishness or shame. Now officially stigmatized, smokers are exposed to a level of harassment that would have been considered shocking a few years ago. Ashtrays have vanished. Lighting up anywhere is likely to draw a withering glance. Studies will continue to find that smoking a cigar, even in an open field on a breezy day, endangers the lives of innocent children for miles around. More and more pressure and regulation will be bought to bear on tobacco addicts. That is the way stigma works.

Another duel that is currently going well for the stigmatizers revolves around animal rights. The fur industry is very vulnerable because it is not in a position to mount a serious counterargument. Furs are not necessities, just status symbols, and such symbols change with blinding speed in America. Yesterday's glamorous mink-wearer is tomorrow's accomplice in the mass murder of tiny furry creatures. Wealthy women are sneaking out the back of fur salons. How long can such furtive departures be associated with high status?

Mothers Against Drunk Driving have taken a light stigma and converted it into a very heavy one. The flurry of interest in how much jail time Michael Milken would serve involved a muddled and inconclusive stigma contest over the economic buccaneering of the 1980s. And the increasingly loud argument over gay rights is not really about rights, but about stigma. The straight majority has no stomach for isolating or penalizing gays, but it is not willing to grant that homosexual behavior has the same value and meaning as normal heterosexual sex. The logic of this, which many straights feel somewhat embarrassed about, is a faint stigma against homosexuality. For some, it leads to a high-wire act—an attempt to stigmatize homosexuality as a condition, without penalizing homosexuals as people.

Efforts to stigmatize drug taking have always run afoul of the sixties generation and its tendency to identify drugs with liberation and now nostalgia. At the moment, the issue is not greatly relevant. The drug destroying us is crack, and it is consumed by people who are not known to respond well to middle-class stigma contests.

Stigma is considered a dirty word partly because a group of influential social scientists changed our understanding of the term. In the sixties, sociologists began to look at society from the bottom up. A huge number of studies appeared focusing on outsiders and "deviants"—prostitutes, homosexuals, transvestites, hoboes, winos, gamblers, addicts, beach bums and carnival workers. The studies were done from the outsiders' point of view. Before long, the stigmatization of bad behavior and low-life activities came to be seen as oppression by an intolerant majority.

"There is only one complete, unblushing male in America," wrote Erving Goffman, the most influential of the sociologists who studied stigma. "He is a young, married, white urban, Northern, heterosexual, Protestant father, of college education, fully employed, of good complexion, weight and height, and a recent record in sports." This was powerful rhetoric. What Professor Goffman and others were doing then, and what the cultural-diversity people are doing now, is reducing all stigma to prejudice, or illegitimate social control of individual behavior. In fact, this position is not consistently held—many who say they oppose all stigma are trying to stigmatize many activities, from animal experimentation to smoking and drinking.

Stigma contests, which clarify and define social values, go on all the time in every community, at every level. There's no need to fear a process that all societies engage in to protect themselves from behavior that weakens or disorders social life. Let the stigma contests flourish.

AN END TO WELFARE

Welfare did not cause the rioting in Los Angeles, but the rioting caused a shift in thinking about welfare.

Before L.A., most analysts seemed to think that the Family Support Act of 1988 should be given time to take hold. That law basically requires a tenth of welfare recipients to accept training or part-time work. It's a real reform, but one with lots of loopholes that's unlikely to cut the caseload by more than 6 or 7 percent. And Senator Moynihan, author of the plan, says it will take until the year 2000 to show results.

In the wake of L.A., that looks too leisurely and small-scale. We have seen a sudden upsurge in demands for a plan of national service, and for government-sponsored work programs based on FDR's Works Progress Administration and Civilian Conservation Corps. Since makework programs are a hard sell, even in a recession, it makes sense to hook this idea to the national aggravation over long-term welfare dependency.

One result is that a WPA-style program by Senator David Boren, greeted with yawns when first introduced, is suddenly a hot item. It would create jobs—ranging from road building and infrastructure repair to park maintenance—and require people on welfare to take them. Only mothers of small children would be exempted.

Before L.A., many people dismissed this sort of plan as "slavefare." Now there is more willingness to say that work must be found—or created—on a large scale. It is too late in the day simply to hand out checks and allow the abilities of millions of Americans to atrophy into second- and third-generation welfare dependency.

The logic of this kind of thinking is to avoid the mincing half-steps and go all the way: spend a great deal of money on jobs creation and totally dismantle the welfare system.

By coincidence, a very good book suggests this: Mickey Kaus's *The End of Equality*. Kaus, a senior editor at *The New Republic*, talks about junking the whole welfare apparatus—Aid to Families with Dependent Children, food stamps, housing subsidies—and replacing it with a single, simple offer from government: employment for every able-bodied American citizen over eighteen who wants it, in a useful public job at a wage slightly below the minimum wage for private-sector work.

Kaus's argument is a simple and direct one that avoids the long debate about whether welfare incentives encouraged family disintegration and the rise of various social pathologies. He says this: regardless of what caused the creation of underclass culture, that culture is kept alive by welfare payments. If you are serious about shutting down a culture based on welfare and saving those trapped inside it, you must shut down welfare. "You have to somehow deny benefits to one-parent families, unplug the underclass culture's life support system."

Would this apply to mothers of young children? Yes. Two-thirds of American mothers are in the workforce. Since most single mothers work, it is hard to argue that certain selected single mothers should be paid to stay home. Day-care centers would be required, but perhaps not on a grand scale. Kaus points out that a large percentage of single mothers who move off welfare prefer to make their own child-care arrangements.

Jobs would vary, depending on abilities. If someone refused a job, there would be no penalty, but also no check. Welfare recipients would be in the same position as everyone else—work, or find some other way to get along. There would still be homeless shelters, soup kitchens and help from charitable organizations. Kaus writes: "This aid will be stigmatizing (as it must be if work is to be honored) and frankly paternalistic, but it could also be compassionate." The government should offer job training and counseling, but no cash handouts.

It's easy to think up a dozen serious objections to the plan. Unions would fight it tooth and nail. WPA-style results would be unlikely from a new batch of demoralized workers with few or no good work habits. What happens to the children of those who fail? Possibilities of leaf-raking boondoggles would enrage the public. How many families could survive on pay kept below the minimum wage? And the cost would be staggering. Kaus thinks it could run $50 billion, minus the value of work produced. (On the other hand, welfare has cost more than $900 billion over the last eight years.)

By making work the norm, the program would bring dignity to new workers and take the edge off much social strife. A lot of that friction looks like class or racial antagonism but is actually a resentment of the dole generated by the nation's strong commitment to the work ethic. And the new workers would gain skills and something to put on resumes that would make them attractive to the private sector.

Kaus says his idea is an obvious one "combining as it does the ancient Democratic dream of a guaranteed job with traditional antipathy to a dole." A left-right consensus has already appeared on the failures of welfare, and another left-right consensus may now be forming on the value of some WPA-style job programs. It's time to talk about whether we should combine the two and put welfare out of its misery.

ADDICTED TO ADDICTIONS

The social sciences have their fashions, and a current one is to view habits as addictions. To many psychologists, and to the flotilla of self-help writers bobbing in their wake, yesterday's womanizer is all too often today's sex addict, and a man or woman who seems to fall in love too often, by the standards of psychologists who monitor such matters, is said to be suffering from "relationship addiction." Besides love, sex, gambling and procrastination, the addiction label has descended upon jogging, fitness and even the overconsumption of chocolates.

Trends such as this are usually harmless, but this one has consequences. A habit is something a person is responsible for, but the word "addict" vaguely implies an innocent person thrashing about helplessly in the grip of a powerful outside force. This effect is heightened when the linguistic sleight of hand escalates from "addiction" to "disease," which neatly converts the person with a dismal habit into a full-fledged victim of medical disaster, like a cancer patient or a hemophiliac. Here is a book reviewer in the *Los Angeles Times* thrilling to the idea (in

Robin Norwood's books) that yesterday's habit and today's addiction is tomorrow's true medical ailment: "Simply by postulating romantic obsession as a disease, a progressive disease like alcoholism, that, if left untreated, can literally cost you your life, sends electric shocks through the reader's brain."

In this passage, the writer makes the rather large assumption that alcoholism, widely considered a disease a century ago, has been the subject of some backsliding, and after being laboriously demedicalized, is ready to emerge once again as a true disease. As it happens, the 1993 style guidelines of the L.A. Times announce that alcoholism is a disease. This drive to reposition problem drinking as some sort of medical ailment is one of the more controversial attempts at social definition now in progress. It is also one that the Supreme Court has recently refused to address in a case brought by two recovered alcoholics, both ex-GIs, against the Veterans' Administration. In effect, the vets said they missed the entire ten-year eligibility period for veterans' educational benefits because they were too drunk to notice the time slipping by. So they asked for an extension, on grounds that the disease of alcoholism was to blame. In ruling four-three against the veterans on narrow jurisdictional grounds, the Court neatly reflected the debate it declined to settle. In the minority, Justice Blackmun cited genetic factors at work in alcoholism and scoffed at the VA's contention that the plaintiffs' heavy drinking was "willful misconduct," while Justice White's majority opinion dryly noted that "the consumption of alcohol is not regarded as wholly involuntary."

In defense of the disease theory, some point to recent evidence of genetic and biological predispositions to problem drinking. But a predisposition is not a disease, or many teetotalers, who have never had a drink in their lives, would have to be defined as alcoholics. Besides, some of the same evidence is turning up in research on tobacco use, and no one thinks heavy smoking is a disease. Genetic markers might one day be found for nail-biting and violent behavior, but if they are, no one will consider them diseases either. They are simply some possible behaviors that are more or less under conscious control.

To defend the notion of disease, proponents tend to glide lightly from predisposition to full-blown alcoholism. Those of us who believe that people often drink heavily to escape or relieve conflict are told we have it backward: the conflict and stress are a consequence, not a cause of this "disease." Dr. Nicholas Pace, who treats a great many problem drinkers at Pace Health Services in Manhattan, says that the soul-sick drunks of Eugene O'Neill and Tennessee Williams are disappearing behind the curtains: "If we thought that yesterday's alcoholic was haunted by internal conflict, we know that today's is primarily haunted by his liver." The real protagaonist in A Moon for the Misbegotten, Jim Tyrone's liver, never made it onstage.

In part, the idea that alcoholism is a disease is shaped by the requirements of insurance plans. Without a diagnosis of some specific ailment, insurance companies will not pay. In psychiatry, this means that doctors often go through the motions of gravely diagnosing such officially listed disorders as oppositional defiant disorder and developmental expressive writing disorder.

Alcohol dependence is listed, and so are inhalant abuse, nicotine dependence and caffeinism, also known unofficially as being hooked on coffee or cola. Psychiatrists and psychologists do not imagine that these are real ailments, but something must be written down so a troubled client can be helped. Occasionally, though, the polite fictions go too far.

Paraphilic rapism, or the disposition to commit rape, was briefly suggested as an official diagnosis. Here the excuse for bad behavior, latent in terms like alcoholism, was too obvious and gross. It also had ominous legal implications as yet another "ism" that makes a perpetrator not responsible for his actions.

Compassion, as well as insurance needs, pushes the disease theory. It seems much less moralistic to talk of heavy drinking in clinical language, as if it were a real medical entity. But the language of medicine leads to the passive expectation of an outside cure when the alcoholic desperately needs to take charge himself. In his book A New Language for Psychoanalysis analyst Roy Schafer makes a similar point: action language prepares a patient for taking control of his life ("I am very angry"); the use of nouns ("I am filled with anger") makes it seem that the real culprit is an outside personified substance.

A good many odd legal cases have already been brought as a result of the last linguistic booby trap erected around the alcohol problem. The Rehabilitation Act of 1973, which banned discrimination against physically or mentally handicapped persons, was reinterpreted in 1977 to include alcoholism as a handicap. Thus alcoholism was repositioned legally as a natural deficiency like blindness or lameness. Quirky law and diffused ideas of responsibilty can flow directly from semantic confusion. Cancer is a disease. Blindness is a handicap. Alcoholism is a personal and social problem.

FIRE HYDRANTS AND SCHOOL BLOCKADES

Youngsters open fire hydrants in the summer and firemen close them to keep water pressure up. It's an age-old urban ritual, but New York City has just changed the ceremony. Now the kids open the hydrants, and if they are pugnacious about it, the firefighters back down and the kids win.

In certain areas, rocks and bottles are tossed whenever hydrant-closers arrive. The standard practice of offering free spray caps hasn't worked. In one case, a hard spray was aimed at the cab of a firetruck, causing it to crash. It's not just about access to water during a heat wave. There's a sense that turf is somehow being invaded by the fire department, and that firefighters are authority figures worth rebelling against.

So the fire department issued a new directive. Firefighters are under orders to back off from confrontations, though they are allowed to try closing the hydrants "at a later time." (Perhaps in the fall?)

In effect the city has "solved" its hydrant problem by turning control of the hydrants over to potential troublemakers. On the street, everyone now knows that firefighters will fade away if growled at. A letter to the editor of the *Daily News* correctly called it a scary precedent that borders on anarchy. What's next, the letter-writer asked, police avoiding gun-bearing thugs?

Policies like this are as demoralizing as major crimes. Cities are haunted by the fear that no one is really in charge, that the nominal government can't or won't keep order, that it is willing to cede any ground and collapse any standard to avoid trouble. Authorities keep backpedaling. Menaces aren't confronted. They are adjusted to and become part of the system.

Guns in school? Just buy metal detectors. Schoolgirls getting pregnant? Just hand out condoms and work out a day-care system for high-school mothers. Residents, too, adjust to ever-higher levels of disorder.

If your children are mugged on the way to school, just give them their daily "mugger money" to offer up on the streets. It's a sort of semi-organized psychic retreat from city life.

That's why former police commissioner Raymond Kelly called for "a new level of intolerance" in New York. "No Radio" signs, he said, are flags of urban surrender that really mean "Please break into somebody else's car." "We need to tear up our 'No Radio' signs and reclaim some dignity," Kelly said. "We can be slaves to our metal detectors and car alarms, or we can stage a revolt. I'm for staging a revolt."

Judge Jack Weinstein got the city's full attention, and irritated two ethnic groups, by coming out for his own brand of urban intolerance. Sentencing three Mafia killers, he called on Italian-Americans to discourage the young from joining the mob. And sentencing a largely Dominican group of defendants for welfare fraud, he called on Dominican leaders to discourage the spread of techniques for milking the welfare system.

Naturally, the judge was attacked on the dread charge of insensitivity. He was accused of ethnic stereotyping and of implying that Dominicans seem to have a higher tendency to commit crime than other people. But he didn't say that. He just said every community has to create standards and stand up against the crime of its members.

Here's another example, outside the city, of a crippling refusal to preserve basic order. In his syndicated column, Nat Hentoff reports that black students at Roslyn High School on Long Island sometimes block a school hallway near the gym. They let nonwhite students and white females pass through, but not white males.

The story came to light when a student who was pushed and punched wrote an article in the school paper about the blockade. Amazingly, the school administration has not acted. "They want to keep ignoring this," an editor of the school paper said to Hentoff. A teacher told Hentoff that the school won't come down on the blockaders because "they're disadvantaged. Some of them need more attention than most of the white students."

The administration doesn't seem to understand that it is undermining its own authority and promoting an expectation of social chaos. What rules can be taken seriously if students are allowed to conduct racial blockades? And if the school won't protect access for its students, how does it have the moral authority to teach anything at all?

The Roslyn case seems like a miniversion of what has happened on so many college campuses—authorities find themselves ignoring certain kind of outrages and gradually endorsing double standards, all out of fear about racial strife.

But the belief that large disasters can be averted by tolerating more and more small ones never works. Bonnie O'Neal, now retired, was an unusually effective police officer in the Mount Pleasant section of Washington, D.C. She cracked down hard on public drunkenness and rousted drug dealers and prostitutes from apartment stairwells. "There are rules of civility we all must embrace or there will be a perception of the neighborhood breaking down," she told *The Washington Post*. "If you give the impression that anything goes, sooner or later it will."

WHY GRAFFITI MATTERS

Graffiti is a big issue in Los Angeles. Litter is a major issue in downtown Philadelphia and panhandling is emerging as a dominant issue in a dozen cities. New York Mayor Rudy Giuliani has declared war on intimidating "squeegeemen" who wash windshields whether drivers like it or not. *Question:* Why should this be so? Aren't most of these cities swamped with far more urgent social problems?

Likely answer: the cities are displaying a significant shift in public attitudes. This shift is strongly in the direction of the "broken window" theory of social decline and decay.

The theory was outlined in a 1982 *Atlantic* article by political scientist James Q. Wilson and criminologist George Kelling. It says this: the key to social decay is a rising level of disorder that residents fail to challenge in time. When broken windows are not fixed, when graffiti and uncollected garbage become regular features and winos begin to doze off on stoops and sidewalks, a powerful signal goes out that the residents of the area have ceased to care about conditions. This leads to a break in morale and a feeling that events are out of control. Landlords don't make repairs. Vandalism spreads. The stage is set for prostitutes, druggies and criminals to drift in and the neighborhood goes under.

The "broken window" theory is upheld by a new book, *Disorder and Decline*, a study of forty urban neighborhoods by Wesley Skogan, professor of political science at Northwestern. But mayors and councilmen and city administrators haven't needed to wait for academic proof. More and more, they grasp the idea intuitively. That's why Los Angeles is aggressively trying to keep up with the flood of graffiti, why Philadelphia businessmen spent so much money to get the litter out of an eighty-block downtown area and why New York spent tens of millions of dollars to wipe graffiti from its subway system and keep it out.

The major lesson of the "broken window" theory is that the crucial battles to save a neighborhood must be fought over apparently minor social infractions, well below the threshold of police response. By the time the offenses are great enough to justify police time and effort, the struggle is often lost.

This is the real reason—not "the new war on the poor" or "compassion fatigue"—why panhandling has mushroomed into a sizeable political issue. In many cities, the life of downtown areas and the remaining stable residential neighborhoods is clearly at stake. Polls in cities such as Nashville and San Francisco show that large numbers of people are beginning to feel too intimidated and coerced by panhandlers to shop in downtown areas. Even in cities where almost nobody walks, such as Miami, the drifters who clean windshields at red lights have become a serious issue.

One political response has been the launching of a movement to encourage people not to give money to panhandlers, but to donate money instead to agencies that serve the poor and homeless. Part of this is a new realization that a great many beggars are con artists or addicts collecting money for wine or drugs. But part comes from a gut feeling, often confused and unarticulated, that things have gone too far, and that the quarter given to a panhandler is helping to finance the downward spiral of cities. A study by social scientists at Columbia University shows that 69 percent of Americans think the homeless should not be allowed to panhandle. But this appears to be "broken window" sentiment: the study also shows that most people are willing to pay more taxes to solve the problem.

The New York City Transit Authority went to court to ban beggars from the subways. It lost in district court but won on appeal. This was an important victory. It was not a triumph of the well-to-do over the poor. A large percentage of riders are blue-collar or poor themselves. It was not a victory for "compassion fatigue"—polls showed that sympathy for the plight of beggars and the homeless actually increased among the ridership after the court decision. Felonies decreased 15 percent.

A New York report said the public's attitude was this: "Get the homeless and the beggars out of the subway so they do not threaten the public (or one another) or interfere with other people's enjoyment of public spaces." The Authority listened to New Yorkers—polls were showing that 80 percent of city residents felt that begging and homelessness were serious, pervasive problems on the subway.

It acted on the proposition that the majority is right in claiming that public spaces must be kept open for orderly public use, free of hassles or coercion. Ten years ago, the suit probably could not have been filed in New York. It would have been out of bounds politically as an attack on social victims or individual freedom.

As usual, the American Civil Liberties Union doesn't even acknowledge the problem. "Sleeping is an innocent activity," says Helen Hershkoff of the ACLU. "I can't see that government has the right to regulate sleeping."

Hershkoff, who is in charge of the homeless docket for the ACLU, means that towns and cities have no right to keep vagrants, winos, addicts, mentally ill drifters, and the homeless from sleeping (i.e., living or camping) in parks, bus stations, on sidewalks and in other public spaces.

Alas, "Sleeping is an innocent activity" is not an example of clear thinking. It is an airy abstraction, far removed from urban reality. Fred Siegel, a historian at New York's Cooper Union specializing in urban affairs, calls the ACLU policy on the homeless "principled ignorance." He asks, "How can they keep sealing themselves off from the consequences of their action?"

But time marches on. I think we are coming to the end of a twenty-five-year experiment to see whether we can tolerate the consequences of social policies based entirely on individual rights and compassion. In my opinion, the answer is in: we can't. The disaster of deinstitutionalization is part of this. So is the gradual surrender of parks, bus depots, train stations and other public spaces. There is now a drive to reclaim those spaces and to find a better balance between the rights of the community and the rights of the individual. No one knows how this will develop, but the impatience with the old policies is all around us and it is starting to flow into the political mainstream.

OUR MISGUIDED SPEECH POLICE

Reformers have just unfurled a sweeping plan to eliminate all expressions of prejudice among California's 128,000 lawyers: a ban on words or conduct reflecting any bias in race, sex, religion, national origin, disability, age, sexual orientation or socioeconomic status.

Does this sound familiar?

It should. It is an off-campus version of the now notorious college speech codes. Muzzlers are on the march. Just when we thought we had the speech police pinned down on the college campuses, they have broken out into the real world, moving down into the high schools and up into the professions.

We are living in the golden age of censorship. The right wants to censor pornography, rap and rock singers, military news, J. D. Salinger's *Catcher in the Rye*, photos showing Robert Mapplethorpe's idea of a good time, and the burning of the American flag. The left wants to censor tobacco ads, girlie calendars and sex jokes in the workplace, Saturday morning TV, overly Eurocentric schoolbooks, Andy Rooney, many college newspapers, all sorts of speech, and the waving of the Confederate flag. (Sometimes the American flag too. During the Gulf War, the sensitivity-prone University of Maryland briefly forbade display of the American flag as hurtful to people in the peace movement. Though the flag is always burnable, it is not always waveable.)

The itch to censor will always be with us, but has the urge to control the speech of ordinary Americans ever been so popular? By examining the college codes, we can see the modern method for accomplishing this control. First, skip over any attempt to appeal to decency, leadership or nonpunitive community standards that might moderate conflict or bring touchy groups together. Instead, adopt the victimization model, portraying the client groups as amazingly weak, resourceless and fragile students in a sea of permanently hostile bigots. This will justify serious penalties, including expulsion. (It will also enrage those depicted as permanently hostile bigots.) Combine these harsh and very specific penalties with a list of offenses kept as generic and misty as possible. The vagueness of the offenses and the possibility of ominous, compli-

cated proceedings will create the desired air of uncertainty and intimidation, even in private speech with another student who might report
to the speech police.

Note how the California plan follows the campus ones. Penalties are
very clear, ranging from public reprimand to disbarment. Offenses are
vague. No one knows which remarks are trouble or whether the program
covers private as well as professional speech. Would a lawyer's overheard
comments in a restaurant count? What about "He's too old for her"
(age bias) or "The rich are so greedy" (socioeconomic bias)? How about
an off-color joke, or criticism of a church for its abortion policy? The
California code piously exempts "legitimate advocacy" from its new
surveillance, but then, what is "legitimate"?

The state bar association should look at what the codes have done
to colleges, where authorities monitor dormitory posters, wisecracks,
comments on physical appearance and such forbidden classroom opinions as "I think men are better than women in this field." To its credit,
the ACLU of Southern California, which had waffled on college codes,
came out instantly against this speech-control plan. But it is still alive,
and doubtless we will see many more like it before the fever of censorship
passes.

Why does the left behave this way? Because it has only one model
for coping with prejudice and group conflict: the emphasis on victimization, citation of a "hostile environment," followed by litigation and
punishment. This approach clearly doesn't work. It seems spectacularly
counterproductive, increasing antagonism, splitting campuses apart and
crippling academic freedom. Now similar ruin will apparently be sought
in the nonacademic world.

In a different but related context (feminist antipornography laws),
political scientist Jean Bethke Elshtain of Vanderbilt University argued
that liberalism is absolutely locked into this losing strategy. Lacking
any language of public morality, she says, and equipped only with a
pinched view of society as a set of rights-bearing individuals, liberals
must use overinflated rhetoric, unrelenting victimization and a parade
of aggrieved individual litigants having to prove damages in order to
make anything happen.

Of all the campus speech-code incidents, the only one in which I
thought a fairly strong case could have been made for the college was
the recent one at Brown. The university expelled a student accused of
shouting antiblack, antigay and anti-Semitic slurs during a drunken

late-night stroll across campus. The case could have been made that as a repeat offender on probation, he had twice failed to observe minimum community standards of decency at a private university. But the university president, Vartan Gregorian, chose not to go that route. Instead he argued that although the student was entitled to free speech, his few drunken words had constituted harmful action. This was universally known to be preposterous. The bigoted midnight musings of a largely unheard drunk had harmed no one at all. But locked into the language of victimization, what else could Gregorian have done?

THROW THE KEY AWAY

The life story of Warren Bland is one of those tales evenly divided between the viciousness of the criminal and the folly of the criminal justice system.

Consider this career.

In 1958, Bland stuck a knife in the stomach of a man in a Los Angeles bar and got off with probation. In 1960, he was arrested in a series of sexual assaults on women in Los Angeles County. Three women fought back and avoided rape. One had her jaw broken in the process. Originally charged with one rape, three attempted rapes, a kidnaping and a robbery, he plea-bargained down to one rape and one kidnaping, and was sent to a state mental hospital under the state's "Mentally Disordered Sex Offender" program, since abandoned. The hospital warned that Bland was a sexual psychopath who would be "assaultive and/or homicidal toward women" if released.

For seven years, Bland was studied, interviewed, counseled, psychoanalyzed and "treated." In the process, the hospital disregarded its own warning. Always expert at simulating rehabilitation, Bland was hailed in a probation report for his "complete change and attitude toward his problem," and the hospital set him free.

Within months, Bland was back at his chosen life's work, violent sexual attacks. He was convicted of two more rapes. At his sentencing, another dark report announced that Bland was "clearly a dangerous individual who warrants segregation from society for the longest time that is possible under existing laws."

Existing laws being what they are, Bland served just seven years. Shortly after his release, he kidnaped an eleven-year-old girl and her mother. The mother was molested. The girl was sexually assaulted and tortured. In yet another of those compassionate criminal-justice breaks that kept coming his way, Bland plea-bargained and served only three years for these crimes. The crimes were growing more violent; the jail terms were getting shorter.

Eight months after his release, Bland was back in jail, this time for sodomizing and torturing a small boy. At this point, in any sensible society, Bland would have been tossed into a dungeon for the rest of his life, but in California, he plea-bargained down to nine years and served four and a half. He got out again in early 1986. In December, Phoebe Ho, age seven, disappeared while walking to school in South Pasadena. She was found dead in a ditch in Riverside County, raped and mutilated with the kind of instruments Bland had used before. A fourteen-year-old girl in Orange County died the same way, and an eighty-one-year-old San Diego woman was found bound, nude and strangled to death, with Bland as the chief suspect.

Sought in the Ho murder, Bland fled and was found by police working under an alias in a McDonald's in Pacific Beach. He was wounded in the buttocks while trying to escape. In his car, police found a gun and evidence linking him to Ho's murder. He was charged in the case.

Enter the Feds. Larry Burns, an assistant U.S. attorney in San Diego, filed federal charges against Bland under the Armed Career Criminal Act, the brainchild of Senator Arlen Specter (Republican, Pennsylvania). This fairly new, fairly obscure legislation passed in 1984. As originally written, it provided that anyone caught with a gun after three burglary or robbery felonies would go to jail for a minimum of fifteen years to a maximum of life imprisonment, with no possibility of parole or probation. In 1986, the law was amended and enlarged to include any three crimes of violence or serious drug offenses.

In his brief to the court, Burns noted dryly that "a public perception has arisen, in California in particular, that the stewards of our criminal justice system have failed to come to grips in a realistic and common-sense manner with the mounting crime wave." This is lawyerly under-statement. What he might have said is that the state of California botched the Bland case for three decades and is implicated by its in-competence in the savage murder of little Phoebe Ho. It has known for twenty-nine years that Bland was a violent sexual psychopath, yet it let him go five times. This casual approach did not end with Bland's latest arrest. Nearly three years after Ho's death, the Riverside County prosecutor still has not managed to hold even a preliminary hearing in the case. The case could go another three to five years.

As Burns notes, if the criminal justice system fails to protect the citizens, the public will lose confidence and turn to vigilantism. Yes. And if the nation is serious about crime, it will not release sexual monsters like Bland every few years and simply let victims pay the price for the next brief round of confinement.

The lack of seriousness about violence was the real source of the outrage over Willie Horton, just as it was in the outrage over the misguided policies at Patuxent, Maryland, where a triple murderer serving a life sentence was allowed an unsupervised furlough. The Patuxent program is being revamped, a straw in the wind. Another such straw is the announcement by New York governor Mario Cuomo that he now favors a lifetime sentence without parole for some hardened criminals, a position he adopted when opponents of his seventh annual veto of the death penalty appeared to have enough votes to override.

The Armed Career Criminal Act also fits this new realism. Under this act, it took only thirty minutes in court for Larry Burns to accomplish what the state of California failed to do for thirty years, take Bland off the streets permanently. With no fanfare at all, the sentencing came in 1989. Warren Bland is in federal prison for the rest of his life.

Keeping career sexual predators behind bars is the goal of Washington state's sexual predator law, passed in 1990 in the wake of the Earl Shriner case. Shriner raped, stabbed and strangled a seven-year-old Tacoma boy, then cut off the child's penis and left him for dead. The boy survived.

Shriner was a career sexual predator with a twenty-four-year record of attacking children. In 1966, after being apprehended for choking a seven-year-old girl, he led police to the body of a missing fifteen-year-old girl. The girl had been strangled and tied to a tree. He was committed as "a defective delinquent" and psychiatrists said he was too dangerous to be at large.

But Shriner was let out again and again. He served ten years for abducting and assaulting two sixteen-year-old girls. After his release in 1987, he served sixty-six days for stabbing a sixteen-year-old boy, then sixty-seven days for tying a ten-year-old boy to a fence post and beating him. The children couldn't be made to testify, and the charges were plea-bargained down.

At every step along the way, authorities knew very well that they had an extremely dangerous predator on their hands. Before his 1987 release, officials knew that he "had hatched elaborate plans to maim or kill youngsters" when he got out. But he couldn't be committed because he wasn't mentally ill and hadn't performed recent and overt acts that might put the community in danger. (The major reason he hadn't, of course, was that he had just spent ten years in prison, where there are no children to attack.)

David Boerner, author of the sexual predator law, says the system obviously failed, but "the failure was not caused by a mistake on the part of some official. . . . The legal system seemed to work as it was designed." It basically operated like a game: vicious predators were set free periodically, and to get them back in prison for a few years, authorities usually had to wait for another woman or child to be mutilated or killed.

It's a system that makes no sense, not even to the predators. Andrew Vachss, a lawyer who represents children, has spoken to many predators over the years. He writes: "They always exhibit amazement that we do not hunt them. And that when we capture them, we eventually let them go."

If Washington's law had been in place in 1987, the state would not have been forced to release Shriner. He would have been brought to trial (a jury trial, at the prosecutor's option), and his plans to maim and kill would have been introduced as evidence. He would have been stashed away (as he is now, finally, for a 131-year term) without making a seven-year-old victim pay the price for getting him off the streets.

The law avoids current psychiatric categories and speaks broadly of "a mental abnormality or personality disorder." The legislature spoke of "a small but extremely dangerous group of sexually violent predators . . . who do not have a mental disease or defect."

In other words, though the legislature used some pseudopsychiatric jargon, it was outlining a way to commit people who aren't mentally ill. It produced a law that focuses on danger to the public and not mental incapacity, because research shows that most predators are simply violent criminals, and not ill at all.

What's wrong with such a law? Obviously jailing people for what

they might do in the future cuts across the grain of American jurisprudence. And there is always the danger that the law will be applied
broadly to people who are not hopeless career predators. Vance Cunningham, a three-time rapist jailed under the sexual predator law after
serving his time, has been making the rounds of talk shows (by phone)
pressing this argument. There's a court challenge, partly based on the
Cunningham case.

But as the Washington legislature said, the true target is not every
sexual offender but a small group of extremely dangerous predators. It
is not rocket science to figure out who these hard-core people are. The
record of Earl Shriner, filled with sadism and escalating violence, is a
common one in this group. So is the phenomenon of the predator
telling authorities what he will do next. Westley Dodd, hanged in
Washington for torturing and killing three boys, said in one of his court
briefs, "If I do escape, I promise you I will kill and rape again, and I
will enjoy every minute of it." Donald Chapman of Wyckoff, New
Jersey, is now free after serving twelve years for a grisly rape and torture
of a twenty-three-year-old woman. His psychiatrist says Chapman has
vowed to rape again, and has called himself a failure for letting his
previous victims live.

No sane society can let these people roam free. Society has rights
too, and one of them is the right to protection from nonstop predators.
Let's have more sexual predator laws.

A "VICTIM" CENSUS FOR AMERICA

As everybody knows, victim production is one of America's few remaining growth industries. Indeed, leading economists (and many trailing economists) warn us that the nation now turns out only three
products that the Japanese can't duplicate without breaking a sweat:
rock music, gory movies and social victims.

This victim boom is a special source of pride in a time of national
doubt, yet no one is making any effort at all to keep track of America's
impressive output.

For instance, Spike Lee wrote that the government invented the
AIDS epidemic to kill off blacks, Hispanics and gays. This isn't just

another reminder that playing with a full deck is optional among successful directors. It is also a wake-up call for the statistically minded: it means that year-end victim estimates must be rejiggered—and soon.

So let's get to work on victim statistics. Here is one industry-watcher's attempt to gauge production (no picky letters please; these are just estimates):

- HIV positive and AIDS victims, created by secret government murder plan (1.4 million victims).

- Victims of the press, including Bill Clinton, George Bush, Hillary Clinton and Barbara Bush (25 million).

- Victims of rock music and pornography (includes serial killer Ted Bundy, who said pornography made him do it) (10 million).

- Victims of codependency and warped family upbringing—96 percent of the population, according to codependency industry sources cited by Wendy Kaminer in her book, *I'm Dysfunctional, You're Dysfunctional* (240 million).

- Official minority victims (blacks, Latinos, Indians and gays) (79 million).

- Unrecognized striving-for-victim-status minority victims—Jews (victims of rising black anti-Semitism, denial of the Holocaust), Greek-Americans (Dukakis and Tsongas jokes), Arab-Amerians (terrorist movies), Irish-Americans (parades and cathedrals invaded by maddened gay youth), Italian-Americans ("fascist" comment by Bob Abrams, Cuomo jokes, demeaning Mafia references in Clinton phone call to Gennifer) (61 million).

- Asian-Americans, oppressed by "model minority myth" (7.5 million).

- Affirmative action victims (resentful whites, 50 million; nonwhites resentful of affirmative action labeling and stigma, 50 million).

- Unhinged males who beat drums in the woods and, for some reason, are frequently laughed at (5,000).

- White-guy victims ("Young white men feel oppressed," writes the editor of *Reason* magazine. "They have spent their entire lives officially marked 'undesirable' ") (97 million).

- Victims of the patriarchy (129 million women and prewomen).

- Victims of sexual harassment, defined as all those who have had unwanted sex, crude comments, propositions, proposals, invitations to go to a movie, low marks or frowns from male professors, faulty hellos, or smiles or gazes not explicitly welcomed in writing (129 million women and prewomen).

- Victims of enforced cheerfulness. In *The Managed Heart*, Arlie Hochschild wrote that flight attendants sometimes suffer minibreakdowns because of the cheerful smiles they are forced to wear. Similarly, in *Revolution from Within*, Gloria Steinem said that teenaged girls who dot their *i*'s with little hearts are acting in obedience to "a smiling, always cheerful mask" the patriarchy forces them to wear (total of smile victims: 45 million).

- The poor, the unemployed, those on welfare (44 million) and the middle-class, "forgotten Americans" bitter about being pre-empted by concern about the poor, the unemployed and those on welfare (149 million).

- Vietnam-era veterans, "now commonly depicted in the press as 'victims' of an evil or unthinking system," according to *The Washington Post* (8.3 million).

- Artists victimized by not getting NEA grants to carry on about victimization. Karen Finley (remember her?): "I basically go through various victims in our society, showing that people are born into victimization" (100).

- Everyone in jail (social victims or political prisoners) plus alcoholics and other drug abusers (victims of addiction or their own genes) (21 million).

■ Smokers—"victims of an alarming—yet socially acceptable—public hostility," says a disinterested source at Philip Morris (67 million).

■ Deviants—the happily married, children with two parents, people praised by Dan Quayle (50 million).

■ Victims of anti-nerd bias. Though few Americans know or care, nerds are callously barred from fashionable urban clubs for failing to be famous or for wearing nerdy clothes. Nerd activists have fought back with bias suits against clubs (60 million nerds).

■ Bald Irish singers who feel abused when people boo them for tearing up papal photos and who then allege that the booing was sexist ("If I were a young man and I was on TV saying these things, I would not be as brutalized") (victim pool: one).

Thus, America's victims exceed 1.2 billion, not bad for a population of only 251 million. Now, if we could only export our victim surplus, we would revive the economy in six months.

PART FOUR

"If I Could Be Like Newt"

Some of Our Best Friends Are Pols

THE GINGRICH WHO STOLE CHRISTMAS

Before the 1990 elections, GOPAC ("The National Grass-Roots Organization Building Republican Leaders for America's Future,") sent out a list of 134 buzzwords for Republican candidates to use in campaign speeches. Like faulty Pintos, two of the words—"traitor" and "betray"—had to be recalled, and rightly so, since GOPAC chairman Howard "Bo" Calloway pointed out that these terms "could be used in a context that would question the motives or patriotism of an opponent." Bo knows prose.

Many readers will ask why the Republicans decided to ship so many highly volatile buzzwords around the country, when they must have realized that some were bound to prove defective, and worse yet, fall into the wrong hands and wreak severe damage. Well, the reason is that GOPAC was tired of hearing what it called "a plaintive plea": "I wish I could speak like Newt."

Newt is, of course, Congressman Newt Gingrich, GOPAC's presiding spirit, and the truth is that there are only two ways to sound like him: either take years of expensive voice and speech lessons (hair treatment optional), or simply use a list of audience-tested, Newt-recommended, brain-freezing buzzwords.

Sensibly enough, costwise, GOPAC chose the latter course, and sent out two word lists, a list of "Optimistic Positive Governing Words" (courage, moral, children, candidly, caring, choice, passionate), and a list of "Contrasting Words" suitable for trashing vile Democrats (decay, collapse, corrupt, bizarre, self-serving, unionized bureacracy, punish the poor, sensationalists and antiflag). Presumably these can be combined in any order at all: morally courageous profamily children, perhaps, or collapsing antiflag sensationalists.

Some buzzwords are old chestnuts (machine, bosses, red tape). Others are newly irradiated chestnuts, like "empowerment," an old-left buzzword that the Republicans are striving to coopt. I phoned Tom Morgan at GOPAC, who said that ten or fifteen of the words came from focus groups, and the rest were culled from Newt speeches. "Permissive" was a strong focus group word. But what is "pristine" doing on the list? "I stuck that in because I like it," Morgan said brightly. "It's a pretty word, and I think Republicans should be concerned with the environment." One term, "eliminate good time in prison" sounds like a bad Monopoly card, but Morgan explained it all: focus groups disliked the idea of time off for good behavior in prisons, and preferred the concept of a shorter sentence with extra time for bad behavior instead. One of the buzzwords turned out to be a whole buzz-sentence: "Compassion is not enough," which vaguely refers to radical chic types who emote about the poor but don't help much.

Newt himself inspires awe. Last August he produced a majestic five-buzz sentence ("We must replace the false compassion of our bureaucratic welfare state with a truly caring humanitarian approach based on common sense") while effortlessly delivering a hearty 139-buzz speech to the Heritage Foundation. That was nothing compared with the brilliant note he once buzzed along to Santa Claus. Here it is, reprinted, of course, with permission.

Dear Santa,

As we hard-working freedom-loving children envision you mobilizing your humane pioneer reindeer this pristine holiday season, let us congratulate you on your uniquely principled commitment to sharing your North Pole prosperity with tough but caring profamily, pro-Christmas children such as myself and the GOPAC kids. Like you, we believe in truth, peace, light and preservation of the American way.

If I may downshift briefly to my Contrasting Words, I might say that I respectfully disagree with the sick, pathetic, destructive, self-serving, obsolete, radical, sensationalist liberal tax-and-spend Democrats (many of whom do not even believe in you, although they bizarrely and permissively believe in criminal rights and incompetent, insensitive, shallow, stagnating flag-burners who urgently threaten the danger of a deeper collapsing crisis).

Some say these people are traitors to the Christmas spirit. Myself, I do not use the word "traitor," since it might be misunderstood to imply some sort of betrayal. But I will say this: given half a chance, these hypocritical destroyers of the holiday dream would probably unionize half your elves, and turn the rest into corrupt welfare cheats, cynically dependent on patronage from big-city machine bosses.

What a wasteful new paradigm! What a selfish and shameful abuse of elf liberty and empowerment!

Reverting to my Optimistic Positive Governing Words, I trust you will express to us your profamily citizen activism through the proud incentive of tons of precious holiday gifts, all tied nicely in festive red tape. These should include an imposing new flag, a somewhat larger vocabulary, and the strength and moral courage to lead a passionate new pro-something-or-other crusade or movement. Please eliminate the good time that so many jailbirds seem to be having in prison these days. And while you may be briefly tempted to bring presents to the poor, remember that this would clearly help sap their moral strength and destroy their initiative. Compassion is all very well and good, but in my opinion, it is not enough. This is just common sense.

Regards to the family, the children, the courageously non-union reindeer,

Newt

BILL CLINTON'S LOST SPEECH

The following document, found on the floor of the Democractic convention by an alert reporter, is apparently a discarded first draft of Bill Clinton's acceptance speech.

My fellow Democrats,

As you know, we are living through a period of convulsive change. Among other things, we are forced to cope with the stunning collapse of a once-powerful ideology that set out to transform the world for the better, but which came to pitch itself against the moral and economic aspirations of the masses it presumed to speak for.

I am speaking, of course, of liberalism. May it rest in peace.

Let us admit that this now departed ideology gave us Social Security, the civil rights movement, Medicare, fair labor relations and deposit insurance. For that we are grateful. Even some Republicans are.

But that was a long time ago. In its crabbed old age, it gave us more dubious gifts: divisive race-based remedies, advanced victimology, group rights, quotas, litigiousness, a tendency to identify only with angry fringe groups, and an unmistakable disdain for what Robert Coles calls "the everyday moral struggles of ordinary people." That's why it died. Ordinary people got the drift and either stayed home on election day or stampeded toward the GOP.

I realize that this is not news to you. In one form or another, the message has been found in a steady stream of book-length autopsy reports written by authors from left and right. But not everyone is emotionally ready to acknowledge that the thing is dead and that we must move on. As you may have noticed, Jesse and Teddy are still in denial. They will need our help getting back on their feet.

Talking about it is still the best path to recovery. That's what Mickey Kaus does right there on page one of his new book *The End of Equality*. He says he joined the Carter administration as a young leftist lawyer with high hopes, but bailed out after nine months to work for a magazine.

"From there I had watched as the best minds of the Democratic party ran the liberal enterprise into the ground," he wrote. "They had put liberalism on the side of welfare rather than work. They funded housing projects that were among the most hellish places on earth. They defended absurd extensions of criminals' rights. . . . They let the teachers' unions run the education department and the construction unions run the labor department."

(This might be a moment to depart from this text and to note, without comment, that the unions laying cable at our convention are charging us two dollars to five dollars per foot, compared with the twenty cents per foot rate the Republicans are paying for their convention in Houston.)

Let me be frank. I realize that some people at this convention think we are pretending not to be liberals so we can fetch some votes from the suburban middle class. But this is no pretense. Campaigning under the banner of liberalism would be like the Castilian army fighting behind the propped-up but regrettably dead body of El Cid.

Liberalism is currently battling rigor mortis because it became obvious that no national political majority can ever again be built around it. And that's because it maneuvered itself into the incredibly stupid position of pitching itself against the core values of the American people. In doing so, it invented the "values" issue and handed it to the Republicans.

Americans are deeply committed to the work ethic, self-reliance, self-discipline, family-building, rules and a stable social order. So if you are trying to build a political majority, it makes no sense to develop yourself into a giant launching pad for attacks on all those values. But that's what liberalism did on the way down. It refused to match rights with obligations. It invented welfare "rights" and rationalized away worklessness, welfare dependency, drug abuse, illegitimacy and crime among the underclass. And this helped fragment the party. By 1984, Thomas Byrne Edsall and Mary Edsall write in their book, *Chain Reaction,* "For a crucial segment of the white electorate, to be middle class, to hold traditional values, to endorse work, family, responsibility, achievement and the like, meant not supporting the presidential wing of the Democratic party."

I support those middle-class values, and I think you do, too, because they are basic American values. If we say unequivocally that we are for social justice, racial justice, and those basic values I believe the American people will back us. They want the race problem solved. But it will not be solved by guilt-inducing victim politics, a racial spoils system or judicial end runs around the electorate. We will favor coalition building and policies based on merit and need, not skin color. And we want integrated election districts, not the one-race Bantustans that liberal policies are currently creating.

In conclusion, we must try to avoid recriminations against those not yet prepared to accept liberalism's demise. I urge you to let Jesse and Teddy move freely among us, just as the Russian people graciously allow Gorbachev to come and go. Perhaps with the aid of a twelve-step program or two, they may even join us. Never give up on rehabilitation. Just look at the progress we're making with Mario.

HILLARY AND THE CHILDREN'S CRUSADE

The Republican attempt to demonize Hillary Clinton is a shameful business. She is not a "radical feminist." She did not say that marriage is like slavery or the Indian reservation system. (She wrote that the relationship of child to parent, like that of wife to husband until modern times, has been a legal dependency relationship, in the same category of law as the relationship of slave to master—a prickly, but accurate, statement.)

Still, beneath the partisan attacks, there lies an actual issue. It has to do with the conflict of advocates for "children's rights" (the belief that children should have an array of legally enforceable claims against parents and the adult world) versus traditionalists who believe that this is a sure-fire formula for undermining what's left of the American family.

In traditional terms, the family is a politically exempt institution into which the state should not intrude, except in instances of total breakdown (chiefly abuse and custody cases). Once you start talking about "the rights of children," of course, you inevitably arrive at very different conclusions about how families should operate. Parental authority begins to seem like an arbitrary constraint of the powerless by the powerful—something lawyers should step in and rectify, just as they do in other civil rights cases.

Clinton's three articles on the subject, published between 1973 and 1978, were comparatively mild versions of what the children's rights movement wanted at the time. The mid-1970s were the high-water mark of the post-1960s campaign against adult "oppression." Books like John Holt's *Escape from Childhood* called for the liberation of children from parents. New York University installed a course on children's liberation. A *Youth Liberation* magazine was publishing in Ann Arbor, and a Young People's Liberation movement began resistance to "ageism" at Berkeley High School in California. Children's liberation was widely assumed to be the logical successor to the other antiauthority liberation movements being codified in the seventies.

Amid all this clamor, Clinton turned out three quietly reasoned articles. Writing in the *New York Review of Books,* Garry Wills twice uses the word "radical" to decribe Clinton's ideas. But the real radicals of the era were forever pounding the table and demanding full adult rights for all children. Clinton merely argued that courts should stop assuming that all children are legally incompetent until they suddenly become fully competent at age eighteen or twenty-one. She said courts and other tribunals should decide on a case-by-case basis, starting out with the presumption that children are competent to make their own major decisions unless proven otherwise.

Clinton is certainly right in arguing that some older teenagers are locked into dependency relationships long after they are ready to strike out on their own. But there's little sense of the enormous cost and conflict of measuring the competence levels of all children who would wish to haul parents into court. Clinton wants to limit these hearings to major matters, such as surgery, abortion and school selection: "I prefer that intervention into an ongoing family be limited to decisions that could have long-term and possibly irreparable effects if they were not resolved." But there is no way of stopping ever more trivial cases coming to court. This would, I think, vastly increase the amount of family chaos and virtually guarantee full employment for the nation's lawyers.

Clinton is obviously dedicated and very smart, but there's something overly abstract and unsatisfying about these articles. Margaret O'Brien Steinfels, the editor of Commonweal, wrote that the most important of the three pieces was "historically and sociologically naive." Even allowing for the fact that these are law articles, there is no real acknowledgment of how families actually operate. In Clinton's pieces, functioning families are not organisms built around affection, restraint and sacrifice. They seem to be arbitrary collections of isolated rights-bearers chafing to be set free. And there is no real indication that what children want and what they need are often quite different.

In the world of public policy, the children's rights movement is still alive, but not thriving, largely because it is essentially irrelevant to the current crisis of the family. American children are not suffering from too much parental authority, but from far too little. Rich or poor, children are much more likely to be ignored and psychically abandoned than they are to be "oppressed" by parental fascists.

A great many people now understand that the rights approach will exacerbate friction in the home and open the door for lawyers, judges, bureaucrats and "the helping professions" to make a further mess of the family. And some are worried about the character children would develop if granted the legal right to go their own way without interference. In her new book, In Their Best Interest?: The Case Against Equal Rights for Children, feminist author Laura Purdy argues that they would tend to grow up without self-control and restraint, which come from parental limits. She also thinks compulsory schooling would have to be eliminated. This is a brave new world we can do without. We already have enough problems.

HILLARY, FROM THE PULPIT

What is "the politics of meaning"?

However it comes to be defined, Hillary Rodham Clinton came out in favor of it in a speech in Austin, Texas, a day before her father died. *The New Republic* mockingly came out against it. "What on earth are these people talking about?" wrote the magazines's editors, referring to Clinton and other "politics of meaning" advocates, including Michael Lerner, editor of the Jewish magazine *Tikkun,* who coined the term.

Lerner has been writing about alienation, lack of community and the emptiness and pain of ordinary life. That's what Clinton spoke about too, referring to "signs of alienation and despair and hopelessness" so deep and broad that it amounts to a "crisis of meaning."

Her speech, and a remarkable profile of her by Michael Kelly in *The New York Times Magazine,* may have changed the public's perception of what Clinton is all about. Just when much of the nation has settled into a general view of Clinton as a hard-edged, rights-oriented liberal activist, she reveals herself as heavily concerned with the spiritual realm and many of the themes sounded by social conservatives.

"We need a new ethos of individual responsibility and caring," she said. Elsewhere she said there should be no doubt that "our family structure is in trouble" (refreshing talk from a liberal). On the health-care front, she wants to get rid of micromanagement, regulation and the bureaucracy.

She endorses Senator Pat Moynihan's thesis that America has disastrously come to accept more and more deviant behavior. Clinton says: "By gosh, it *is* deviant! It is deviant if you have any standards by which you expect to be judged." Michael Kelly writes that she not only sounds like a social conservative, "she sounds like just another angry, sincere, middle-aged citizen, wondering how everything went so wrong."

In the profile and speech, Clinton seems to drop in and out of different vocabularies—including the language of political liberalism and the New Age tongue of growth and wellness. But her dominant rhetoric is religious. She speaks of standards, the existence of evil and the Golden Rule. "She's speaking a language they can hear in the black Baptist churches, in Catholic churches, in mainline Protestant churches," said Margaret O'Brien Steinfels, editor of *Commonweal* magazine.

Quoting the dying Lee Atwater in her Austin speech, Clinton talked of "this spiritual vacuum at the heart of American society, this tumor of the soul." Like Michael Lerner, she paints a picture of American life spinning on without much love, connection or purpose. Lerner writes about "the debilitating depression that shapes the consciousness of daily life in a privatized society."

Clinton and Lerner seem to be saying that it's not just politics and the economy, stupid, it's also selfishness and the hollowness of everyday life.

"The politics of meaning" turns out to be big and gauzy enough to irritate *The New Republic,* but perhaps accurate enough about "society's ethical and spiritual malaise" (as described by *Tikkun*) to attract converts.

Any movement willing to retreat from the dead end of entitlements and rights-talk deserves our full attention. But there are some problems with the currently sketchy content of "the politics of meaning." It isn't very clear how meaning is created and supplied to converts or how much the political process properly has to do with all this.

In the May/June issue of *Tikkun,* Lerner has a few suggestions for the Department of Labor. One is for the department to declare an annual "Occupational Stress Day" to highlight worker stress and its impact on the family. Another is for each workplace to draw up "a mission statement" outlining the proposed contribution to the common good. An "Honor Labor" campaign would salute workers for this contribution. Many of Lerner's ideas are sharp and thoughtful, but not these. They sound like proposals rejected by Fidel Castro's Department of Sugar Production.

Nothing like this has been set forth by Hillary Rodham Clinton, though she occasionally strums an odd New Age theme or two. "It is not going to be easy to redefine who we are as human beings in this post-modern age," she says, without telling us why such redefining should be on anybody's agenda. She also wants "a new definition of civil society which answers the unanswerable questions posed by both the market forces and the governmental ones as to how we can have a society that fills us up again and makes us feel that we are part of something bigger than ourselves."

But many of her constant critics are going to come away from this profile and speech liking her more. Hillary-bashers may lose heart when they notice that she stands for a form of liberalism that believes in standards and actually opposes deviance.

How far she intends to go with her "politics of meaning" is anybody's guess. At the moment it seems like a hodgepodge of theory from *Tikkun* magazine and Protestant theology. What will it look like when she works it all out?

MIGHTY MOUTH MARIO

Mario Cuomo called me in November of 1989. Until then, I had never been Mario-ed. Though "to be Mario-ed" is not in most dictionaries, it refers to the common experience of New York journalists who innocently pick up the phone and hear the booming voice of Mario Cuomo, challenging some news article or wrestling some idea to the ground.

The governor wanted to talk about abortion. As a Catholic he embraces the Church's position. ("You teach it; I accept it. I'm in the club.") But as an elected official, he doesn't think an antiabortion law or amendment should be shoved down the throats of people who do not share Catholic principles.

Many names floated by—Cardinal Spellman, George Will, Father Hesburgh, Gloria Steinem ("I tried to tell Gloria, wherever you are on choice, 1.5 million abortions a year is way too many.") As Howard Kurtz of *The Washington Post* says, it is virtually impossible for the best note-taker to scribble more than half of the words that pour by during telephonic Cuomification. I began jotting down five-word summaries of each aria, hoping I could reconstruct the whole libretto later.

About ten minutes into the phone call, I began to feel as though my arm was being kneaded, my elbow cupped and my face affectionately patted. A lot of Italian men do this in face-to-face conversation. Cuomo can do it over the phone. (No ethnic complaints, please. I'm half-Italian myself.)

After another ten or twelve minutes, I dimly sensed that Cuomo was circling closer and closer to something he wanted to say. He left it for me to figure out, and finally I did. I had just written a column that mentioned Cuomo in passing. Although the governor had always described abortion as a complex moral issue, I wrote, moral nuances seemed to be disappearing, since the Cuomo of late 1989 "felt embarrassed, as a male, to be saying anything about abortion at all." Cuomo told me that this impression came from a truncated wire-service report of an Arizona speech. In the next line of the speech he had added the "however": as a morally concerned person and elected official, he must speak out.

This was said with no hint of complaint or grievance. It was tucked away in a rolling upbeat monologue. Quickly activating my vocal cords during a brief pause, I said, "Governor, if I got it wrong, I'll make a correction." "No, no!," Cuomo replied at quite a high decibel level. "I don't want to look backward, I want to move ahead."

Cuomo gave me his home phone number, told me to call any time for a chat, then hung up. The governor of New York had just spent three-quarters of an hour not asking for a correction. This is nowhere near a world's record for being Mario-ed. As Mary McGrory says, "Cuomo will argue with a reporter for hours over a single sentence in a story." He has been known to call the same reporter three times in a single day.

Cuomo's phone calls reveal him as very smart and utterly without pretense. He likes reporters and engages them directly, though, of course, he thinks he's lots smarter, and most of the time, he's right to think that. Mario doesn't go behind your back or over your head. He comes right at you. Most politicians are fearful of speaking three unscripted sentences. Cuomo is happy to let his reputation ride on long, daily orations.

But the obvious downside of his phonomania is the staggering amount of time it takes. If it amounts to four or five hours a day—no one knows—that is a huge chunk of the workday not devoted to running the state. This problem is magnified by Cuomo's unwillingness to delegate. Just as he acts as his own press secretry, he acts as his own everything, which means problems that should be solved at lower levels pile up on his desk while he is schmoozing with Jimmy Breslin of *Newsday* or Jack Newfield of the *New York Post,* or composing jingles to put on Mary McGrory's answering machine. He has little taste for administration or the kind of arm twisting and head banging required to push strong legislation through a divided legislature. He is primarily an inspired talker, trained in the two most nit-picking yakety-yak polemical occupations the world has yet devised: theology and law.

Call this his Jimmy Carter side: high idealism, remoteness from the carrot-and-stick process of getting laws passed, little delegation, few management skills. Like Carter, he started to think about running for president just when the magic was wearing thin at home. The editorial writers of *New York Newsday* criticized him in conventional anti-Carter language for his "wilful, contentious, suspicious, self-righteous, short-sighted way of governing."

But he also has a Ronald Reagan side: he is a superb communicator who actually stands for something. No one can quite calibrate the market value of that, though Reagan gave us a pretty good idea of the number of deficits it can overcome. By the time I got around to writing about Cuomo's call, the 1992 campaign was starting and I thought the Democrats would be wise to shove aside all the Peter Profile candidates and roll the dice with Mario.

Later I had second thoughts. The Mario who stays in Albany all the time, who whiles away so much time gabbing with reporters, has a serious flaw we can only speculate about. Though confident and loquacious, he is somehow a profoundly reticent man stuck at the level of talk and ideas. He really doesn't want to reach outside Albany for any brass rings, and so his moment has passed. Too bad.

BUSHSPEAK: GOOD CAKE, NO VERBS, GOODBYE

Maybe it's too early to get nostalgic about President Bush, but some of us are going to miss his valiant struggles with the English language.

Right up to the end of his term, he was giving us great sentence fragments, mostly because he hates verbs as much as broccoli. In the final days, Senator Alan Simpson dropped by the White House, said goodbye and waited for the president's last words. He says Mr. Bush replied, "Over and out."

Reporters asked Mr. Bush how he enjoyed his sixty-eighth birthday party. He replied: "good cake, good card, not bad." No American president has ever done more without verbs. During the campaign, he said of Bill Clinton "not without redemption . . . in terms of personal kind of guy, nice fellow."

The sections of his diary dealing with the Iran-contra scandal show that Bush stamped out verbs in private too. "Great speculation in the press about what did or didn't happen. Enormous national interest out there. . . ." On and on it went, just like a Dana Carvey impression.

Once you have mastered the Bush fragments, you are ready to tackle a whole Bush sentence. Though not verb-free, the sentences are usually cryptic too. During the 1988 campaign he observed: "It is no exaggeration to say that the undecideds could go one way or another."

Someone asked him what he thought about after his plane was shot down at sea during World War II. Bush replied, "I thought of my faith, the separation of church and state." There he was in shock, drifting helplessly in icy, shark-infested waters, thinking, "Should we help Quaker schools, or what?"

Saying goodbye on his last day in office, Mr. Bush attempted to quote a line from a familiar Kenny Rogers song. Referring to poker, the song goes, "you gotta know when to hold 'em, know when to fold 'em." Only Mr. Bush's version came out, "there's a time to stay, a time to go, a time to fold 'em." He thus became the first American president to confuse Kenny Rogers with Ecclesiastes.

But your basic Bush sentence is one that has a way of trailing off helplessly at the end: "We have to catch this wave that's moving through Eastern Europe, and indeed around the world, of freedom and democracy and things of that nature." And he once spoke of Lincoln "going to his knees in prayer at times of trial and the Civil War and all that stuff."

He praised Vaclav Havel, then president of Czechoslovakia, for "living, and dying, whatever, for freedom." And he said, "I'm all for Lawrence Welk. He's a wonderful man. He used to be, or was, or wherever he is now, bless him." What Mr. Bush was telling us here is that he firmly believes Vaclav Havel and Lawrence Welk are dead, but if they turn out to be alive, that's okay too.

Same thing with Meir Kahane. When Kahane supporters showed up to demonstrate in Kennebunkport one summer, Bush quipped: "Look, look, there's Kahane protesting on the boat. I thought this guy was kind of dead." Actually he was kind of dead. Whatever.

If you wish to listen to a Bush sentence, and many say they are still eager to do so, it is best to tune in quickly to the front part of the sentence, delivered when Mr. Bush is still fresh. This is your best chance to wrest some meaning from what he says.

"We believe strongly in separation of church and state," he once proclaimed, "but when you get into some questions, there are some moral overtones. Murder, that kind of thing, and I feel a little, I will say, uncomfortable with the elevation of the religion thing." Mr. Bush is telling us plainly here that the murder thing makes him uncomfy with the religion thing. (As if he were the only one.)

Then there's his habit of dropping g's. Like the pork rinds and the horseshoes, this is designed to give us the impression that Mr. Bush is an average guy from Texas with a gun-rack on his pickup, not a skull and bones prepster from Connecticut.

There's a theory that Bushspeak is not a personal failing, but part of the secret skull and bones ritual at Yale. Nobody knows for sure, but rumor has it that skull-and-boners lie in a casket and swear a blood oath to eat pork rinds, declare war on verbs and, at the point of death, think hard about vexing problems of church and state.

We will miss the language and the man. As someone once said, he is "not without redemption. In terms of a personal kind of guy, nice fellow." Good thought. Good grief, and stuff of that nature. Over and out.

Bob Kerrey's Little Joke

Have you heard the one about Jerry Brown and the two lesbians?

Chances are you haven't, though you might have read a lot about it. This is the joke that Senator Bob Kerrey told Governor Bill Clinton at a political roast in New Hampshire during the 1992 campaign. A crew from C-SPAN recorded the story, but the tape was shelved because the conversation was private and therefore out of bounds.

The astonishing thing is that lots of people in Washington seem to know the story but no one is willing to tell it, even off the record to an earnest, high-minded columnist. One reason is that some are not sure they really have the original version. (For understandable reasons, Kerrey has not announced what he actually said.) And because the joke involves gays and women, others think it is just too toxic to say aloud. This was the position of Gregory King, an otherwise impressive spokesman for the Human Rights Campaign Fund, a gay lobby. King wouldn't come close to describing the story, though he told me, in hushed tones, the joke is so horrific that women in his office cried when they heard it.

Get ready now. Send the children out of the room and brace yourselves. Having laboriously pieced together the wording of the actual joke, I am about to tell it, somewhat sanitized.

Jerry Brown walks into a bar and ogles two women. A bystander tells Brown to forget about it—the women are gay. The man describes a sexual act that the woman with large breasts likes to perform on the woman with small breasts. Jerry Brown replies that he would enjoy performing this act too, and wonders if this makes him a lesbian. End of joke. Bring children and sensitive people back into room. Commence optional laughter.

Let's put this story through rapid joke analysis. It is remarkably unfunny. Washington jokes don't come any dumber. Two objectionable terms were used, the common vulgar term for breasts and the common vulgar phrase for oral sex performed on a woman. That's all, my sources say. Many women may be offended by the reference to breast sizes, but there were no nasty terms for lesbians, no put-downs of gays or women. One of the more incensed critics of the joke, Patricia Ireland of the National Organization for Women, said: "I gather the joke was extremely and terribly degrading toward women." No, it wasn't. It was an ordinary off-color story with only one target—Governor Moonbeam—told in the normal language of dirty jokes. Like them or not (I think they are juvenile and generally humor-free), off-color stories usually feature crude Anglo-Saxon words for genitals, male or female. This does not make them antimale or antifemale. It just makes them naughty. That's the whole point of a dirty joke.

Activists and the press worked very hard to miss this point. So did Jerry Brown, who said loftily that it's wrong to make fun of people's sexual orientation, neglecting to add that no one had done so. Gays are free to resent being used as props in Moonbeam jokes, but this is by no means an antigay story.

Still, gay organizations took the opportunity to explode in rage. "Kerrey is anti-lesbian" signs appeared. The board cochair of the National Gay and Lesbian Task Force complained of "sexist and homophobic implications." Lamentations and threats filled the air. Kerrey offered a brief statement of regret, calling the joke "inappropriate" and saying "If it offended anyone, I apologize." A reasonable move. But gays immediately announced that Kerrey "needs to do more than send a one-paragraph apology." Several groups made clear what they had in mind. To make amends, he would have to become cosponsor of a gay rights bill.

At this point, Kerrey had a chance to say something important to his party. He could have said, look, I said I was sorry and I meant it, but by trying to turn a joke into a pork-barrel opportunity for special-interest legislation, you are recapitulating all the narrow pressure-group politics that has brought our party to its knees and alienated all the mainstream voters we need if we actually want to win the presidency someday.

Instead, Kerrey issued a stronger self-abasing apology, calling himself temporarily stupid, and "in a barely audible voice," according to one report, "said he had spent the previous twelve hours examining his own feelings and attitudes in an attempt to learn a lesson." This is the sort of straightforward groveling and the embrace of official re-education that we have learned to associate with students apologizing for being in the vicinity of Tiananmen Square.

Like many politicians, Kerrey doesn't know how to cope with the current wave of militant utopian puritanism. My favorite example of this expansive philosophy is the image of the press collapsing on Bill Clinton, demanding to know whether he had laughed at Kerrey's joke. This was no laughing matter. An Arkansas feminist, Kerry Lobel of Little Rock, announced gravely, "This is going to be a clear example of Governor Clinton colluding in an act of bigotry." Clinton's campaign hung in the balance. Even the slightest upward twitch of a left smile muscle could have implicated him in a career-ending hate crime. But he dodged the bullet. An aide emerged with crucial news—he hadn't laughed. Nobody bothered to get a court order to check the C-SPAN tape for bigoted smiling; the matter was closed. That's the way it goes in big-time campaign politics.

PART FIVE

"A Cloak of Silence and Denial"

Race, Ethnicity, and Immigration

GERRYMANDERING, RACIAL STYLE

Whenever the left and the right agree wholeheartedly about any issue, the strong likelihood is that an amazing disaster is about to be jointly sponsored. That was true of the dumping of tens of thousands of mental patients on the streets of our cities. The right wanted to save money by closing asylums. The left imagined it was freeing snake-pit prisoners of the psychiatric bureaucracy. Working together, they created much of the urban disaster that goes under the label of "homelessness."

Now they are at it again. The ACLU, civil rights groups, the Bush Justice Department and selected Democratic and Republican pols are busy institutionalizing a system of racial gerrymandering. Many Democrats want a lot of safe black and Hispanic districts in which to run black and Hispanic candidates. The Republicans want to pack minorities into electoral homelands, thus "whitening" surrounding districts and increasing the likelihood that black and Hispanic gains will be more than offset by increased numbers of white Republicans in Congress. This is ethnic cleansing American-style.

There's another advantage for Republicans. Racializing the districts pits blacks against Hispanics as well as against the white majority. This enables Republicans to use a civil rights cover for a campaign to lure Hispanics into the party and separate them from alliances with blacks.

Abigail Thernstrom, author of *Whose Votes Count?* had this to say about John Dunne, the Republicans' point man on these matters in the Justice Department: "He can embrace legislative quotas, make civil rights groups happy and line the political pockets of Republicans while hardly making a political ripple."

Each side gets its short-term gain. The only losers are the American people, who will have to cope with an even higher level of racial polarization, now being built into the electoral system in a notably high-minded bipartisan manner.

On the left, at least, the impulse toward the new racial gerrymandering was a fair one: to overcome the old racial gerrymandering that diluted the voting strength of minorities, particularly blacks. In eleven southern states, where about 25 percent of the population is black, only 5 of 116 congressional seats are held by blacks. This goes on in the North too. Compact communities of Latinos in Philadelphia and blacks in Brooklyn have long been carved up to keep white politicians in power.

But the problem is this: instead of removing barriers to minority participation in politics, the reformers have in effect launched yet another system of racial set-asides, carving up real communities as cynically as the older gerrymanderers once did.

New York City has a preposterous X-shaped district, slashing through a dozen different school districts and police precincts to connect scattered Hispanics in Manhattan, Queens and Brooklyn. For much of its meandering length it is only a few blocks wide. At one point it's just one block wide. But this fulfills the new racial etiquette. A Hispanic won the Democratic nomination last week. Even so, Representative Stephen Solarz, an unpopular Jewish incumbent, nearly won. Certain Hispanic spokesmen were outraged: how dare a non-Hispanic run in an offically designated Hispanic district? Presumably he should have searched out an officially designated Jewish district, where he belongs.

The assumption in all this is that racial voting is all that can be expected of the American voter, and if minorities are to make it, they must be handed safe seats because whites won't vote for nonwhites. This is an extraordinary assumption on which to base an entire policy. One study shows that Asian-Americans in California already have a substantial share of political power, and they got it the old-fashioned way by winning the votes of blacks, Hispanics and whites.

The racial gerrymandering has this in common with reform efforts of the past generation: it disdains coalition building (the normal work of politics) in favor of a quick fix, either administrative or judicial. As in other end runs around the political process, there has been almost no public discussion about what is happening. It is being pushed through as quickly and quietly as possible on the basis of a vague Supreme Court ruling on an ambivalent congressional amendment to the Voting Rights Act.

We are seeing a replay of what happened in affirmative action. A program that began with the idea of equal opportunity (remove the obstacles) shaded over into a slight edge for equally qualified minorities, then to a system of clear racial preferences and quotas. The only difference this time around is that the new gerrymandering is colored by the new multicultural ideology, which assumes that race and gender are the dominant issues of the day. While normal politics tries to blur race and find common ground, the multicultural approach keeps the racial barriers high and assumes that racial groups must be empowered, not individuals.

The relentless search for monoracial districts is a sorry business. It makes too much of tribal identity and may usher in an era in which people get elected primarily by making racial appeals. Instead of encouraging minority candidates to rise to power by seeking the votes of all groups, it will tend to isolate them in racial enclaves and further fragment our politics. This is one voting reform that should be unreformed as quickly as possible.

SENATORS 2, HACKER 0

Here's a clear indication that a significant shift is under way in thinking about racial matters: in the same week, two Democratic senators gave strong speeches that deviated sharply from what white liberals normally allow themselves to say in public.

On the floor of the Senate, Bill Bradley said we cannot "make race an excuse for failing to pass judgment about self-destructive behavior." He specifically named the 65 percent rate of out-of-wedlock births among black women and said that fear of violence at the hands of young urban black males "covers the streets like a sheet of ice."

Speaking at Yale, John Kerry of Massachusetts sounded many of the same themes in the same stark language: a high illegitimacy rate, families "on welfare for far too long," a reality "ruled not simply by poverty but by savagery," a crime rate that is "the most deadly poison there is to improved relations between black and white Americans" and the desperate need for "the simple restoration of order."

Pulling these quotations out of long speeches may make it seem that the senators were hostile to the cause of racial justice, but that is not the case. Both were pleading for the rebuilding of our cities and both were straightforward about the sins of whites.

But here is what is significant: in their use of blunt language and their repeated calls for honesty in racial matters, both senators were acknowledging that the discussion has been basically dishonest for some time. Bradley said Republicans have Hortonized the race issue, while Democrats have "suffocated discussion of self-destructive behavior . . . in a cloak of silence and denial."

In fact, public discussions of race have been basically dishonest for twenty-seven years, ever since the Moynihan Report. The denunciation of Daniel Patrick Moynihan as a racist (for reporting on the apparent breakdown of the black family) ushered in a defensive and narrow orthodoxy built around the insistence that all problems of blacks are the products of white racism. Any criticism of behavior has been off-limits, a form of "blaming the victim" that can only give aid and comfort to racists.

That orthodoxy, policed for decades by the civil rights establishment, is now breaking down. Kerry's speech reveals, at last, a liberal senator vividly acknowledging the downside of affirmative action and challenging the whites-are-racists rhetoric so popular among black spokesmen. Kerry told the Yalies: "We cannot equate fear of crime and concern about deteriorating schools with racism and then expect those we have called racists to invest in the very neighborhoods they have fled."

Another sign that the long post-Moynihan period is ending is the reception now being given to Andrew Hacker's new book, *Two Nations.* Hacker is a political scientist at Queens College. His book, written entirely in the approved prose of post-Moynihanism, is basically a long argument that blacks are nothing but victims and whites nothing but victimizers. It is an uncomplicated appeal to white guilt and shame. Even the killing of blacks by blacks is mostly the fault of whites. ("While in one sense these are 'free' acts . . . it is white America that has made being black so disconsolate an estate.")

Tom Wicker gave the Hacker book a glowing review in *The New York Times.* Ten years ago, this would have been the standard reaction among liberals. But times are changing, and the book is being hammered. Alan Wolfe of the New School for Social Research took it apart in a devastating *New Republic* review. Jim Sleeper, author of *The Closest of Strangers,* a study of liberalism and race in New York City, wrote in *New York Newsday* that Hacker's book reveals a mindset "profoundly offensive to most whites and insufferably patronizing to blacks." Both reviewers insist that blacks, like everyone else, are accountable for their own behavior. They cannot be depicted as spectators in their own lives. Sleeper writes: "We are well past the time when anything will be gained by denying blacks a larger measure of credit and responsibility for their own liberation, even in the teeth of racism itself."

Hacker's prose reflects the ossified thinking of an older white liberal elite that has just finished spending a quarter-century placating an older black liberal elite. Along the way, this alliance has spent much energy ignoring or explaining away the disorder, illegitimacy, crime and urban chaos that Americans of all colors desperately want to have addressed. The coalition has bred a dead-end politics based on grievance and guilt that no longer has a hold on any significant part of the electorate. Instead of undertaking the hard work of building a black-white coalition around common goals, it has endlessly pursued a backdoor legal strategy to make the courts force unwilling and often uncomprehending majorities into line. It has racialized standards, breeding its own opposition. And it has greeted every dissent from the party line as a message from David Duke.

Bradley and Kerry are political harbingers of a different body of thought that has been gaining ground in academic circles. That thought assumes that old strategies have been exhausted and new ones must be tried. Whatever these strategies are, they will have to avoid all the dreary stereotyping of white apprehensions and build broad, nonpolarizing multiracial alliances. There is no other way to go.

COUNTING BY RACE AT GEORGETOWN

Timothy Maguire wrote an op-ed piece in a campus newspaper that nearly got him tossed out of Georgetown's law school just three weeks short of graduation. This was just after "Diversity Day" on campus, with arguments that blacks are held back on campus by racism, a lack of black role models and a hostile environment. Not so, Maguire wrote, rather testily—the problem is that "at every level of postsecondary education black achievements are far inferior to those of whites." This, he said, "explains minority underrepresentation far more convincingly than the vague racism incessantly decried."

Maguire, who had worked briefly in the school admissions office, said that among a sample of students admitted to Georgetown Law, whites had scored an average of 43 (out of 48) on the law school admission test, while blacks had averaged 36. Furthermore, he wrote, if bias and hostile environments are the problem, how can we explain the very low LSAT scores from graduates of historically black colleges?

The explosive reaction to Maguire seemed to depend as much on the unpleasant tone as on the unwelcome numbers. "That was a mean-spirited piece, wasn't it?" I asked him. "That's accurate," he said. "I apologize for the tone of it." Charging racism, the campus Black Law Students Association demanded the expulsion of Maguire and the editor of the paper, Claudia Callaway. In response, the law school named a "prosecutor" who has filed an indictmentlike complaint against Maguire for using confidential information from the admission files.

National figures show what Georgetown seems to be trying to keep out of sight: that blacks accepted into law school have not yet caught up to whites in either grade point averages or LSAT scores. In fact, whites rejected by law schools score slightly higher than blacks accepted by the schools. The reason so many apparently underqualified blacks are making it into law school is obvious enough: a lot of schools are moving aggressively to recruit blacks as a matter of social justice. Georgetown law, with 11 percent black enrollment and 23 percent minority, is apparently one of these schools. Father Robert Drinan, Georgetown law professor and a former congressman, said, "When I graduated in 1951, Georgetown law had not accepted a single black in its eighty-one-year history. We have a lot of reparations to do." Also: "If you oppose affirmative action, how else are we going to get blacks into the system?"

Good question. The problem is that while Georgetown seems to be doing what Father Drinan wants it to do, it is not owning up to it. Nothing about reparations or social justice is in the admissions vocabulary. On the contrary, Georgetown law argues that all incoming students, every year, are already fully qualified to be accepted on nonracial criteria before final decisions are made on the basis of regional, racial, ethnic and gender diversity. Whether any campus official actually believes this is not certain. I know I don't. I agree with Maguire's lawyer, Michael MacDonald of the Center for Individual Rights, who says Georgetown is embarrassed by this case because it wants to have it both ways: "They want to be able to say that everyone is on an academic par while they are really running a race-based admissions policy."

The advantage of Georgetown's policy is that it keeps inside the

Baake guidelines (race cannot be the determining factor in admissions, but diversity can be one factor). Georgetown says it determines who is qualified by looking at three loose subjective factors in addition to the more objective ones of college grades and LSAT scores: recommendations, personal statement and activities or work experience. Marks and test scores are good predictors of law school success. But some subjectivity is fair, particularly when candidates come from a difficult background. Yet if it is widely known that the grades and LSAT scores of blacks as a group are fairly low, people will want to know how the three subjective factors are scored so high that whites and blacks seem to be on a par before racial considerations are brought in (supposedly for the first time) in the final cut to shape the first-year class. Therefore it makes sense to suppress the numbers, not just to protect black self-esteem, but to fudge how the admissions process really works.

Georgetown is hardly alone here. ("If you feel there's a wall of secrecy, it's nationwide," said the PR director for the Georgetown Law Center.) In my opinion, everything legally possible should be done to pump more black lawyers and judges into the system. But let's have it all out in the open. Georgetown ought to tell us how it weights its five criteria, and it mustn't try to hide racial data. It ought to be able to demonstrate that it is not running a two-track racial system, which would be a clear violation of *Baake.* Referring to the five criteria and racial data, Mary Ann Glendon, professor of law at Harvard, said: "In the current climate of opinion, it's not healthy to have this crucial data locked away in a box." Amen.

THOSE WELLESLEY WOMEN IN LONG WHITE DRESSES

The president of Occidental College says that many blacks on predominantly white campuses "face a level of hatred, prejudice and ignorance comparable to that of the days of Bull Connor, Lester Maddox and Orval Faubus." Now, let's stop and think about this very dramatic statement for a minute. Connor, Maddox and Faubus—obvious racists all—used police, axes, clubs, dogs and water hoses to abuse or exclude blacks. A few of their supporters used bombings and lynchings. Which predominantly white campus, exactly, is doing this to blacks today?

A few years ago, a college president who made wildly inaccurate charges about race on campus would have been challenged immediately. Now, however, race relations are so touchy that a good deal of overblown rhetoric sails by without comment. Better not to risk a confrontation. In this case, the rhetoric plays to black pessimism and separatism. If mainstream colleges are so hopelessly racist, why would any sensible black want to attend?

Are our campuses hotbeds of racism? Many people seem to think so, but this is based on the belief that the sporadic horror stories that make the AP wire are reflective of the tone of campus life at hundreds of different colleges. This is a bit like judging life in New York City by counting the number of Manhattan mugging jokes in *Tonight Show* monologues.

Until about six months ago, I assumed from news reports that race relations were turning ugly on one campus after another. Then I noticed that stories on the subject tended to start with the same few examples— the mock slave auction, the racist jokes on a campus radio station, the shocking graffiti, the black-white melee after the Red Sox–Mets World Series. Some examples were fresher, and a few were alarming. But there was no way to judge how typical they were. Then I came across a very revealing quotation, buried deep in *The New York Times*. It was from Howard Ehrlich, research director of the National Institute Against Prejudice and Violence, a group based in Baltimore. Ehrlich, who monitors racial incidents on American campuses, said there is no way of knowing whether any upsurge of racial harassment at colleges is actually occurring. It may simply be, he said, that minority students are showing "strength and self-confidence" to file more reports and demand changes.

If you believe Mr. Ehrlich, and there is no reason not to, then we are a long way from the hate-filled, Bull Connoresque campuses envisioned in the fevered statement by the president of Occidental. Of course, it all depends on those reports filed by minorities on campuses. Since reading Mr. Ehrlich's comment last May, I have tried to collect and read some of these reports. So far, those I have read have been massively unconvincing.

At Wellesley College, the *Report of the Task Force on Racism* contains zero evidence of any racist incidents, harassment or intimidation. Two years in the making, the document is so weak and vague that the normal response may be to wonder why it was published or whom it is supposed to convince. The nearest thing to evidence is a collection of some three dozen anonymous and offhand remarks, five of which seem to me either racially stereotyped or prejudiced (for example, "My roommate refers to African-Americans as chocolate candy drops," "Black students are routinely late to class because they are not taught about time at home"). "Although these clear and direct expressions of racial prejudice are not numerous," the report says gravely, "stories about them are so often repeated that they are important because they generate widespread perceptions and may influence behavior. They haunt the community."

Oddly, the report gives Wellesley high marks for trying to treat everyone alike, regardless of race and class, and says the college has "a pervasive therapeutic mentality which is hypersensitive to those in need." What really annoys the authors is that Wellesley seems so WASPy. Differences are politely noted, not argued about openly. "Wellesley is not a community which tolerates conflict or disruption very well. It suppresses differences beneath a veneer of gentility which is experienced as oppressive by many black, white, Hispanic and Asian members."

Instead of evidence about racism, the report features complaints about loneliness, isolation, the "impenetrability" of the college and the "unconsciously white" campus culture (that is, much of the food, music and artwork are new and unsettling to minority students). The book-store does not feature enough posters of black athletes, and travel posters show Bavarian castles but not beautiful Third World settings. The report calls this a "racially based environment," but as the text makes painfully clear, the real problem is that blacks and some other minority members do not yet feel at home at Wellesley, with its pictures on the wall of white "women at the turn of the century playing tennis in their long white dresses." One staff member says the campus looks so homogenized that "I often get the feeling I should straighten my hair." Setting out to find "institutional racism," the report merely collects expression of discomfort, similar to those of the first Jews and the first Catholics to show up on campus.

Those earlier outsiders felt the same pain of entry that blacks do now. I hope blacks at elite colleges stick it out and resist the currently fashionable temptation to quit, transfer to Morehouse and denounce the game as rigged. The whole point of going to a place like Wellesley is to join the mainstream, not to attack it.

RACIAL DISASTER WITHOUT RACISM

Is there a great upsurge of racism on college campuses? Many media accounts seem to say so. But that conclusion may say more about the limitations of journalism than it does about the campus. In reporting on campus racial tensions, journalists tend to focus on the most dramatic incidents, often stringing them together to create the impression of broad and open conflict.

The view from campus is often different. "More often than not, suggestions of racism that are so frequently reported in the press offer excitement at the expense of truth," according to John Bunzel, former president of San Jose State University, now at the Hoover Institution at Stanford. "Most thoughtful observers acknowledge that the 'redneck' racism of fights, slurs, property damage and other acts of 'ethnoviolence' does not describe the character or atmosphere of campus life today."

Bunzel's book, *Race Relations on Campus: Stanford Students Speak,* based on hour-long interviews and student questionnaires, reported little hard-core bigotry. Despite "pervasive racial anxiety," the book says, surface conditions between blacks and whites are very good. Close to two-thirds of all seniors thought that "most people on campus are fair to all racial and ethnic groups." Very few whites have stereotyped views of black academic ability.

That's the good news. The bad news is that tensions between blacks and whites are high and rising.

Blacks and whites aren't even speaking the same language. To whites, the race problem is one of personal relationships and individual fairness. Blacks, or at least the black student leaders, view it as a black struggle to change the system of white control of the university. Half of black students agreed that "institutional racism" exists on campus, but only 28 percent of that group could come up with a concrete example.

White students are frustrated by the way blacks try to bring about change. Almost half of the white seniors agree that "the black student leadership is made up of people with their own political agenda who are devoted to simply *seeing* racism."

To gather strength and stand against white control, blacks more and more segregate themselves and whites resent it. Bunzel writes: "But a great many blacks, inclined to think of racism in institutional terms and therefore as firmly fixed in the university, insist that the real problem is oppression, not segregation."

The result is that black students define progress in terms of more power, rather than education or reconciliation, and in turn, frustrated whites become less interested in reconciliation, too.

The more Stanford tried to do—aggressive affirmative action, sensitivity training, ethnic theme houses, changing the "Eurocentric" curriculum—the worse matters became. One of the most liberal campuses in America is now turning out more and more racially alienated graduates. Seventy percent of seniors said racial tension had increased during the years they had spent on campus. Whites are leaving Stanford less sympathetic to minority causes than when they arrived.

How does a major university manage to produce a disaster like this?

One explanation is that university administrators have no wish to see angry protesters on their lawns, carrying highly telegenic signs about racist policies. To show support for minorities, to send the "right" signal to liberal activist constituencies, they end up caving in to demands they should be opposing on principled grounds.

These demands include freshman orientation programs that amount to heavy indoctrination, "sensitivity" seminars that assume whites are bigots, and some highly dubious classes (Stanford has offered a course called "Black Hair as Culture and History," for instance).

The most serious offense committed by colleges is the failure to do anything about the relentless trend toward segregation on campus. At various campuses, blacks have their own segregated dorms, student centers, tutorial programs, yearbooks, pages in college newspapers, dances and fraternities. Some schools have freshman orientation programs exclusively for minorities and others even hold some black-only graduation receptions. At many universities, it is possible to go through four highly segregated years without having much contact with white students at all. "If you didn't know the context," says Glenn Ricketts of the National Association of Scholars, "you would say this is a Klansman's delight."

Brunetta Wolfman of George Washington University calls this the "warm, dark cocoon of resegregation." The cocoon is comfortable, but it requires conformity and keeps students on the margins of campus life, says Wolfman, an education professor. Colleges, she says, find "it's easier to say OK, they want their own house, let's give it to them; it's a caving in."

Black students created the push for resegregation. But the scaffolding that put it in place was provided by college administrations. Nothing important will happen to improve racial relations on campuses until administrations admit the disaster and start pulling the scaffolding down.

LEO'S FIRST LAW OF RACIAL FOLLY

For five years, Washington debated whether the Smithsonian's major new project on black heritage would be a "free-standing" building or "a major wing" of the National Museum of American History. The Smithsonian's secretary, Robert McC. Adams, argued for a wing, so that black experience could "join its presence with the broad themes of American history and culture as a whole." Translation: let's avoid the disastrous symbolism of a separate-but-equal black-only museum standing apart from the national history museum on the mall. But black leaders disagreed and won the argument. Nobody in Congress seems to have objected. Neither *The Washington Post* nor *The New York Times* even bothered to mention the "wing" versus "free-standing" debate in their reports announcing the new black museum. Yes, the emphasis on black culture is welcome and overdue, but the separatist symbolism is appalling. It means that fewer whites will be exposed to black exhibits, and fewer blacks to those of the main museum. More important, it plays into the hands of blacks and radicals who argue that American history of any kind is either irrelevant or permanently skewed white propaganda. A bad piece of work.

The uncomprehending huzzahs that have greeted the museum decision lead me to announce Leo's First Law of Racial Folly in the Nineties: all setbacks for integration will immediately be hailed as triumphs for diversity. Immutably, this will be true of all manifestations of the new separatism, large and small. The University of Pennsylvania sponsors an all-black yearbook—a pictorial view of campus clubs, teams and faculty members with all the nonblack faces removed. Just when the campus had reached the point where a lot of black faces were appearing in the real yearbook, Penn was financing the allegedly wonderful diversity of yearbook apartheid. Anybody has the right to publish monoracial picture books, black or white, but why should a major university subsidize them?

Separatism at Syracuse University came under fire but remained intact. A complaint filed with the U.S. Office of Civil Rights charged that a blacks-only membership policy of the campus African-American Society is discriminatory and illegal. Pending a federal ruling, the university managed to defend this exclusionary policy, citing its "legitimate purposes and its role in enriching diversity."

A case can be made for racial societies on campus as a haven for students facing an intimidating new environment, something like an American club at the Sorbonne. But the costs are high. They open the door for irritated or racist whites to establish white student unions (Temple had one; the University of Florida has one now). They become complaint factories, polarizing the races. And they are key building blocks in the new separatism that high-minded, liberal, integrationist universities have allowed to rise on campus with almost no complaint. It is now possible for a student to live in an all-black dorm or frat, hang out at all-black student unions, take mostly black courses in the African-American Studies Department and spend four years at a major campus recreating the conditions of a blacks-only college. This is integration?

Sometimes the separatism is constructed along "Third World" lines. The most dubious program here is probably the "Third World Transition Program" at Brown University. Each year all nonwhite freshmen are invited to school three days early to meet and interact under the helpful ministrations of nonwhite advisors and teachers. It passes for a routine attempt to make Asians, blacks, Hispanics and Native Americans at home (but not Italian-American or Russian Jewish kids who may be feeling the same culture shock at a rich, traditionally WASP campus). According to many witnesses, including two friends with offspring at Brown, this has the predictable effect of bonding the nonwhites together before any whites set foot on campus, thus providing the basic structure for a race-based class rift that some say lasts the full four years. The TWTP literature makes clear that the program aims at defining and unifying all available "Third Worlders" as nonwhites. One student gushes about the "special bonding that we as people of color share," and another about the "extra sensitivity" of nonwhites, although the exact nature of what students from Hong Kong and Harlem share in the sensitivity and bonding departments is left obscure. Oddly, it does not seem to occur to anyone at Brown that this is racist claptrap. Perhaps Vartan Gregorian, president of Brown and a famous in-group intellectual in New York, can explain this all to us. Or maybe whites should be hauled on campus early to make up that melanin-based sensitivity deficit.

Brown's program is the most embarrassing but hardly the only entry in the field. The California state system, for instance, says it is committed to "building a sense of community among minority students," without explaining why this is preferable to building a sense of community involving everybody, or at least one not based solely on ethnic divisions. This is the fashionable rhetoric of the day. It is perverse and separatist, but then again, it's probably a great triumph of some sort for diversity.

THE FREE-AGENT MARKET IN BLACK STUDENTS

It's not news that colleges have been trying hard to attract black students, but it's news that the effort is now turning into a competitive scramble.

A story by Fox Butterfield in *The New York Times* describes an overheated free-agent market in black high school seniors. To attract them, various colleges are offering scholarships, refunds of application fees, free trips to campus, fringe inducements like tickets to rap concerts and football games and cash. "Many [colleges] do this by offering them extra money in the form of grants, which need not be repaid," Butterfield wrote.

The key fact in the *Times* story is this: almost half of the blacks admitted last year to Harvard's freshman class never went there. They rejected the most famous university in the hemisphere "overwhelmingly for financial reasons," Harvard announced. Translation: other colleges put more money on the table and simply outbid Harvard.

What sets any free-agent market spiraling upward is demand vastly exceeding supply. In this case, colleges want at least 10 percent of students and faculty to be black, but only 1 to 2 percent of blacks have good enough marks or SAT scores of 600 or above on both math and verbal, the minimum level that top colleges normally require.

This is the kind of story guaranteed to bring conflicting emotions and high anxiety to most readers. On the one hand, something must be done to bring more blacks onto the campus and into strong positions in society. On the other hand, an open bidding war for selected minorities is bound to increase racial resentments. After all, nobody flung open the gates of Harvard for the Irish, the Jews, the Poles and the Italians and then paid them to walk through.

The free-agent market has other unsettling effects too. Since it is not based on need, some of the chief beneficiaries are members of the black elite. They are being courted and sometimes paid to do what they would have done anyway: send their sons and daughters to elite colleges.

Are colleges simply buying black students? "The answer is yes," said Fred Hargadon, dean of admissions at Princeton. "There's a very delicate balance to maintain when diversifying student bodies. Some schools seem to have crossed the line." Hargadon also said that at some colleges, recruitment efforts send the sorry message that minorities needn't work hard at their studies.

After all, if recruiters pursue both the students who work hard and the students who don't, why is effort important? A number of awful lessons are being taught by the current aggressive pursuit of black students—that blackness has a higher commercial value than personal traits or achievement and that blackness may be able to buy acceptance of a lower work ethic.

Obviously it is a disservice to black youngsters to teach them that they can get by without full effort. High school seniors know what's happening on campus: that the same forces pushing colleges to recruit minority students who may not work very hard also push them to look the other way if those habits persist at college. A flood of writing and seminars has raised enormous pressure on administrations to do something about their "retention rates"—that is, to make sure that black students, brought to campus at such a high cost in money and energy, not be allowed to drop out or fail. Some colleges have worked hard on remedial programs. Others have just changed grading systems and softened curricula to make sure almost no one flunks out. It's the easiest way to keep the diversity numbers up.

The original conception of affirmative action was that minority group members would be given a slight edge among roughly equal applicants. But we are way beyond that now, wandering in the world of "diversity," which requires college presidents to do anything to produce a roughly 10 percent black student body.

In prediversity days, there still was a vague expectation that it was the student's job to measure up and meet standards. Now it is the college's job to court and hold black youngsters, even if it means cutting corners and accepting low output from students. There's an important shift of power here too. Since black students are pursued so avidly, they gain leverage over college administrations, which cannot afford to let them fail.

The free-agent scramble is nothing new, but the current fevered level of competition shows the power of the new diversity ethic. Diversity is no longer viewed as the expected by-product of youngsters of all races and backgrounds striving to achieve. It's an end in itself, basically a quota system of group representation, with little or no talk any more about merit or standards.

All this well-intentioned special treatment has had a devastating effect on campus race relations. A professor at the University of Texas Law School, Lino Graglia, says white students "have become convinced that ordinary standards just don't apply to blacks—they are a very special group." The special treatment ensures that the campus is divided by race, and that affirmative action has emerged as the number-one topic that can never be discussed openly by faculty or students.

Does anyone really think this system is working?

TUSKEGEE: "RACIST TO THE CORE"

Twenty years ago, a whistle-blower in the public health service had a chat with a reporter from the Associated Press. Headlines blossomed on the front pages of the *Washington Star* and *The New York Times.* As a result, the American public finally learned about the Tuskegee study, a shocking and profoundly immoral research project. Some four hundred men, suffering from syphilis, were deliberately left untreated for forty years so researchers could study the disease.

How could people have done this? Writing in a special section on the subject in the *Hastings Center Report*, a prominent journal dealing with medicine, biology and ethics, Columbia law professor Harold Edgar says the best answer to that question is the most obvious one. The researchers "did not see the participants as part of 'their' community or, indeed, as people whose lives could or would be much affected by what the researchers did." In other words, they were poor and black and therefore alien.

The study focused on four hundred males living in Macon County, Alabama, most of them poor, all of them black. They had been promised "special free treatment" for syphilis but in fact effective treatment was withheld so that the course of the disease could be studied. As incentives, the men were promised free transportation, free hot lunches and free burial after autopsies were performed.

The "special free treatment" consisted of spinal taps, conducted without anesthesia, so that researchers could check the neurological effects of syphilis as it spread. An article by two public health experts calls the study "the most notorious case of prolonged and knowing violation of subjects' rights" in medical history.

Others have cited the study as the longest-running "nontherapeutic experiment" ever conducted, but that is not quite accurate. At the outset of the project in 1932, the men were treated with mercury and arsenic-based remedies. These crude and inadequate medicines were the best available at the time. But when it became clear in the 1940s that penicillin was a safe and effective treatment, it was withheld.

The study was, in Professor Edgar's words, "racist to the core, in that no such program could possibly have continued so long but for the central fact that participants were African-Americans." But he calls this an irony, since the researchers involved, far from being vicious racists, were personally committed to expanding public health services for blacks, and had, in fact, gone to the trouble of getting research help from the black community.

The news that many of the researchers were high-minded do-gooders only adds to the horror. The research was undertaken, or stumbled into, in the wake of an earlier study of untreated syphilis done in Oslo, Norway. That study suggested that nothing adverse happens to two of every three men with syphilis who take no treatment at all. This notion that nontreatment of syphilis would work most of the time was a beguiling one for health officials with limited funds in the midst of a depression.

Step by step, the researchers headed into a moral swamp. At first the plan was to visit Alabama for a brief look at a population with secondary syphilis. Later, doubts about the data led officials to return to Macon County. They set up a control group of uninfected men for comparison, and decided to "bring the material to autopsy" (wait for the men to die).

This meant keeping the subjects away from medicine that worked. So as word of penicillin's effectiveness spread in the 1940s, the men with syphilis had to be sealed off from the news. Newly infected men were switched into the group of study participants, while no effort was made to protect them or their families. The project glided from research to deadly manipulation to coverup.

Today strict controls are in place to prevent such off-the-rails immoral research, but the issues raised by Tuskegee are still with us. Is it moral, for instance, for current researchers to use the results of the Tuskegee study? Citing the results not only seems repugnant. It can be viewed as a posthumous reward to those who produced the evil in the first place.

But Arthur Caplan, director of the Center for Biomedical Ethics at the University of Minnesota, writes: "Too much of what is known about the natural history of syphilis is based upon the study, and that knowledge has become so deeply embedded that it could not be removed." Caplan urges that every time the research is cited, the ethical shadow over it should also be cited.

But that will not deal with the pain many black Americans continue to feel about Tuskegee. The conspiracy theory about AIDS—that it was deliberately introduced by whites to kill off blacks—is emotionally rooted in what happened in Macon County. In his book on Tuskegee, *Bad Blood,* James Jones argues that hidden within the anger and anguish over Tuskegee is a plea for governmental authorities and medical officials to "hear the fears of people whose faith has been damaged . . . and to acknowledge the link between public health and community trust." Tuskegee will be behind us only when that trust is restored.

THE REDS AND THE BLACKS

Could Major League Baseball have handled the Marge Schott case any worse than it did? Probably not.

The lords of baseball knew about Schott's racist remarks for years and no one got her to shut up. Schott, principal owner of the Cincinnati Reds, has been quoted as referring to two of her stars as "million-dollar niggers," and saying that she would "rather have a trained monkey working for me than a nigger." She owned a swastika armband and has been quoted as delivering many anti-Semitic slurs, including "Jew bastards," "money-grubbing Jews" and "Hitler had the right idea for them, but went too far."

By the time the owners finally responded, they had no commissioner to exert moral leadership. The last commissioner, Fay Vincent, had been fired and not replaced. So when the council of owners got around to punishing Schott, it looked as though one used-car dealer was being censured by other used-car dealers for her ethical lapses.

There was also a heavy whiff of hypocrisy and coverup. Other owners and high executives make racist comments too. Without naming names, Ira Berkow of *The New York Times* quoted one owner talking about having "too many niggers on the field," and another owner saying, "The Jews are ruining baseball." Can it be that Schott got off lightly, because, if she had sued, a great deal more bigotry would have come out?

After months of dithering, the owners let Schott negotiate her own punishment, which turned out to be a brief and toothless suspension (eight months to a year), a tiny fine (twenty-five thousand dollars), a ridiculous seating rearrangement at Reds' home games (she is supposed to sit away from the dugout, not in the owner's box) and a re-education program (she must take some multicultural training).

The only serious mistake that the owners managed to avoid was trying to remove Schott as Reds owner. This idea has automatic emotional appeal. But in America, we don't take people's property away for indecent remarks. We march, picket, shame, boycott, but we don't reach for a legal hammer when we hear offensive speech.

Here we have arrived at the core of the mess created by Major League Baseball. Because owners and officials were reluctant to respond morally to Schott's racist comments (meeting speech with speech), they backed into the currently fashionable position of punishing speech. Major League Baseball is a private association with an antitrust exemption, so it can get away with this. But it's a dangerous habit to get into.

The owners should properly focus on behavior—how minorities are treated in major league ball. Until recently, Marge Schott had hired only one minority staffer for the front office in eight years, and he spent much of his time working on the grounds crew.

A game heavily dependent on black stars has pitifully few blacks in its upper ranks. When the owners started looking around for a black to put on the committee to investigate Schott, all they could come up with was Bill White, the National League president. White has been a strong and impressive figure for decades, but in recent years he has been best known for his acid comments on baseball's racial practices. Having promoted so few blacks, the owners are hard-pressed to come up with one to defend the fairness of the industry. Now it has to sit by as one of its greatest stars, Hank Aaron, refers to baseball as "a country club."

The narrow focus on Schott's speech, instead of baseball's behavior, has introduced baseball to a familiar campus tactic: an official re-education program designed to purge the offender of offensive thoughts. This seems to be the brainchild of Jesse Jackson, who wrote a December column calling for Schott to undergo some sensitivity training. By dragging its heels for so long, baseball found itself responding, not to Schott, but to Jackson, who had been casting about for an issue to push.

So Schott will submit to a mandatory multicultural training program of some sort. The details are vague but she will apparently propose the program herself, which may consist of lectures, reading and watching movies. Nobody seems to think it's odd that the offender is in charge of her own deprogramming, or odder still that baseball is in the deprogramming business at all.

Here we go again. An attitude born on the campus (speech is action and can be punished as action) has been leaching into the real world. In 1988, under the old University of Michigan code, a student who ridiculed homosexual acts during a classroom discussion was forced to attend a gay rap session and had to write an essay, "Learned My Lesson."

At the 1991 St. Patrick's Day parade in New York City, someone threw a beer can at the mayor, who was marching with a gay group. Instead of being fined, the offender was sentenced to work for the mayor's office on gay issues. The writer Jonathan Rauch, who is gay, correctly complained of the "overtones of forced re-education."

The same overtones are obvious in the Schott case. Forced re-education is something we properly associate with communist regimes. What's it doing in baseball?

SEND US MORE HMONG

Visiting New York? See the Statue of Liberty and Radio City if you must, but the most interesting thing you can do here is hail a cab and chat up the driver. Among the cabbies who have hauled me around Manhattan in the past few months are these: a Thai actor; several Russian Jews; a Baptist minister from Haiti; a Hindu from Calcutta who is studying to be a corporate economist; a young Uruguayan woman who said she left her university and her country one step ahead of the secret police; a stolid Yorkshireman who moonlights as a security guard; a professor from Ghana; a Hong Kong immigrant who brought me up to date on the turf wars between the Chinese and the Italians in lower Manhattan; a native of Eritrea who thinks New Yorkers are too negative; a Bangladesh man who loves country music and (somewhat alarmingly) steps on the gas in time with the beat; many Palestinians and other Moslems; a chipper Samoan; an Iranian who misses the shah; and one homegrown fellow with a defiant sign on his visor that reads "BORN HERE—a genuine native born American white."

To climb the ladder, the new cabbies are willing to work hard for fairly low pay, clearing between $60 and $110 per twelve-hour day during this recession, not a lot of money if you have to pay New York prices. But then, as they are quick to tell you, they are free—no boss hovering around and they can quit or keep driving whenever they want. Some have not quite cut ties with the old country, flying back to Moscow or Manila or Port-au-Prince when they can afford to. They are good at what they do, picking the right routes almost every time and moving in rhythm with the city's quickness and hustle.

They seem like classic New Yorkers, shaking their heads like everybody else when they see a blue-and-yellow New Jersey license plate (a frightening warning sign that means "wretched driver" to knowledgeable natives). And they are relentlessly optimistic. No matter how carefully I explain that the city is going down the tubes, the drivers see only a bright future. That's why they are here. One burly Haitian said: "Many difficulties, yes, but in America, we always handle our problems." He's not a citizen yet, here only three years, and America is already "us." I love it.

New York City has close to a million newcomers. California has over 3 million, mostly Hispanic and Asian, mostly in the south. Though we hardly seemed to notice at the time, roughly 8 million arrived during the 1980s, a huge injection of new energy and talent at a time when the nation desperately needed it.

Labor Secretary Robert Reich keeps reminding us that our workforce is just not good enough to compete internationally. Here in New York, businesses complain that most new high school grads don't have enough skills. At New York Telephone, for instance, less than a quarter qualified for low-level jobs over the last several years. Reich estimates that only 20 percent of U.S. workers have the skill and training to meet world competition. He wants to spend $2 trillion on our schools to get that figure up to 55 percent within twenty years. Does anyone think we can get anywhere near that level without immigration?

We have an aging, undertalented workforce. Our students are performing worse relative to the rest of the world. A group of our high school seniors, better than the national average, tested thirteenth among thirteen nations in biology, twelfth in chemistry and tenth in physics. "The globalization of labor is inevitable," says the *Harvard Business Review*. A good thing, too, given our predicament.

Think of it as a free agent market. The Bobby Bonillas and Rickey Hendersons are workers from countries where schools are better developed than their national economies—Argentina, Poland, Korea, the Philippines. The Steinbrenners who need players are the mature economies, Germany, Canada, the United States and Japan, which refuses to bid for players. But as in baseball, no one really knows who the future MVPs will be. They often come from the ranks of the unheralded and unwanted.

Has anyone heard of the Hmong? The United States is now home to ninety thousand of these refugees from Laos. About twenty thousand settled in Wisconsin and had great difficulty coping. Half are on welfare, more than half unemployed. By traditional western standards, these are people from a remote, isolated and primitive part of the world. "Rarely have we absorbed a population that had so little initial understanding of the meaning and purposes" of a modern economy and American ways, said a Wisconsin Policy Research Institute report.

But apparently nobody told this to the Hmong children. Their grade scores are usually 40 percent higher than those of native Wisconsin students. Almost no one drops out. High school graduation rates are close to 100 percent, and a huge percentage of Hmong youngsters is heading on to college or technical school. This is an amazing story in the making, the national myth of immigrant success acted out by new players at blinding speed. Send us more Hmong.

I thought of the white cabbie's "BORN HERE" sign when I read Pat Buchanan's column the other day on how threatening the current wave of immigration is. He's right that Southern California is currently being overwhelmed. And it is far wiser to revive the collapsed economies of Mexico and Central America than to plan on making room for everyone here. At some point, immigration must slow. Still, Buchanan's column seemed like the first distant sound of nativist honking. We haven't had that yet, and The Economist gracefully complimented us about it: "In most other rich white countries, such waves of brown, yellow and black newcomers produce a frightened shout for tighter immigration laws. The United States is different." Yes, we are. That's why they come.

A POT STILL MELTING

The award for the most dubious op-ed article published in the month of June goes to David Hayes-Bautista, a doctor; Edward James Olmos, the actor; and Gregory Rodriguez, a writer.

The three Latinos published an article in the Los Angeles Times informing readers that Anglo culture is dying in the city, with Latinos poised to take over. (No mention of Asian-Americans, who are apparently cast as bystanders in this drama.) "Destiny takes hold of Los

Angeles in silence," they wrote. "No one has been imagining a post-Anglo world, and until someone does, we will be doomed to watch passively the slow social disintegration of a departing society."

The authors evidently thought it was useful to depict the rapid rise in immigration as triggering some sort of Latino cultural putsch and a new "post-Anglo era." This is, of course, exactly how the people in the English-only and anti-immigration movements tend to look at the issue.

The militant Latino talk is the product of activists and official Hispanic organizations that have fashioned a Latino identity around language and disadvantaged status. By pushing the analogy with blacks, the activists managed to get Latinos included under the Voting Rights Act and various affirmative-action programs. In this view, Latinos are locked in a struggle with an oppressive, colonizing Anglo culture.

One trouble with this worldview is that most Latinos don't seem to share it.

Is there a common Latino identity? The recent Latino National Political Survey, polling people of Mexican, Cuban and Puerto Rican origins, said no. Members of the three groups didn't acknowledge having much in common. Only a few called themselves Latino or Hispanic. In fact, more people wanted to be called "American" than "Latino." Those polled didn't much care about Latin America or even know much about it. Each of the three groups was fonder of Great Britain than of Latin America.

Do Latinos feel oppressed or alienated from Anglos? Obviously many Latinos have been treated badly in America. In parts of Texas, Anglo-Latino relations still look like a caste system. But Latino opinion is upbeat. Most said they had not been discriminated against because of ethnicity. Over 90 percent said they are treated as well as anyone else by Anglo officials. About 90 percent said they were "proud" or "extremely "proud" of the United States.

Do Latinos resist learning English? No. Over 80 percent support bilingual education, but as a means of learning English, not as a way of maintaining a separate cultural identity. Ninety percent say anyone living here should learn English. And more than two-thirds of American-born Hispanics are better in English than in Spanish, or speak no Spanish at all. On the other hand, a large majority strongly resists the idea that English should be designated as the official American language, possibly because it looks like a slap at Latinos.

A great deal of other evidence shows that Latinos are following in the footsteps of earlier immigrant groups, moving up and out of the barrio, intermarrying and blending into the general population at approximately the same rate.

Then why do we constantly hear about Latino oppression and exclusion? Two conservative authors, Linda Chavez in *Out of the Barrio* and Peter Skerry in *Mexican Americans: The Ambivalent Minority,* have an answer: the activist elites, with access to media, are out of touch with the communities they allegedly represent. One finding in the Latino survey backs that contention: 90 percent of Latinos do not belong to any of the ethnic Hispanic organizations that claim to speak for them.

Skerry gives one example. During the debate over possible legal sanctions against employers who hire illegals, the Latino elite adamantly opposed any sanctions, but various polls showed that between 42 and 60 percent of Latinos favored them. In fact, many polls show Latino values and attitudes are not very different from those of other Americans. Three-quarters of Latinos, for instance, think we have too many immigrants.

Poverty statistics are quite high, but skewed by the continuing arrival of semiskilled workers who arrive poor and not knowing English. As Chavez notes, Latino males are strongly attached to the workforce, and when salaries are adjusted to reflect schooling and experience, Latino males now make 93 percent of the money earned by non-Latino white males.

Assimilation is a dirty word these days, but Latinos are assimilating anyway. Studies show that Latinos do not wish to avoid the mainstream or brush aside Anglo culture, as the *L.A. Times* op-ed piece implies. The Latino National Political Survey said, "There is no evidence here of values, demands, or behaviors that threaten the nation's cultural or political identity." That's putting it negatively. The director of the project, Rodolfo O. de la Garza of the University of Texas, said he is "really stunned by how supportive Latinos are of American values."

Keep that in mind when listening to fearful opponents of immigration or Latino activists eager to conscript their people into the army of the alienated and oppressed.

INDIANS BEFORE KEVIN COSTNER

What were the Indians like when the first Europeans arrived? My old, dog-eared copy of A Pocket History of the United States by the famous historians Allan Nevins and Henry Steele Commager, has a crisp answer right there on page two. The natives were "a warlike, cruel and treacherous people still in the Stone Age of culture." Their numbers "certainly did not exceed 500,000," and since they had "shown little capacity to subdue nature," they "were too few and too backward to be a grave impediment to colonization."

Historians no longer write like that. A broad debate about the nature of Indian civilizations and the coming of the white man, percolating in the universities for twenty years, is surfacing in the popular culture, from movies (Dances with Wolves) and popular fiction (the best-selling potboiler The Crown of Columbus) to the Smithsonian's highly ideological art exhibit about the Old West. Get ready for more of this.

Were the Indians a Stone Age people? Yes, sort of. They had no writing systems, no metal tools, no looms, no useful domesticated animals. They hadn't gotten around to inventing the wheel. On the other hand, "Stone Age" usually refers to hunter-gatherers, not farming cultures. The natives had fancy irrigation systems, some complicated urban cultures, a knowledge of natural medicines and agricultural methods that beat anything Europe was capable of at the time.

How many Indians were there? The answers given here are crucial to the debate. The low numbers offered by Commager and Nevins make colonial America seem almost unoccupied and ripe for the taking. After all, if only half a million people were rattling around in all of the current United States and Canada, how could they justify hogging the whole place? Estimates have inched higher over the years, now ranging from a conservative 30 million for the hemisphere in 1492, to a high of around 100 million, the number used by the fictional professor of Native American studies in The Crown of Columbus. This high total nearly equals the population of Europe and Africa combined in the year 1500, estimated to be 127 million. Higher estimates (unproven and political) sustain the argument that Europeans didn't "settle" America—it was already settled.

The revisionists argue that "treacherous" "Stone Age" and "fewer than five hundred thousand" amount to propaganda designed to justify what happened to the Indians. Historian Francis Jennings calls this "the cant of conquest." Revisionists and their off-campus allies are using some tough words: invasion, genocide, ecocide. One academic sourcebook is titled *American Indian Holocaust and Survival.* These terms colored the debate about what to call the five hundredth anniversary of Columbus's arrival. "Discovery" is out and "invasion" seemed unthinkable. The Smithsonian tiptoed by with "encounter," as in, "My car just encountered a large truck going eighty miles an hour."

Well, was it an invasion and conquest? Sure. What else could it be called? Motives varied, from the crude and squalid conquistadors to the more careful English, but the results were the same. The Indians were stripped of their lands. Values crumbled and whole societies fell apart. An astounding 90 percent of native populations died off, mostly from imported European and African diseases.

Here comes the yes-but part. The revisionist work is not emerging in a vacuum, but in a context of great unhappiness about industrial pollution, American power in the world and rising complaints from domestic minority groups. When the *City Paper* of Washington, D.C., reviewed the Smithsonian's revisionist exhibit, it did not merely point out the sins of European settlers. It ranted a while about "business-suited white males." The depiction of Indians as unremittingly noble is simply the flip side of the current depiction of the West as totally evil. The cultures here when Columbus arrived were approximately as devoted to torture, slavery and cruelty as the rest of the world. And the positioning of the Indian as an environmental hero, living in perfect harmony with nature, is something of a stretch. America was a hard place, and Indians mowed down small forests and drove lots of buffalo over cliffs whenever they had to or could. Many tribes just messed up the place and moved on. There is no reason to believe that with better technology they wouldn't have made just as big a mess as more advanced cultures have. After all, Europeans and Asians at the same stage of development weren't major environmental villains either.

In much of the popularized literature, the deadly diseases brought by Europeans are either counted as "genocide" or implicitly used as an antiwhite political paradigm (whites equal disease and death). Novels and plays (like *The Kentucky Cycle*) perpetrate the myth of whites deliberately giving Indians blankets infected with smallpox. But the tragic deaths of so many Indians occurred because the natives had been isolated for thousands of years from the rest of the world's cycle of diseases and immunities. The incredible die-off would have happened if the Europeans had come in peace and remained on the coast, or if Asians or Africans had been the new settlers. Besides, historians rarely assign blame and guilt as diseases are transported around and around. Nobody says that the Mongols were genocidal killers for passing on the Black Plague to Europe.

But these are cavils about the more fevered attempts to politicize the new historical research. The scholarship itself seems basically right to me. European (and American) treatment of the Indians was a horror and the die-off of tens of millions of natives was one of history's greatest catastrophes. The least we can do is to say this plainly in our textbooks.

PART SIX

"Protecting a Roomful of Fruit from Venereal Disease"

Our Wayward Schools

OVER THE HEADS OF PARENTS

In his new book, *Free Speech For Me—But Not for Thee*, Nat Hentoff tells the story of a Pennsylvania high school pressuring two fundamentalist students to read *Working*, a Studs Terkel book with a chapter on prostitutes and a good deal of blasphemous language. Supported by their parents, the schoolboys asked, in conscience, to opt out from reading it. The school said it would withhold diplomas if the students didn't read the book. The two families hired a lawyer and won a settlement. Vengeful to the end, the school gave the boys Fs in the class that assigned the book. Along the way, the school board said haughtily that "with all deference due the parents, their sensibilities are not the full measure of what is a proper education."

That's a rather conventional attitude among educational bureaucrats: we are the professionals; parents are the nettlesome amateurs to be mollified or brushed aside. These days the attitude is on vivid display in the debate about condoms and AIDS prevention programs, with school and health officials cutting many corners to get the programs they want.

A friend reports that his eleven-year-old daughter came home from school one day and announced that she had put a contraceptive on a banana in her fifth-grade class. My friend was not consulted, or even told that the preteens were learning how to protect a roomful of tropical fruit from venereal disease. These things have a way of happening without parental input, possibly because the sensibilities of parents, poor yahoos that they are, aren't as good as the sensibilities of enlightened bureaucrats in instructing the young about sex. Besides, you can get a lot more done if parents don't know what's going on. At least my friend had the advantage of dealing with a private school he could yank his daughter out of. At public schools, the stakes are higher. When you send a child to a state school, do you yield all authority over the child's sexual education?

In New York City, some parents noticed their children coming home from school with a pamphlet outlining a sexual "bill of rights" for teenagers, including "I have the right to decide whether to have sex and who to have it with." Parents were surprised to learn that all children had the inalienable right to sleep around, and wondered who, exactly, had bestowed it. As it turned out, the new "rights" sprang full-grown from the head of someone at the City Department of Health. They were printed up there with federal money and made their way into the schools.

The list includes "the right to ask for help if I need it." This sounds harmless, but it has the effect of inviting a student-school alliance on sex, with parents cut out of the loop. A critic of these alleged new rights, Dr. Irene Impellizerri, vice-president of the city board of education, translated it as "I can go behind my parents' back." She argued that ethnic groups get ahead by not allowing schools and other institutions to get between child and parent: "Any school policy that shields children from their parents' traditional values and authority—any practice of addressing children over the heads of their parents—tends to hinder the progress of the group and to 'emancipate' more and more of its children into the underclass."

Washington, D.C., has just acted firmly to emancipate students from parental objections to condom distribution. Dr. Mohammad Akhter, the city public health commissioner, overrode an arrangement allowing parents to get their children exempted from the condom program in district schools. The superintendent of schools said parents could opt out of the condom program by writing him a letter. But Akhter ordered school nurses to disregard any such notes. The head of the district Congress of Parents and Teachers complained, in effect, that parents with moral or religious objections had been mugged. Columnist William Raspberry complained too, writing that Akhter's "doctor-knows-best arrogance" in brushing parents aside will have the effect of weakening the authority of mothers in the eyes of children.

Many school systems are notably honest and open with parents about sex programs. The city of Baltimore, for example, has that reputation. Partly as a result of working closely with parents, it has avoided the uproar over contraceptives that has hit New York, Los Angeles and Boston. But other school systems like to hide from parents the exact details of what their children are being taught and offered.

Dr. Impellizerri says she found out about New York's teen "bill of rights" only because a teacher slipped it to her privately, asking her not to tell where she got it. She says graphic material on how to perform anal sex is showing up, unapproved, inside city schools. Under various other programs around the country, children can be taught the use of "dental dams" for oral sex or referred for counseling to a gay activist without parents knowing.

David Blankenhorn, president of the Institute for American Values, thinks parents are quite intentionally kept in the dark. Educational bureaucrats, he says, "accept the proposition that parents are kind of backward, repressed, held back by religion, and have to be handled." Look for more stealth programs in schools.

HEATHER'S EXTRA MOMMY

Heather Has Two Mommies is a children's book about a lesbian couple having a child through artificial insemination. It is one of many books listed in the first-grade teachers' guide for New York City public schools. So is *Daddy's Roommate,* which features a happy youngster with two male parents who concludes that "being gay is just one more kind of love."

New York Newsday had some sensible things to say about *Heather*: it is "almost a parody of political correctness," but it shouldn't be used to discredit the city's entire multicultural curriculum, and no children should be made to feel ashamed because they come from "nontraditional" families. All true. So is the argument that gay-bashing is a serious problem in the schools. Surely the schools must do something about this.

Still, this does not explain why the curriculum is pushing stories like *Heather Has Two Mommies* and *Daddy's Roommate.* These are not books about tolerance—letting people alone and not picking on others because of sexual orientation or family structure. They are books celebrating the wonders of double-mommy and double-daddy households. But surely schools can generate respect for Catholic children, let's say, without putting *Heather Finds Peace as a Nun* on the reading list. They can promote respect for all children without endorsing all the different beliefs, lifestyles or orientations found in their homes.

So how did these books make it onto the reading list?

The answer is tucked away on page 145 of the city's *Children of the Rainbow* first-grade curriculum: teachers must "be aware of varied family structures . . . including gay or lesbian parents," and "children must be taught to acknowledge the positive aspects of each type of household." A line is being crossed here, in fact, a brand-new ethic is descending upon the city's public school system. The traditional civic virtue of tolerance (if gays want to live together, it's their own business) has been replaced with a new ethic requiring approval and endorsement (if gays want to live together, we must "acknowedge the positive aspects" of their way of life).

Four of the city's thirty-two school districts erupted over the issue and rejected the offending passage on page 145. With emotions running high, many people on both sides pumped out dubious arguments. The New York Civil Liberties Union, always the most eccentric of the ACLU chapters, professed to see censorhip in the rejection of Heather's two-mommy book. Some protestors hid behind age-appropriateness, arguing that five- and six-year-olds are too young to learn about lesbian artificial insemination (which is surely true, but a side issue).

The key question goes something like this: schools have a duty to promote decent behavior toward gays, but on what basis can a public school system insist that homosexuality must be approved? Under the traditional pluralism that New York City schools have now decided to reject, questions like this do not come up. The system has always been agnostic, asking diverse groups to park their conflicting value systems at the door so education can proceed with some degree of peace.

A letter-writer to *Newsday* had this to say: "If my wife and I choose to believe in what the Holy Scriptures say about homosexuality, it is not up to teachers, or any municipal or political group, public or private, to refute these teachings." His letter amounts to a case for traditional pluralism. He approves of banning religion from the schools, that is, he is willing to park his values at the schoolhouse door, but he wants the gays to park theirs outside too. But under the new city school curriculum, this sort of tolerance is gone. The letter-writer's beliefs are not just ignored by a value-neutral curriculum. They are overridden by newly imposed values. This touches off a destructive battle over public norms at a time when the schools desperately need to focus on academics, not intergroup warfare.

Journalist Richard Vigilante, writing in *The City Journal*, a conservative New York magazine, says that "to ask people to accept in their own children's schools a curriculum that undermines or contradicts their own deeply held moral beliefs is to ask of them an enormous sacrifice. If Americans do not have the right to maintain, for themselves and their families, moral beliefs taught for millennia by the religions to which between 70 and 90 percent of the population subscribe, then a lot of us are living in the wrong country." To slough off the distress of parents who learn that their six-year-olds "are to be taught the positive side of homosexuality," he says, "is not tolerance but moral and intellectual imperialism."

This is only one skirmish in the cultural war. The new multicultural ethic, shown clearly in doctrinal writings both inside and outside the school systems, is contemptuous of tolerance and "information-dominant" (that is, neutral) teaching. The key words, "positive teaching" and "appreciating diversity," mean that certain sets of ideas are about to be "infused" as valuable, whether parents think so or not. If that happens, home schooling and the school choice movement will empty out many schools. Mary Cummins, president of a Queens school district that strongly resisted page 145, said, "If they try to impose it on us, they won't have any kids in the public schools."

HERE COMES SCHOOL CHOICE

School choice, the six-hundred-pound gorilla of domestic politics, looms larger every day. The surprising new status of this old issue is largely due to the efforts of one politician: Polly Williams, a black Wisconsin state legislator who pushed through a bill allowing up to one thousand poor children to attend private, nonsectarian schools with the state paying twenty-five hundred dollars per year for each pupil. That plan, struck down by the courts on a very minor technicality, is being appealed, but the point is that Williams, almost singlehandedly, converted a languishing, middle-class, right-wing issue into a new and potent one of minority empowerment.

By lashing out at "the poverty industry," "the entrenched school establishment" and "our liberal friends" who want to control the poor, Williams won the hearts of the right. ("Some Democrats are upset because their whole lives revolve around taking care of dumb poor people," she told me last week. "We're very able people. We just need a little help.") By asking that funds and power be granted directly to the poor, she appealed strongly to the left. As a result, school choice is warmly supported by the *National Review* and *The Nation,* the liberal Brookings Institution and the conservative Heritage Foundation, libertarians, Catholics, Afrocentrists, radicals, the business elite (twenty-six articles and opinion pieces on Polly Williams in *The Wall Street Journal*), minorities (72 percent of parents in favor of some form of choice, Gallup says) and Americans in general (62 percent in favor). This is an astonishing coalition that will produce change and ferment from coast to coast. Predictably, the only major naysayers are the educational bureaucrats and teachers' unions. Reacting like the owners of any company store, both are officially shocked to find that many consumers wish to shop elsewhere.

Since I endorse school choice, including the right to apply vouchers or tuition credits to private and religious schools, let me first raise some reservations about these plans. First, if the free-market model of school choice is accurate, schools may appear and disappear from the market as fast as brands of cake mixes. This problem is a long way off, but it would mean a period of great disruption and instability, with a psychological toll on children shuffled from school to school every year or two, and rich opportunities for financial scandals and educational versions of consumer fraud.

Second, there is the possibility that choice will further balkanize American society by in effect funding schools with a strong separatist tint. This would include schools run by cults, by some of the loonier Afrocentrists, and by Hispanics who do not wish their children to learn English. One need not romanticize the public school system to worry about this kind of institutionalized fragmentation.

I think we should face up to the fact that school choice in effect downgrades the goal of integration by focusing sharply on quality and the right to pick any school at all. When I asked Polly Williams, are excellence and empowerment more important than integration, she said, "Definitely. If they are priorities, integration will follow." Maybe so, but it isn't obvious. It is true that many experiments focus on "controlled choice" (that is, choice limited by racial balance), but the logic of the movement is to let parental choice rule, and choice leads just as easily to more segregation as to less. Attempts to restrict choice by quotas will produce a blizzard of lawsuits. It probably is time to make excellence and choice the primary goals in education, but if so, it would be nice to discuss openly what happens to the goal of school integration that America has spent so much energy and money to pursue for two generations.

The most important argument for school choice is the collapse of the public school system. We seem to rank at the bottom in most studies of scholastic achievement in western nations. Our high school students don't seem able to find China on a map. In one survey, 45 percent of high school juniors didn't realize that nine is 9 percent of one hundred, and in another, 95 percent of seniors couldn't figure out a bus schedule. American business is said to spend as much money each year teaching basics to high school grads as the public schools spend on high school education and miseducation.

While school choice is no panacea, as the National Endowment for the Humanities recently argued, "Simply because of the forces it sets in motion, choice does have primacy among reforms." Since Polly Williams's experiment was approved, the public school system in Milwaukee has been hustling to carry out its own reforms. That's what competition does. It also unleashes the energies of parents, who have smaller, more accessible schools to deal with and no glacial bureaucracy to cut through. The most celebrated example of this within the public school system was in East Harlem's District 4, which successfully splintered into four different schools, many of them housed in one building, along the way raising reading scores from dead last in the city to about the middle of the pack.

But if the challenge to a bureaucratic and monopolistic school system is something like the breakup of communism (the analogy is irresistible), offering choice only within the public schools is something like a timid reformer offering Russians the right to shop at different state stores. For competition to work, we should respect the right to apply our own tax funds to any kind of school that can help. Seeing that some sort of choice is inevitable, the teachers' unions will likely try to contain it within the public system. But I think that breaking out of that shell is the only way to guarantee widespread change and put the poor on the same footing as the well-off.

THE SORRY TEACHING OF TEACHERS

Anyone who thinks that a new crop of young teachers will rescue our public schools should take a look at Rita Kramer's book *Ed School Follies.* Kramer, a New York writer, traveled around the country to more than twenty schools of education to find out what the teachers of tomorrow are being taught. She came away thinking she was watching a gigantic train wreck in slow motion.

The cream of the crop of ed students tend to go to Harvard, Berkeley and Columbia's Teachers College and most become sophisticated bureaucrats who never go near a classroom. At less famous schools, many of the apprentice teachers were astonishingly inarticulate. When they could express themselves, a large number sprinkled their sentences randomly with the word "like," just as teenagers do. And they knew so little that Kramer wondered how or what they will be able to teach. A professor at the State University of New York, Plattsburgh, said that half of his ed students did not know what the suffix "ism" means. "We can't assume our students know anything," he said. "They've never even learned the states and their capitals."

Kramer's technique was to sop up the ed school culture by sitting in on classes and talking to professors and students. Threading through all this talk is the reigning doctrine of the schools, which almost everyone seems to take for granted. It is "child-centered." This means it is the teacher's job to interest the students, not the students' responsibility to buckle down and learn. There was a startling amount of emphasis on teaching children about themselves and their feelings, rather than about the outside world. Kramer learned that one sixth-grade curriculum about sex and reproduction, under discussion in an ed school class at Eastern Michigan University, is titled "Figuring Out What's Best for Me." With that reasoning, a class on auto mechanics could be called "Figuring Out What's Best for My Car."

As Kramer reports, ed school theorists seem to think their students are so fragile that one low mark, one discouraging comment will turn a child into a druggie or a dropout. In another new book, *The Learning*

Gap, a comparison of Asian and American schools, psychologists Harold W. Stevenson and James W. Stigler tell the story of a Japanese youngster who was having trouble drawing a picture of a cube. The teacher asked the child to go to the blackboard and keep at it until he figured out how to produce the picture. The children in the class were unconcerned and no humiliation was involved. The Japanese assume that not every task comes easily, and the only humiliation is not trying hard. In America, the same youngster might have been shielded from effort by a flurry of fretting about hurt feelings and the dire threat to self-esteem.

Ed school theory these days is tightly focused on feelings and hostile to standards and the idea of competition. Grades and marks are bad too, since they characterize and divide children. The good side of this doctrine is its insistence on equality, community and treating poor children and outsiders with respect. But the emphasis is lopsided and its cost is high. In ed-school theory, "equity" is something of a Trojan Horse. Smuggled in along with equality is the notion that performance and learning shouldn't really count—they elevate some children at the expense of others. This produces a philosophy of leveling that is indifferent, sometimes antagonistic to achievement. Kramer writes: "What happens to those more capable or motivated students is hardly anyone's concern."

In fact, there is more than a hint that the bright achievers must be tamped down somehow as part of the campaign for social equality. A professor at Texas Southern makes this clear, calling for teachers to "promote equity in student achievement." Kramer finds that this strange demand "for equality, not of opportunity, but of outcome" is widespread in ed schools. Lurking behind "equity" is a socially destructive resentment of children who work hard and achieve something that the rest of the class doesn't.

Everywhere there is the whiff of ideology. At East Michigan University, a grim professor discusses the children's book *Tootle* as an example of the plight of workers manipulated by the dominant class. (Tootle, a train, learns to stay on the tracks.) The villains in this discussion included "meritocracy" (discussed as a self-evident dirty word) and the idea of working hard, which the professor said "covers up a whole set of social, structural issues." The professor asks for an example of an activity that supports the dominant class. "Going to the doctor," one aspiring teacher answers brightly. "That's an ideology. It benefits the group of doctors at the expense of native healers and herbalists."

Most of these ideas percolating through the ed schools are leftovers from the 1960s. "In every conceivable fashion, the reigning ethos of those times was hostile to excellence in education," Professor Daniel Singal wrote recently in a memorable *Atlantic* article. "Individual achievement fell under intense suspicion, as did attempts to maintain standards." Those notions were discredited long ago in the real world. How long will it take to clear them out of the ed schools?

DO SCHOOLS VICTIMIZE GIRLS?

How Schools Shortchange Girls, a report from the American Association of University Women, landed with a loud thump on the front pages of our newspapers. It has received unusually heavy editorial support and the stampede is on to push its forty recommendations into elementary and high school curricula as soon as possible.

But there's a problem. As Anne Bryant, executive director of the AAUW Educational Foundation, acknowledges, almost nothing in the report is new. It is a rehash of studies—some dubious, some trivial, some out of date—assembled to make a point. The report could have said something like this: we have more to do, but we have come a very long way in a very short time. Our textbooks and expectations have changed; sex differences on tests are narrowing; females generally get better grades than males, go to college in greater numbers than males, get more MA degrees, and are catching up on the Ph.D. level.

That story would have wound up in the back of the weekly education section. But when the bias-victimization button was pressed—"Bias Against Girls Is Found Rife in Schools, with Lasting Damage" was *The New York Times* headline—the story catapulted to page one.

The trouble is, neither this highly polemical report nor the research behind it can justify that headline. The report brings up subjects that have generated exhaustive and ambiguous research and quickly rounds them off to fit the charge of bias. For instance, boys outscore girls by about fifty points on SAT math tests. The report says "no efforts have been made to balance" this test. Not true. The Educational Testing Service has been pulling, adding and analyzing test items in pursuit of balance, but boys keep outscoring girls. No one knows for sure why this is happening. It may be that boys tend to show heavier interest in abstract matters. Whatever the reason, to fob this off as a simple bias issue is wrong. At the heart of this report is a dubious instinct: where girls do better than boys, the disparity is accepted without much comment; where boys do better, it's always bias. (Girls with high marks and low test scores may be suffering "test bias." But we can look at it the other way too, as "marks bias" against males who score high on objective tests but get lower classroom grades.)

The same sort of packaging is provided for another well-known phenomenon: teachers call on boys more often than they do on girls. The report simply chalks this up to discrimination. Could be, but there's another factor. At all levels, boys are typically more restive and unruly in class, and teachers tend to call on boys as a kind of behavioral control to keep them from blissing out or acting up. Swagger and aggressiveness also help boys dominate classroom talk. In the words of Myra Sadker, coauthor of a study cited in the AAUW report, "One reason teachers give boys more attention is they are more aggressive in grabbing it." This finding suggests a call for single-sex schools, where male behavior will no longer be able to set the tone for female learning. But the report doesn't go that way, or even deal directly with the differences in classroom behavior. It just complains about bias.

There's another disturbing aspect: on page after page, schools are depicted as if their major role is to function as social agencies and feelgood therapy centers. Other reports talk with alarm of how our schools have declined academically. This one is heavily concerned with feelings ("Classrooms must become places where girls and boys can express feelings and discuss personal experiences." "Children must have a safe place to acknowledge their pain and vulnerability.") It calls for installing "the evaded curriculum," a term it coins for a social agenda of teaching on battered women, gender bias, emotional abuse, sexuality, rape, drug abuse, sexual harassment, body image, depression and the affirming of groups as well as individuals through multiculturalism. The form of multiculturalism it has in mind is revealed when it endorses the most radical and irresponsible of existing reports on the subject, the New York State plan prepared for Education Commissioner Thomas Sobol.

The report was prepared by feminists at the Wellesley College Center for Research on Women. While some recommendations make sense, the report is pervaded by fringe feminist ideas. Violence against women is called "an increasingly accepted aspect of our culture." The fact that heterosexuality is taken to be the norm in America is called unfair. ("The assumption of heterosexuality is a form of discrimination.") Sexual stereotyping, the report says, leads to teen pregnancy. And "gender-equity experts" should be installed in Washington "to foster gender-equitable education."

The team of federal gender-equity experts may turn out to include Peggy McIntosh of Wellesley, one of the report authors, whose criticism of "vertical thinking" is highlighted in the text. Perhaps wisely, the exact nature of "vertical thinking" is left vague, but in a videotaped lecture she once said it involved "exact thinking, or decisiveness, or mastery of something," which is triggered in students by words like "excellence, accomplishment, success and achievement." Instead of achievement-mongering, McIntosh wants to promote "lateral thinking" in the curriculum, the aim of which is not to win or excel, but "to be in a decent relationship to the invisible elements of the universe." Consider that an alarm bell. This report needs a full vertical analysis.

EXCLUSIVE: BARBIE SPEAKS UP

Barbie will probably survive, but the truth is, she's in a lot of trouble. It seems that the new Teen Talk Barbie, the first talking Barbie in twenty years, has shocked many feminists with a loose-lipped comment about girls and math. Each twenty-five-dollar doll speaks four of the 270 programmed one-liners. In one of those messages, Barbie says, "Math class is tough." This was a big error. She should have said "Math is particularly easy if you're a girl, despite the heavy shackles of proven test bias and male patriarchal oppression."

Because of this lapse from correctness, the head of the American Association of University Women is severely peeved with Barbie, and you can no longer invite both of them to the same party. Other feminists and math teachers have weighed in with their own dudgeon.

Since this is Barbie's darkest hour, I placed a phone call out to Mattel,

Inc., in California to see how the famous long-haired, long-legged forerunner of Ivana Trump was holding up. To my astonishment, they put me right through to Barbie herself.

"Barbie, it's me," I said. As the father of three girls, I have shopped for thirty-five to forty Barbies over the years, including doctor Barbie, ballerina Barbie, TV news reporter Barbie, African-American Barbie, animal-rights Barbie, and Barbie's shower, which takes two days to construct and makes the average father feel like a bumbling voyeur. So I figured Barbie would know me.

Barbie spoke: "Do you want to go for a pizza? Let's go to the mall. Do you have a crush on anybody? Teaching kids is great. Computers make homework fun!"

In a flash, I realized that Barbie was stonewalling. These were not spontaneous comments at all. They were just the prerecorded messages that she was forced to say, probably under pressure from those heartless, controlling patriarchs at Mattel.

At the same time, I began to appreciate Barbie's characteristic subtlety—by reminding me that she was recommending the educational use of computers to young girls, she was, in effect, stoutly rebutting the charge of antifeminist backlash among talking toys. I had to admit it was pretty effective.

So I pleaded with her to speak honestly and clear her name. I heard a telltale rustle of satin, and then she spoke. "You're the one who took three days to put my shower together. That was ugly."

"Two days," I said, gently correcting the world-famous plastic figurine. I asked her about the harsh words of Sharon Schuster, the awfully upset head of the AAUW. Shuster had said, "The message is a negative one for girls, telling them they can't do well in math, and that perpetuates a stereotype."

"That's a crock," Barbie replied. "Just because a course is tough or challenging doesn't mean my girls can't do it. Weren't your daughters a little apprehensive about math?" I admitted that they were. "Well, how did they do?" "Top of the class," I replied. This seemed like a good time to brag, particularly after Barbie's wounding comment on my shower-construction skills.

"Then tell Sharon Schuster to stop arguing with dolls and go get a life." Her remark was an amazement. This was not roller-skating Barbie or perfume-wearing Barbie. It was the real thing, in-your-face Barbie.

"The first time I open my mouth after twenty years, and what happens? I get squelched by a bunch of women." At this point, I mentioned that my friend M. G. Lord, the syndicated columnist who is doing a book on Barbie, is firmly on her side. M. G. told me: "Math class *is* tough, but it doesn't mean you have to drop out and go to cosmetology school. These people are projecting a lot of fears onto Barbie."

Barbie was grateful. "Thank M. G. for me. I'm looking forward to her biography of me. And tell her that if she ever fails in life, she can always become head of the AAUW."

That remark may have been a trifle sharp, I said. "Well," said Barbie, "I'm just tired of taking all this guff from women's groups. They're scapegoating the wrong girl. I'll match feminist credentials with any of them. I worked my way up from candy-striper to doctor. I was a stewardess in the sixties, and now I'm a pilot. Ken is one of my flight attendants. You can buy me as Olympic athlete, astronaut and corporate executive."

Barbie was on a roll now. I was writing furiously to keep up. "In the summer of 1992, they put out a presidential candidate Barbie, and two days later, Ross Perot withdrew. Figure it out," she said. "As far back as 1984, my ad slogan was 'We girls can do anything.' I've done more than any other doll to turn girls into achievers, and still they treat me as a prefeminist bimbo. What's wrong with the women's movement?"

I knew enough not to touch that one. Besides, it's a very short column. But I was struck by her comment that Ken was now employed as a flight attendant. "Didn't he used to be a corporate executive?" I asked. "We didn't vote for Bush again," she replied bitterly.

Then I heard a muffled side comment: "Ken! Be careful with those dishes." I said I felt bad about Ken's comedown, but Barbie brought me back to reality: "Remember, he's only an accessory." This was tough to take, but the issue was settled. Barbie is indeed a feminist. Over to you, Sharon Schuster.

SINGLE-SEX COLLEGES—WHY NOT?

At first glance, the successful student rebellion to keep males out of Mills College seems merely modish. This is not an age in which college protests have much to do with the outside world. Instead, group indignation erupts over parochial and tribal issues: tuition increases (bad), installing speech codes (good), dividing up the curriculum like a spoils system (wonderful), or admitting males to all-female colleges (formerly good, now bad).

Then too, the Mills protest against coeducation eerily echoed black protests against traditionally white colleges, talking about "institutional gender bias" and "subtle sexism" at coed institutions, and severely trashing "the male element." (The correct word here should have been "ilk"—males and their ilk.)

A few of the protesters made the female-black parallel explicit, arguing that women should turn away from coed colleges to be with their own kind, just as many blacks are turning away from Michigan and Harvard and going to traditionally black institutions such as Morehouse and Howard. This also makes the Mills protest a child of the times: it is plugging in to the touchy tribalism of the day and the growing impulse toward segregation.

There is also the richly enjoyable spectacle of feminist hypocrisy. After arguing for years that one-sex clubs, bars and associations are dastardly betrayals of the American dream, many feminists are nimbly managing to defend exclusion by sex at college—at Mills, that is, not at all-male VMI.

Having said all that, however, and after fretting about the rampant separatism among collegians, I am bound to say that I think the Mills protesters have a strong case. A fairly large body of evidence now indicates that women learn more, learn faster and emerge more confidently at women's colleges than at coed colleges. Some of this is attributable to the elimination of sexual distraction in class. But much more seems to depend on the larger number of female teachers, who serve as mentors and role models, and the gearing of education to female strengths and sensibilities.

Most of these studies point to a loss of confidence among many women at mainstream colleges. One survey of high school valedictorians, for instance, showed that upon entering college roughly equal numbers of males and females thought they were intellectually superior to their peers. But after two years of college, 22 percent of the males and only 4 percent of the females considered themselves smarter than the rest of the class. It would be nice to know why so many of our brightest females acquire self-doubt so quickly at college.

One thing that shows up in almost every study is the finding that male students talk more in class and somehow manage to command more attention from teachers. We have all read a lot about teachers looking past females to call on males. But this is not a conspiracy, as many feminists imagine. Most teachers do not set out to shortchange females. It is a clash of classroom styles in which the males, more inclined to interrupt, take risks, show off and talk off the top of their heads, tend to eclipse the more orderly and less aggressive style of females. Still, the fact is that when male behavior sets the tone for female learning, females tend to lose out. Professor Myra Sadker of American University recalls that when women from all-female Wellesley showed up for an exchange program at coed MIT, one resident teacher said he could instantly pick out the Wellesley students—they were the women who spoke up in class. This is not an indictment of coed education in principle, but it is certainly an indictment of coed teaching as currently packaged by males for female consumption.

Educational theory is particularly prone to faddism, and it now seems that we have been as careless in cutting down most of our all-female colleges as the Brazilians have been with the rain forests. Only 94 out of 298 remain, and they have an important function in building confidence and leadership potential. In addition, it seems sensible to view women's colleges as laboratories where we will discover what teaching works best with women. Take one example: the percentage of women in the engineering profession has actually declined in the past six years—from roughly 17 percent to 15 percent. There is no apparent reason why this should be occurring. Is it because of the way math and science are presented and taught to women? There are already indications that women take more math and science and do better at it at women's colleges. But more detailed studies at all-women colleges ought to pin down what is happening and why.

The fact is that we know very little about the education of women. We have simply assumed that one-size-fits-all education will apply equally well to males and females. But this is very likely not the case. Girls entering first grade score higher on virtually every standardized achievement test, and for years their verbal superiority to boys is astonishing. Yet by the time they graduate from high school, they are well behind boys in every area, including verbal. Doesn't this suggest that something is wrong with their schooling? If so, is there any connection between relatively poorer female performance and the declining number of single-sex high schools and junior high schools, which have been disappearing at about the same rate as women's colleges? In 1986 a study of seventy-five Catholic high schools, both single-sex and coed, showed that the girls from single-sex schools were more likely to enjoy math, do homework, show ambition and have higher test scores in vocabulary, reading, math and science.

In New York City, when the last all-female public high school admitted boys, the students, mostly poor black and Hispanic girls, let out a howl of protest similar to the one at Mills. In retrospect, they probably had a sure sense of what was happening. Maybe we should pay more attention to the howls.

STOP BLAMING THE TESTS

Headquartered near Harvard, the National Center for Fair and Open Testing—FairTest, for short—is a group of earnest young reformers who feel certain that the Scholastic Aptitude Test (SAT) is biased against blacks and women. This is a very serious charge, but if you send away for their literature, do not brace yourself for much subtlety. One publication features a cartoon of a black student struggling with this SAT question: "If Tad is supposed to meet Buffy at the country club, but his Volvo breaks down, will Buffy play tennis without him?"

Can it be that FairTest has evidence that nefarious test-makers at SAT are stacking the exam in favor of Tad and Buffy, not to mention Brent and Forsythia? I phoned Sarah Stockwell, a veteran spokeswoman for FairTest, asking for examples of real-life questions loaded against blacks. Well, she said, one analogy question used the word regatta, which is hardly part of black experience. This lamentable use of regatta is by now almost immortal. It pops up all the time as a horrid example of SAT bias without (alas) the information that the question was removed from the test twenty years ago.

Any other examples, perhaps a bit juicier and more recent? Well, Stockwell said, the word pirouette showed up once, and tympanist and melodeon were used in a single question. These examples, also long gone from the test, make up the short list of FairTest's Greatest Hits. Stockwell's one example of bias against women was a two-part math question about calculating the winning percentage of a basketball team.

She felt this was objectionable because more boys than girls play basketball, and students do slightly better on questions dealing with familiar subjects. Always trying to be helpful, I asked if it would be nonprejudiced if we changed it to focus on stats of a women's field-hockey team. No, she said, because girls aren't brought up to figure out what a winning sports record is, and boys are.

This Alice-in-Wonderland quality of FairTest responses has two important sources: a serious shortage of biased questions, since the test, like its competitor, the American College of Testing exam (ACT), is carefully combed for possible bias; and a determination to ignore the questions in any event, since claims of prejudice by FairTest and others are really based on disparity of test results. Whites score higher than blacks and males higher than females; therefore, the test must be biased. (No complaint, however, that the math test must be tilted in favor of Asian-Americans, who easily outscore whites.)

This has been a hard few years for the Educational Testing Service, which draws up the SAT, and the College Board, which sponsors the operation. First they were drawn into the National Collegiate Athletic Association's attempt to use a (very low) combined math-and-verbal-SAT score of 700 as a barrier against academically unqualified jocks getting college scholarships. Given the state of race relations right now, this was probably not a very bright idea, since most of those excluded would be blacks. The College Board protested this use of the test, but it took its lumps when the leading black in the dispute, Georgetown basketball coach John Thompson, offhandedly referred to the "proven cultural bias" of the SAT.

The second blow came when a federal judge ruled that New York state was unfair to women in giving out college scholarships purely on the basis of SAT scores. It is hard to see how the judge could have ruled any other way. Because men consistently outscore women on these tests, the state was giving about two-thirds of its scholarship money to males. The judge wisely found bias in the state's use of scores, not in the test itself. The fact that women's scores are fifty-six points lower than men's is a disaster, and while FairTest sits on the sidelines shouting "bias," the truth seems to be that no one really understands what is happening here or why. The theories include the following: innate sexual differences that pitch males toward spatial and quantitative tasks and females toward verbal ones (but then why are women's verbal scores declining steadily?); the tendency of teachers to take boys more seriously and help them more than girls; the possibility that tests with time limits and multiple-choice questions somehow favor the male mind; the trend among girls to avoid using computers and math; indications that more women than men who take the test are currently coming from disadvantaged families.

Whatever the problem is, it goes well beyond the SAT. The ACT shows the same pattern of declining verbal scores, and according to the College Board, so do 150 other standardized tests. But instead of falling back into the familiar and exhausted vocabulary of bigots and victims, why don't we simply put a hundred or so underemployed sociologists to work and find out what is really happening?

Casting blacks as victims of the SAT is particularly incendiary; it also undermines the real educational progress that is being made. Scores of blacks on the SAT, though still low, are up twenty-one points on the verbal and thirty on the math since 1976, the largest gains of any group. "These kids can learn," said Greg Anrig, president of ETS. "It's like turning a ship; you don't do it in a second. To tell a kid the test is biased is wrong. The spotlight should be kept on opportunity."

SCUTTLING SCHOOL REFORM

Just when it looked as though we would get a serious school-reform plan through Congress, House Democrats have moved in and mugged it beyond recognition.

The heart of President Clinton's "Goals 2000: Educate America Act" was a council that would set up voluntary, national standards on what students should know and be able to do. Other modern industrial nations already do this.

But the plan for measuring and encouraging student performance standards has been undermined in the House bill by a labor and education subcommittee. The emphasis now is on "opportunity to learn" standards, which are supposed to spell out what schools must make available to students. This might include smaller classes, new technology, competent teachers and up-to-date textbooks.

How was the committee able to change the subject so quickly and divert attention away from curriculum standards? The lever was "fairness" and "equity." The argument goes like this: it's unfair to set standards for students until the quality of schools is taken into account and perhaps equalized.

There's a seductive surface logic to this argument. Many students are in fact handicapped by terrible schools and terrible teachers. But it's not obvious that standards must be postponed until every substandard school is fixed and every poor teacher is replaced.

As Albert Shanker, president of the American Federation of Teachers, says: "We don't abolish medical school exams because not everyone has had the opportunity for top-notch pre-med education. Nor do we say that tests for airline pilots shouldn't count because not everyone has the opportunity to do well on them."

House Democrats are undermining the bipartisan effort worked out among the nation's governers, led by then-governor Bill Clinton, and the Bush administration. Why? Turf is surely one reason. Two presidents and many governors built this program without much input from Congress. And old-line Democrats dream of massive school funding from Washington, not commissions on standards with no money to hand out.

But there is also the clash of philosophies. Reformers, such as the National Governors' Association, focus on standards, excellence, measuring job skills and preparing the workforce for international competition. The most powerful wing of the educational establishment focuses on social equality and student cooperation. This camp opposes elitism and advanced programs (which create a student elite) and fears that minorities will not be able to meet real academic standards.

The National Education Association, always a formidable obstacle to reform, is doing its usual job here. "We've been raising the high bar without worrying about who can jump it in the first place," NEA president Keith Geiger said about standards and testing.

Democrats are responding to a wide array of forces that don't want standards at all. Some are loading the bill down with amendments, perhaps hoping it will sink.

The equity language in the original bill was bad enough. It talks of "student performance standards that all students, including disadvantaged students . . . [and] students with disabilities . . . will be expected to achieve." This means standards that brilliant and retarded students will both be able to handle. Someone close to the committee discussions said: "No one can go any faster than the most handicapped person." This is yet another indication that ideology and the suspicion of brains and student achievement are big problems for some on the Democratic side.

Republicans fear that voluntary "opportunity to learn" standards will become compulsory. Diane Ravitch, an assistant secretary of education in the Bush administration, writes: "You do not have to be a seer to predict that the new standards . . . would permit federal regulation of curricula, textbooks, facilities and instructional materials."

An amendment to the bill by Representative Jack Reed (Democrat, Rhode Island) seems to convert voluntary standards into mandatory ones. It would make future federal funding dependent on "corrective action" by school systems that don't meet the standards. Litigation is another route. Parents may successfully sue a school for not meeting the federal "opportunity to learn" standards.

The school-reform bill was not supposed to go through all this. After all, there has been a strong bipartisan consensus on its content for years. The nation's governors, led by Bill Clinton, were in basic agreement with the Bush administration. What it comes down to now is a battle between the so-called New Democrats and old-line liberals.

In a May letter to Secretary of Education Richard Riley, South Carolina governor Carroll Campbell, a Republican, wrote that the revised bill "comes dangerously close to derailing our hard-won emphasis on student achievement . . . and threatens to turn the clock back on four years' worth of bipartisan teamwork." Campbell is right. Too much effort has been invested in much-needed school reform for it to be wasted now. Is the president going to do something about this or not?

A FOR EFFORT—OR FOR SHOWING UP

What is the hardest mark to get at many American colleges?

Answer: C. Like the California condor, it is a seriously endangered species. It may need massive outside help to survive. Otherwise, it could easily go the way of marks like D, E and F, all believed to be extinct.

Harvard instructor William Cole put it this way in an article in the *Chronicle of Higher Education:* A generation or two ago, students who mentally dropped out of classes settled for "a gentleman's C." Now, he says, perfunctory students get "a gentleperson's B," and "a gentleperson's A" is not out of the question, particularly in the humanities. A tutor in English told *Harvard Magazine* "in our department, people rarely receive a grade lower than B minus. Even B minus is kind of beneath mediocre."

As college tuitions have climbed, grade inflation has risen right along with them, perhaps muting complaints about what it all costs. At Harvard in 1992, 91 percent of undergraduate grades were B minus or higher. Stanford is topheavy with As and Bs, too; only about 6 percent of all grades are Cs. At Princeton, As rose from 33 percent of all grades to 40 percent in four years.

Because of grade inflation, outstanding students and average students are often bunched together at the top. "In some departments, A stands for average," Harvard senior Dianne Reeder said at a panel discussion on inflated grades last spring. "Since so many of us have A-minus averages, our grades are meaningless."

The avalanche of As is producing a similar avalanche of students graduating with honors. *Harvard Magazine* cites an unidentified dean of admissions at a top-six law school saying his office ignores magna cum laude and cum laude honors from Harvard because so many applicants have them. In 1993, 83.6 percent of Harvard seniors graduated with honors.

This is a national problem. Outside of economics, science and engineering, collegians are getting such good marks these days that it seems average students are disappearing from the campus, all replaced by outstanding achievers. It's reminiscent of Garrison Keillor's fictional Lake Wobegon, where "all the children are above average."

What's going on here? Market forces surely play a role. Colleges are competing for a pool of students who expect and sometimes demand high marks. "Students complain in ways they didn't before," said Martin Meyerson, former president of the University of Pennsylvania. "Teachers find it easier to avoid the hassle and just give higher grades." And good marks sustain enrollments in academic departments, a sign of success for professors.

Many people think grade inflation started with the generous marks professors gave to mediocre students in the sixties to keep them out of the draft during the Vietnam War. Fallout from the sixties is surely involved; during the campus upheavals, radicals attacked grading as a display of institutional power over the young. And, in general, the postsixties makeover of campuses has been crucial.

"Relativism is the key word today," William Cole said. "There's a general conception in the literary-academic world that holding things to high standards—like logic, argument, having an interesting thesis—is patriarchal, Eurocentric, and conservative. If you say, 'This paper is no good because you don't support your argument,' that's almost like being racist and sexist."

The current campus climate makes professors reluctant to challenge grade inflation. Harvard professor Harvey Mansfield said during the panel discussion on grading that "professors have lost faith in the value of reason and hence lost faith in the value of their status. Their inability to give grades that reflect the standards of their profession is a sign of a serious loss of morale." Boston University professor Edwin Delattre says: "If everything is subjective and arbitrary, and you try to apply standards, you run afoul of the prevailing ethos of the time."

Still, whatever the failings of the academy, inflated grades don't start there. The same virus has afflicted high schools for at least two decades. Since 1972, when the College Boards began keeping tabs on high school seniors, the percentage of college-bound students reporting high marks in school has almost tripled. In 1972, 28.4 percent of those taking the test said they had A or B averages in high school. By 1993, it was 83 percent. This happened while SAT scores were falling from a mean combined score of 937 to the current 902.

For whatever reasons (and the feelgood self-esteem movement is surely one), marks have broken free of performance and become more and more unreal. They are designed to please, not to measure or to guide students about strengths and weaknesses.

Give As and Bs for average effort and the whole system becomes a game of "Let's Pretend." Parents are pleased and don't keep the pressure on. Students tend to relax and expect high rewards for low output. What happens when they join the real world where A and B rewards are rarely given for C and D work?

PART SEVEN

"IF IT FEELS BAD, ATTACK IT"

The Tyranny of the Hurt-Feelings Movement

SELF-ESTEEM UP, LEARNING DOWN

Most people think of the California state task force on self-esteem as yet another California joke, one more zany feelgood perpetration by blissed-out mental surfers. This notion has been encouraged by Garry Trudeau, the *Doonesbury* cartoonist, who poked savage fun at the task force when it was announced, and again when it issued its final report, three years and $735,000 later.

Any report devoted to the idea that the state should go around promoting and monitoring good feelings is obviously open to ridicule. (The task force deflected some gibes and criticism by adding "personal and social responsibility" to its title, and by issuing a few conservative findings.)

But the conception of self-esteem as a public-policy issue is not a Lotusland joke, or a California-only phenomenon. It is an idea that has quietly taken hold all around the country. The self-esteem movement, in fact, is a social force of some strength, particularly in the schools.

Those who push self-esteem in the schools point out that the public school system is in disastrous shape, particularly in the cities. Teachers are expected to cope with the devastating results of poverty, racial discrimination, crime, drugs, broken homes and child abuse. Under these wartime conditions, the schools are de facto social agencies, presumably with nothing to lose and much to gain by building up the egos of their children.

Self-esteem programs use simple exercises more or less frankly borrowed from the "You're-much-too-hard-on-yourself" California therapies. In the curriculum at St. Clement Catholic School in Somerville, Massachusetts, children take part in "affirmation exercises," saying nice things about themselves such as "I am kind; I am friendly," or "I am a good person; I am special." Sometimes they do this silently while imagining themselves atop a windswept mountain, or aloud in front of the class while looking into a mirror. They keep journals of their accomplishments, are encouraged to support the good feelings of classmates (the proper response is "Thanks—I affirm you for being a good friend") and glance up many times a day at the symbol of the program, a "potential bottle," a foot-high jar filled with blue water that represents the untapped possibilities in all children.

The current era of tight money turns out to be a perfect time for self-esteem programs. They cost almost nothing. They offer the light of sunny California optimism at a time of great pessimism. They are simple—easily grasped, easily spread. And in public school systems torn by competing pressure groups, they have no natural enemies. They have only one flaw: they are a terrible idea.

First of all, despite the firsthand reports of many teachers, there is almost no research evidence that these programs work. The book *The Social Importance of Self-Esteem*, which is basically all the research turned up by the California task force, says frankly, "One of the disappointing aspects of every chapter in this volume . . . is how low the associations between self-esteem and its consequences are in research to date." In fact, those correlations are as close to zero as you can get in the social sciences.

This confirms the commonsense judgment that behavior is rarely changed by injections of positive thinking and psychic boosterism. Confidence boosting has a long and important tradition in the schools, but what evidence we have indicates that fear of failure and parental hovering have much more to do with academic success than good feelings about the self.

Second, the self-esteem movement is on a collision course with the growing movement to revive the schools academically. The self-esteem movement is rooted in the California therapies, which are sunny, feel-good and generally hostile to learning and intellect. Fritz Perls, the founder of Gestalt Therapy, set the tone for California therapies by denouncing intellect as "a drag" and "a whore." The California task force report is dedicated to the late Virginia Satir, a charismatic therapist with not much use for the human mind. ("She can fill any hall in the country, but she has great difficulty conceptualizing," one of her colleagues told me after a Satir lecture.)

The self-esteem literature is clotted with dismissive references to achievement. The self-esteem research book mentioned above contains many darts aimed at competition, achievement and success. After all, if people are perfect and lovable just the way they are, why should anyone need to change or strive?

This is why the obsession with self-esteem ultimately undermines real education. When the self-esteem movement takes over a school, teachers are under pressure to accept every child as is, and to maintain each child's self-esteem. To keep children feeling good about themselves, you must avoid all criticism and almost any challenge that could conceivably end in failure. In practice, this means each child is treated like a fragile therapy consumer in constant need of an ego boost. Difficult work is out of the question, and standards get lowered in school after school. Even tests become problematic because someone might fail them.

This becomes a parody of self-esteem. Real self-esteem is released when a child learns something and develops a sense of mastery. It is a by-product of, and not a substitute for, real education. And until we grapple with the real agenda of the self-esteem movement—ersatz therapeutic massage instead of learning—there will probably be no educational reform at all.

THE POLITICS OF FEELINGS

The original guidelines for the University of Michigan anti-discrimination code said "students must be free to participate in class discussion without feeling harassed or intimidated." Penn State is striving to forbid anything on campus that makes people uncomfortable about sexual issues. Law professor Catharine MacKinnon says, "I call it rape whenever a woman has sex and feels violated."

Note that in these three examples, we are far from any objective or social standard of offense. Instead we are in the realm of feelings. Under the Michigan code, since declared unconstitutional, if a student felt intimidated by a professor's remark, even if no one else in the class saw anything objectionable, the student's negative feeling created and defined an offense. Apparently, any sexual discomfort felt anywhere by anyone at Penn State does the same thing. And according to MacKinnon's standard, and some far vaguer than hers, any consensual act of sex can be labeled rape if negative feelings develop. Since rape and sexual harassment are increasingly being viewed subjectively, definitions of these acts can expand indefinitely, and are indeed doing so.

The use of feelings as a trump card is becoming pervasive. The codes and laws generated by the campus-based race and gender alliance are aimed at real problems. But almost all are disastrously rooted in the demand that there must be no negative feelings. If there are, as is so often the case when the individual collides with the real world, then someone must be penalized for it. Jonathan Rauch, a writer concerned with these matters, says this amounts to yet another freshly minted right, "the right not to be offended."

More and more, this means the abandonment of communal standards in favor of subjective, personal ones. In effect, the "right not to be offended" has been widely granted. In the media, many militant groups essentially have a veto power over their own bad press. Even in the best newspapers, coverage of such matters as Afrocentrism, the real ideas of campus feminists, or the guerrilla activities of Act-Up tends to be omitted or carefully softened up to avoid controversy. Editing such stories is thought to be in the same category as defusing a land mine.

The loss of consensus and the rise of the "right not to be offended" explain why "sensitivity" and "insensitivity" have become the nouns of the nineties. Since there are apparently very few social rules that anyone wants to defend, our constant chore is to guess what will trigger negative emotions ("sensitivity") and accuse ourselves ruefully when we accidentally step on another person's emotional land mine and set it off ("insensitivity"). Even the evasive nonapologies of those caught in scandals have taken on this "feelie" quality. William Aramony, stepping down as head of the United Way amid allegations of financial abuses, apologized for a "lack of sensitivity to perceptions." The board, in turn, accepted his "thoughtful and sensitive offer" to leave immediately.

We are hip deep in a bizarre attempt to use feelings as a social standard, mostly thanks to the therapized ethic produced in the sixties and seventies by the human potential movement and other pop therapies. These therapies had very little use for rationality or social commitment—the self was autonomous, virtually independent of culture and properly steered by its own feelings, whatever they happened to be. Carl Rogers wrote: "Doing what feels right proves to be a competent and trustworthy guide to behavior which is truly satisfying." This is the basis of the famous axiom "if it feels good, do it" and its not so famous corollary "if it feels bad, attack or ignore it."

Along the way, a great deal of our educational system has been therapized: self-esteem programs that induce a feeling of success, quite apart from any achievement; history as therapy in the high schools and colleges, featuring feelgood stories about each ethnic and sexual group; an unembarrassed relativism based mostly on feelings—all traditions must be equal lest anyone feel inferior.

The enterprise requires a thorough subjectivity. There are no truths, only different views. An offense is what an individual or tribe says it is. After an insulting racial comment at the University of Washington, a Hispanic professor said that "the abused community [must] define what is or is not acceptable." The implicit argument is that injured feelings, usually under cover of "hostile environment" theory, must be translated into penalties, codes and laws. But as William Galston of the University of Maryland says, "We have to resist the tendency to make feelings normative for definition of a crime." Yes, indeed. Feelings are private and mercurial; laws are not.

LOSING IS BRUISING, SO LET'S NOT PLAY

If you read *The New York Times*, always look first at the bottom of page one. That's where the editors sometimes insert a warm and fuzzy article to get your mind off the real front-page news.

One day the fuzziness and warmth radiated smartly out of an article headlined "New Gym Class: No More Choosing Up Sides." The story was that basketball and other games are disappearing from gym classes across America, mostly because gym teachers think the games damage the feelings of children who aren't outstanding players.

Even games like dodgeball "have fallen into disrepute," wrote reporter Melinda Henneberger, who evidently had a harrowing time in traditional gym class. A subhead to her article sums up its thesis: "Cooperation is in, competition and humiliation out."

Sure enough, right above the article was a photo of six children in a gym, each up on one leg doing an interpretive dance. Nearby a grim phys-ed teacher looks on, perhaps to make sure that none of the kids made a break for it and tried to start an illicit basketball game.

Kids can still shoot some hoops on their own, the *Times* said, but "even then, the goal is not so much to learn to score a basket as to develop body awareness, hand and motion skills and the confidence to try new activities."

This is a New Age approach to sports, drained of fun and skill. "Body awareness," "space awareness" and various concepts and feelings are excruciatingly important to this form of basketball. Actually putting the ball in the basket is not.

The *Times* article carries the implicit message that win-lose games are dangerous. Losing inevitably means humiliation. Kids have such fragile egos that it's better to avoid any challenge or competition that might send them into a tailspin. (Chalk up much of this attitude to the self-esteem movement.) There's also the hint that these games are vaguely undemocratic because the kids who play them are suddenly separated into winners and losers.

A lot of the anticompetition theory made the rounds in the late sixties, when giant earth balls were pushed around by whole classes so everybody could be on the same team. Later, books of noncompetitive games started to appear, with titles like *Everybody Wins*, the first sign that losing at kickball was about to be defined as an amazing trauma.

In fairness, the game theorists who stressed group fun and de-emphasized competition had a point. This is a very competitive hyper-individualistic culture that undervalues cooperation. School sports shouldn't be used to turn out little predators or the screaming Little League parents of tomorrow.

The trouble is that the anticompetition people couldn't seem to hold up the ideal of cooperation without going berserk over team games. Alfie Kohn, author of the 1986 book *No Contest*, argues that competition in the classroom and in the gym inevitably has destructive effects. Even a choose-up game of hoops? Yes, he told me. "There are still destructive effects—anxiety, a sense of failure and lack of interest in exercise. Fun doesn't require adversarial activities. The way we feel about people is affected by the structure of the game."

But kids in a pickup game are not learning the dangerous lesson that "other people are obstacles to my success" (Alfie Kohn's phrase). They are simply playing, and perhaps learning something about cooperation, discipline and excellence along the way.

The attack on competitive sports in schools comes in two new forms these days. One has to do with gender. Since boys tend to grow up throwing a ball against a wall or a stoop, and most girls may not, there's a feeling that girls reach school age with an athletic disadvantage. The schools are addressing this problem, but some people want to avoid the whole issue by downgrading or eliminating team games. Rita Kramer, author of *Ed School Follies,* a book on theories at schools of education, thinks a feminist argument against competitive sports is emerging. "This is one of those hidden agenda items for feminists," she says. "Some of them don't want masculine skills to be valued too highly in the schools."

The other, more serious argument comes from the cooperative learning movement and other school movements that promote "equity issues," and are less concerned with excellence than with equality. The basic teaching, that nobody is better than anybody else, leads believers to oppose any activity that produces winning individuals. From an "equity" point of view, it's better to have everybody hopping up and down on one leg than to risk the inequality of having winners.

There are many obvious things to say here. The antiachievement ethic buried in the "equity" argument is a deadly one. People can lose without humiliation and win without feeling superior. Through sports, children learn how to handle defeat as well as victory—no sulking, gloating or rubbing it in. Aerobics and interpretive dancing have their place, but so do team sports. And it's always best to keep ideologues out of the gym.

Come on. Let's play ball.

TOUCHY, TOUCHY, TOUCHY

For a week now, I have been trying to whomp up the correct degree of indignation over Billy Crystal's little Mafia joke on Oscar night. This is because I happen to be of Italian extraction, and two Italian-American groups have indicated quite explicitly that I should have achieved high ethnic dudgeon by now over Billy's remark that if a certain Italian businessman buys MGM, the lion won't roar, it will take the Fifth Amendment.

Alas, dudgeon keeps eluding me. I have concluded that Crystal's one-liner was a relatively harmless and clunking wisecrack in the midst of a very funny monologue. I have further concluded that no Italian-American should expect to sail through life totally protected from the occasional observation that a prominent sector of organized crime is run by folks whose names end in vowels. And besides, Billy Crystal seems to be a nice guy with no track record for bigotry, and anyone who introduces actual humor into an Academy Awards show deserves to be seen in the best possible light.

This is apparently an eccentric view in the eyes of the two highly incensed Italian-American groups. They have denounced Billy's remark as "racist." (Ten years ago the word "racist" indicated full-time haters, usually those in Nazi uniforms or white hoods; now it is the conventional way that ethnic groups clear their collective throats while preparing to say hello to one another.)

Untold Italian-American man-hours of labor have been devoted to reaching and organizing people like myself who have somehow neglected to become irate. Fifty-two members of Congress solemnly signed a statement accusing Crystal of "soiling the reputations of . . . 26 million citizens of Italian heritage who live throughout this free and loving land." This is perhaps the biggest Italian-American protest since the 1976 suit to stop the Alexander Graham Bell stamp on the grounds that Antonio Meucci, and not Bell, invented the telephone.

Why the overreaction? Well, the answer seems to be that overreaction is the current community standard. Everyone howls like a banshee these days over small and imagined intergroup slights, denouncing everyone in the area as a dreaded "ist" or "phobe" of some sort or another. Even Aryeh Neier, the veteran civil liberties lawyer who is now with the Human Rights Watch, deplores the current "competitive attempt to be more sensitive than one's neighbor." In other words, if I hear Mr. Neier correctly, we are currently in the midst of a grievance olympics, with more and more players joining the game.

One way to play the game is to monitor the media with a hawk eye, burnishing one's image wherever possible and bristling with highly predictable outrage at any TV or movie depiction that is less than perfect. In general, this means that no fictional villain is allowed to come from your group. As producer of *Cagney and Lacey,* Barney Rosenzweig was inundated by letters from blacks, women, Arab-Americans, Hispanics and Italian-Americans, all angry at the way they were occasionally portrayed, even though the show was unusually careful about ethnic sensitivities. He even heard from a few Gypsies outraged by the use of "gypped" in the script, so the word was banned.

The disability rights movement objects to all use of the words "crazy" and "moron" as insulting to the mentally impaired. The movement also generally objects to cartoon characters such as Mr. Magoo (bad eyesight), Porky Pig (stutter), Daffy Duck (lisp) and the wicked witch from Snow White (the implied connection between evil and ugliness). Shakespeare regularly takes his lumps for the real-life hunchback Richard III, Melville for Ahab (who would quickly be changed to a conventional two-legged villain by most alert modern editors), and one woman objects to virtually all blind characters in children's books. The movement has a good argument, of course—physical disability is casually used as a symbol of evil in all sorts of fiction—but at the fringes oversensitivity gallops along. A fuss was raised over this harmless sentence in a health magazine: "The face is the reflection of the soul." Barking at lines like this is the equivalent of founding the Homeliness Liberation Movement. The disability rights people are probably now strong and touchy enough to veto all disabled villains. Disney's *Snow White*, for instance, could not be made today (there's Dopey to worry about besides that wicked witch, and feminist objections too).

Porky Pig probably couldn't make it past the image-censors today either because he is fat and would very likely cause some organized bristling at the National Association to Advance Fat Acceptance, headquartered in Sacramento. The organization is fresh from a triumph over Hallmark, which capitulated to a stout protest from the group and withdrew a card joking about a thin person on a crowded bus being squeezed by a fat man.

This sort of thing goes on all the time, often perpetrated by the same groups that complain publicly about censorship. After a friendly visit by gay lobbyists, a *Midnight Caller* TV script about a homosexual threatening to infect sex partners with AIDS was changed beyond recognition. A villainous Catholic priest in a *Miami Vice* script quickly became a nonpriest. After protests from Native Americans, the depictions of savagery by the Sioux in the best-selling book *Hanta Yo!* were dropped in the TV version and replaced with labored emphasis on tribal spirituality. Rastafarians called for the banning of the movie *Marked for Death* because it portrayed some Jamaicans as killers and drug-dealers. A Halloween mask of an Arab sheik was removed from sale when the Arab-American Anti-Discrimination Committee denounced it as racist. (There's that mandatory word again.) An Arafat mask ("Put on our Arafat mask and terrorize your neighbors") might seem to be fair game, but no, the lobby said the slogan "reinforces the stereotypical view of Palestinians as terrorists."

My favorite example of touchiness is the formal protest filed against Gallo by the Kohlrabi Growers' Association after the two hayseeds in the Bartles & Jaymes TV ad said that their wine cooler goes with every food in the world except kohlrabi and candy corn. The Candy Corn Anti-Discrimination Committee has yet to be heard from.

TAKE TWO LAUGHS AND CALL ME IN THE MORNING

Loretta Laroche of Plymouth, Massachusetts, says that healthy people laugh one hundred to four hundred times a day. Ms. Laroche should know. She is a health educator who runs a company called Wellness Associates, and she travels around staging workshops on health matters, including "Humor: the Healing Power of Health and Play."

Only the churlish would wish to attack such a well-meaning humor-monger. But let us face facts. Yukking it up at Ms. Laroche's recommended peak capacity—25 times an hour, 2,800 times a week, 146,000 times a year—is obviously no laughing matter. Holding it down to 5 seconds per laugh, this would still amount to 200 man-hours (or woman-hours) per year devoted solely to self-help guffawing. After six or seven months of this rigorous regimen, not even the videotape of Geraldo drilling into Al Capone's empty safe would be likely to fetch a thera-peutic chuckle. But as Ms. Laroche knows, the antistress and fitness industries have decreed that laughter is the best medicine, and we had better spoon it down regularly, no matter how unpalatable.

As in any Puritan culture, activities that even faintly smack of fun must be justified by high purpose. Happily, this is so among the humor missionaries. In a properly monitored belly laugh, muscles all over the body contract, the pulse doubles from 60 to 120 and blood pressure shoots from 120 to 200. Although science has not sorted out the chemical effects of laughter, or even figured out why some people think Pee Wee Herman is funny, researchers believe that regular injections of mirth are associated with fewer headaches, reduced stress and even a longer life. This means it can be packaged and sold as a fitness product to high-strung workaholics, who would otherwise have to change their lifestyles or risk expiring of a heart attack at age thirty-five. With a few jokes and an ergometer Air Cycle, scientists believe, many such death-prone workers can confidently expect to reach age thirty-seven.

This packaging is, in fact, under way. Several companies, such as Safeway Stores and Manville Corporation, have installed humor programs. Dr. William Fry of Stanford, usually cited as the leading theoretician of salvific joking, says laughter is like "stationary jogging." This neatly positions the new health product alongside an established one already popular among the target cohort of consumers.

Elsewhere Dr. Fry is quoted as saying that laughing 100 times a day (thus nearly diluting the dose—remember, this is Ms. Laroche's minimum daily requirement) is equivalent to about 10 minutes of rowing. Here we have an estimate susceptible to cost-benefit analysis. A hundred laughs would take only a trifling 8.5 minutes per day, a 15 percent saving of time over the 10 minutes of rowing, not even counting the considerable gain of not having to dress in funny clothes, travel to the boat or shower afterward. The more competitive laughers, of course, would eventually shave a second or two off each humorous outburst, thus boosting the net gain to 30 or 40 percent. This might well put rowing out of business. It could also establish organized laughing as the only endorphin-producing leisure activity that does not lead to shin splints, back pain or criminal charges.

(This is true of your bunny as well, studies show. If rabbits on a high-fat diet are cuddled, fondled and talked to, they are protected against arteriosclerotic heart disease, while similar but friendless rabbits die.)

Laughing is not the only surprising new health product. Here is a good sociologist, James House of the University of Michigan, giving the sales pitch for another one: lab experiments "have demonstrated that the presence of others, especially familiar others, can reduce the adverse effects of experimentally induced stressors or other health hazards on psychological, physiological and behavioral functioning." Whew. What he means is that people are better off if they have friends.

While friendship may well hit much of the country as a revolutionary idea, it is old hat in California. "Friends can be good medicine" bumper stickers began appearing in California in 1982, along with a state-sponsored find-a-friend campaign (Jerry Brown was governor) and a frankly profriendship promotional film starring Ed Asner, who doesn't mind being controversial. *Psychology Today* magazine said that trusting people builds a healthy heart. It even quoted a psychologist who suggested falling in love as a way of averting heart failure.

While that would be a truly radical move, it seems obvious that future health discoveries will be turned up by intrepid researchers, among them the following:

▪ Activities completely unrelated to the workplace, such as stamp collecting or torturing iguanas, will be found to be associated with fewer heart attacks.

▪ Scientists will learn to directly stimulate the joke receptors in the human brain, allowing workers to gain the health benefits of laughing without actually smiling or leaving their work stations.

▪ Sexual activity will be found to be an acceptably time-effective health pursuit, if boiled down to two minutes or less and conducted with throaty chuckles. This can be done by eliminating foreplay, which has been found to have no wellness benefits at all.

▪ Reading this column while eating oat bran, laughing wholeheartedly, and fondling one or more persons of the opposite sex will be found to increase heart strength 14.7 percent, whereas any one of these four health-promoting activities, taken singly, improves heart functioning by only 2.9 percent.

▪ An average of 98.8 percent of Americans who are not related to Jerry Brown will ignore all of the above and just lead normal lives.

RALPH AND WANDA DON'T UNDERSTAND

RALPH: Say, Wanda, where did you get this meat?

WANDA: What's wrong with it?

RALPH: Gotcha, my pet! You have just helped me illustrate Ralph's First Law of Male-Female Conversation. Ask a hundred American husbands where the roast beef came from, they will all name the local butcher or supermarket. Ask a hundred wives who have just cooked a meal, and every single one will turn slightly white, like you just did, and ask, "What's wrong with it?"

WANDA: . . . And I suppose this is because all women are insecure and unable to answer direct questions, is that what you want to say, Ralph?

RALPH: That would be unfair, my love. After all, women constitute one of our top two sexes. It's just that us guys are so splendidly precise and logical. We don't hear "This meat is terrible" if someone is just asking which market we use.

WANDA: Before you break out into a chorus of "Why can't a woman be more like a man?" Ralph, let me admit that you have a point. Men are more direct and literal-minded in conversation, and women are more attuned to the metamessages, the nuances and the emotional tone. That's why men are so abysmal at lamentation talk.

RALPH: What's lamentation talk? And how come I'm so bad at it?

WANDA: Remember the argument we had last week? I said I felt bad because I was putting on some weight, and what did you say?

RALPH: I said what any loving and supportive husband would say: "Why don't you go on a diet?" You got mad, for no reason at all. Then I pointed out, rather kindly, I thought, that you were endlessly worrying the problem instead of dealing with it and moving on.

WANDA: Ralph, believe it or not, I already know that going on a diet is one way of losing weight. I didn't raise the subject with you so you could clobber me with cracker-barrel advice. It was lamentation talk. I wanted reassurance and confirmation of my feelings about myself.

RALPH: Good grief, Wanda. What would happen to the world if guys went around confirming feelings? Most of us break out in hives if forced to talk about emotions for more than forty seconds. We face things directly, in a manly way. We don't just sit around gabbing endlessly about them.

WANDA: That's just what Deborah Tannen, a sociolinguist, says in her new book, *You Just Don't Understand: Women and Men in Conversation.* She says that women engage in lamentation talk all the time, offering matching troubles to reassure one another. This phenomenon seems to be true all around the world.

RALPH: I do that every week with Fred. We meet at the fence. He talks about his crabgrass problem. Then I talk about my crabgrass problem, and we both go back inside feeling better. Lamentation talk about lawns is the very heartbeat of the suburban experience, Wanda.

WANDA: Don't be smart, Ralph. The problem is that troubles talk grates on men, just as the man's standard response grates on women. Men can't wait to change the subject, as you just did with your crabgrass joke, or cut off discussion by saying, "Here's what you do . . ." If you had empathized, you would have sent a calming metamessage: "We're the same, you are not alone."

RALPH: So what was my offense?

WANDA: By giving the obvious advice about dieting, you sent a different metamessage: "We're not the same. You have the problems; I have the solutions." You Tarzan, me Jane.

RALPH: Having a solution is not a character flaw, dearest. How is your average male supposed to know when a wife wants actual help, and when she just wants her hubby to join her in a good wallow?

WANDA: Congratulations, Ralph. You have just illustrated many of Tannen's points about male conversation in a single sentence: it is often abstract, abrupt, polemical and concerned with being one-up, or at least avoiding being one-down. Have you ever noticed that you get irritated whenever I start a sentence with "Let's"?

RALPH: I love all your sentences, my pet.

WANDA: Tannen says women tend to use "Let's" as a way of seeking consensus. "Let's go for a walk" is the opening of a negotiation. But men tend to bristle at the word—they think they're being told what to do. That's also why you never ask directions when you're lost, Ralph. Like most men, you drive around in circles for ten minutes or so rather than take the subservient role of asking for help.

RALPH: So this is one of those books that says men are beasts?

WANDA: Actually not. Tannen says both male and female styles are valid. Men speak and hear a language of status and independence, where women speak and hear a language of connection and intimacy. Basically we come from different planets. This is why so many small parties break down into one group speaking female and another speaking male. You know, the impersonal male stuff—traveling salesman jokes, politics, sports and status.

RALPH: Wanda, have I told you the one about the man who wouldn't ask directions? It seems he and his wife were driving along, totally engrossed in a deeply satisfying lamentation talk about being lost, when all of a sudden . . .

WANDA: A&P, Ralph.

RALPH: What?

WANDA: The meat is from the A&P. Now let's pass the potatoes, if that's OK with you.

SEX, LIES, AND VIDEOHABITS

WANDA: Ralph, why are you clicking your way from Channel 2 to Channel 98 over and over? Is the remote control broken, or do you consider it urgent to see exactly four seconds of every program?

RALPH: None of the above, dearest. The activity I am happily engaged in is known as grazing. When you graze from the lowest channel right on up the highest and around again, it's known as rolling through. It's the highest form of grazing there is.

WANDA: It's a little like watching clothes tumble around in a dryer, Ralph. Do you think it will be over soon?

RALPH: A trend this powerful? Are you kidding? Some guys spend whole evenings rolling through, just checking out every channel, or maybe watching three or four shows at once, shuttling back and forth constantly.

WANDA: This is fun?

RALPH: For your doting husband it is, but not for everybody. *Channels* magazine says a lot of grazers hate what they do and keep doing it anyway. It's addictive, like booze, chocolates or codependency. Tony Kornheiser did a whole column in *The Washington Post* admitting that he's a clickaholic. At that level, you probably wake up in the middle of the night, sweating, with your thumb pressing the air every five seconds. Not a pretty thing to see.

WANDA: Ralph, am I right in thinking that this is one of those numbingly senseless male activities that few women are ever going to understand?

RALPH: Harsh words, Wanda. Let's just say that grazing harmlessly harnesses the natural nomadic promiscuity of your basic male viewer. It probably goes back to the hunter-gatherer phase of human evolution, when us guys were restlessly rolling through in manly pursuit of a mighty mastodon and you girls were back home gathering nuts with the kids, a single-channel activity for sure.

WANDA: You mean women are more attentive, and men are easily distracted. Okay, Ralph, I accept that grazing is a good way for men to work at shortening their attention spans. Everybody's got to keep in shape. But something tells me there's another motive for grazing. Can it be the average male's terrible fear that somewhere, on some obscure cable channel, there's a naked woman dancing and he's missing out?

RALPH: Wanda, I'm shocked. Here I've got a great new hobby, and my very own wife thinks I'm some sort of voyeur. Sure, the possibility of catching a nude woman or two has been mentioned once or twice as a very minor motive for some grazing. But do I go around attacking your TV habits and calling them perverse?

WANDA: Something tells me you're about to. Fire away, Ralph. At least it will give you a chance to put down the clicker before it melts.

RALPH: Made-for-TV movies.

WANDA: What about them?

RALPH: About two-thirds of them are two-handkerchief snifflers for women, and you watch every single one. Every atrocity and ailment that can happen to a woman or child eventually gets its own three-hour home movie. The only conflict is whether to watch Farrah Fawcett being beaten, raped, strangled, stabbed, burned and treated discourteously on CBS or flip on over to NBC, where Jane Alexander wakes up one morning shocked to find that her sweet little daughter has somehow turned into a neo-Nazi transvestite prostitute with scurvy. Either way, there's lots of enjoyable heartbreak all around. Frankly, I'd rather catch a documentary on Canadian fishing rights.

WANDA: You wouldn't understand, Ralph. These stories have to do with women overcoming the sense of their own powerlessness, facing emotional problems that you guys evade whenever you can.

RALPH: Wanda, you don't go down to the morgue on your day off to watch a few autopsies, so why do you curl up happily to watch the death, disease and abuse of women and their small children?

WANDA: And why are you men so allergic to the ordinary business of emotional life? If an emotional scene appears on the tube, you immediately jump up to get popcorn or disappear into the john until the car chase starts.

RALPH: All I have to work with here is male hormones, dearest, but I'm doing the best I can. Even though my heart sinks, don't I point out every single abused-woman movie I see in the listings?

WANDA: For a man, you're really sweet, Ralph.

RALPH: I'm going to graze awhile until Jaqueline Smith's battle with Lou Gehrig's disease at nine o'clock, dearest. She's a plucky woman, and I just know she'll fight like a tigress. Now avert your eyes, my pet, I'm rolling through.

PART EIGHT

"JUST ANOTHER MARLBORO MAN FROM OUTER SPACE"

Our Zany Popular Culture

MOVIES TO FEEL VIOLENT BY

As a critic of violent entertainment, I have a flaw: I've always enjoyed it. When my wife heads for Cinema One to revel in some deeply empathic movie about meaningful relationships, usually starring Meryl Streep or Shirley MacLaine, I meander off to Cinema Two for a film with more action, a higher body count and a few mandatory car crashes and explosions.

This is an absolutely conventional male attitude. If a meaningful relationship breaks out on screen, men usually go for popcorn. Most of us want action stories based on quest, challenge and danger (and therefore the likelihood of some violence). Like many males, I am especially partial to cartoon shoot-'em-ups, such as the *Robocop* and *Terminator* movies. If someone has to die, let it be villainous stick figures rather than recognizable humans.

Now, however, I am bailing out. The dial has been turned up too far on gruesomeness and sadism, even in comic-book films. The most innocent-looking male action movie must be checked in advance for stomach-churning brutality. I knew I would not be going to see *Cape Fear* when a reviewer informed me that the DeNiro character "bites into the cheek of a handcuffed woman and spits out a Dinty Moore Chunky Stew–sized piece of flesh." Over-the-top hair-raising violence that would have been unthinkable in mainstream movies a decade or so ago now seems routine.

What's worse, the attitude toward the justification of violence has changed. At the beginning of *Terminator II*, Arnold Schwarzenegger arrives from the future, naked and programmed for violence. He enters a bar and casually bludgeons a few pool players whose only offense is refusing to give him their clothes and motorcycle. This is uncomfortably close to the common urban crime of attacking youngsters for their bikes or starter jackets. Here that kind of violence is implicitly but rather clearly endorsed. After all, Arnold is bigger, stronger and has a nuclear war to stop. So beating up bystanders is OK.

In the old Hollywood, the code was different. On the whole, violence among heroes was limited and a last resort. The deck was usually stacked to make nonviolence a nonoption at the end. But at least sympathetic characters were rarely shown enjoying violence or overdoing it. Now, the social critic Mark Crispin Miller wrote in *The Atlantic,* screen violence "is used primarily to invite the viewer to enjoy the *feel* of killing, beating, mutilating." The movie is set up for the viewer to identify with the hero and the fulfillment that violence brings him. Often, Miller says, the hero's murderous rage has no point "other than its open invitation to become him at that moment." This is not violence as last resort, but as deeply satisfying lifestyle.

Michael Medved's book *Hollywood vs. America,* is very sharp on another aspect of the new violence: it is often played for laughs. In the first *Predator* movie, the hero impales a man against a tree with a machete, then urges the victim to "stick around." In *Lethal Weapon 2,* Danny Glover jokes, "I nailed 'em both," after holding a nail gun to the heads of villains and puncturing their skulls. And in *Hudson Hawk,* Bruce Willis decapitates a bad guy and jokes, "I guess you won't be attending that hat convention in July." This is hardly hilarious humor, but it serves to suppress the moviegoer's normal emotional response to agony and mutilation. This flip attitude, very common in films now, is an invitation to the joys of sadism.

In response to snowballing protests about screen violence, Hollywood has frequently tried to argue that fictional violence has a useful, cathartic effect. "I think it's a kind of purifying experience to see violence," says Paul Verhoeven, director of *Total Recall.* But a large and growing number of studies point away from this comforting thesis. The studies show that children exposed to violent entertainment tend to be more violent themselves and less sensitive to the pain of others. This makes screen violence a social problem, and not, as Hollywood likes to argue, an individual problem for consumers ("If you don't like the movie, don't go").

Cardinal Roger Mahony, the Roman Catholic archbishop of Los Angeles, terrified the industry last winter by talking about a tough Hollywood film-rating code. But he dropped the idea and instead has issued a pastoral letter defending artistic freedom and asking Hollywood, ever so politely, to clean up its act. When violence is portrayed, he asks, "Do we feel the pain and dehumanization it causes to the person on the receiving end, *and* to the person who engages in it? . . . Does the film cater to the aggressive and violent impulses that lie hidden in every human heart? Is there danger its viewers will be desensitized to the horror of violence by seeing it?" Good questions, and no threat of censorship. Just an invitation to grow up.

Todd Gitlin, a Berkeley sociologist, put it less decorously, talking at a recent conference about "the rage and nihilism" that Hollywood is tossing on screen.

He said: "The industry is in the grip of inner forces which amount to a cynicism so deep as to defy parody," reveling "in the means to inflict pain, to maim, disfigure, shatter the human image." Message to Hollywood from cardinal and sociologist: try something else.

THELMA, LOUISE, AND TOXIC FEMINISM

A friend called to say that *Thelma and Louise,* the new female-buddy car-chase movie, is a very disturbing film, and I must write about it immediately. Since this friend is no faintheart but a strong woman, extremely successful in her field, I saw the film and hereby pronounce her correct, as usual. This is just one of the current bumper crop of woman-kills-man movies, but it is clearly the most upsetting. A colleague here at the magazine said she could not come to terms with the themes and ideas so blithely unleashed in this movie, and that many of the women who sat in the audience with her seemed to leave the theater in something of a daze.

What is producing this sort of anxiety? I doubt that the movie's resolute male-bashing is the reason. Hollywood has such a long and honored tradition of misogyny that few of us would begrudge women two hours of male comeuppance. Nor is it that woman are invading the male-buddy genre. Susan Sarandon and Geena Davis are at least as good at this sort of thing as Redford and Newman. And knot-in-the-stomach violence is not the problem: just one murder, one armed robbery, one exploded oil truck, one Nazilike cop reduced to blubbering at gunpoint and stuffed into the trunk of his police car. By the standards of Butch and Sundance, who shot up screenfuls of totally innocent Bolivians, this movie is ballistically underdeveloped.

The problem, I think, is the dissonance created by manipulation of the audience. Once we identify with the likeable Thelma and Louise and the legitimacy of their complaints about men, we are led step by step to accept the nihilistic and self-destructive values they come to embody. By the time this becomes clear it is very difficult for moviegoers, particularly women, to bail out emotionally and distance themselves from the apocalyptic craziness that the script is hurtling toward. This is precisely the issue that caused the uproar in the sixties over *Bonnie and Clyde,* a far better and much less cynical movie from which this one derives.

Louise and Thelma, sensible waitress and ditsy housewife, set out on a weekend fishing trip to escape an emotionally stunted boyfriend and a buffoonish, overbearing husband. Right from the start, they are hemmed in by and constantly intimidated by huge trucks, director Ridley Scott's symbol of suffocating male oppression. No movie has ever budgeted so many menacing trucks or so many hoses and spraying machines aimed at women—two or three hoses, two street sprinklers, an irrigation system or two and one crop-dusting plane (Calling Dr. Freud: what can all this male spraying represent?)

The scene is set in the Southwest, but the real landscape is that of Andrea Dworkin and the most alienated radical feminists. All males in this movie exist only to betray, ignore, sideswipe, penetrate or arrest our heroines. Anyone who has ever gotten to the end of a Dworkin essay knows how this movie will turn out—there is no hope for women, or for any truce in the battle of the sexes, because the patriarchy will crush all women who resist or simply try to live their own lives.

Now for the really bad news about this film: though the situation for women is hopeless, a form of presuicidal spiritual liberation is possible, and the key to this is violence. Killing the would-be rapist makes Louise momentarily ill, but it makes her stronger, giving her, finally, the power to ditch her insufferable boyfriend. Thelma, the scatterbrained near-victim of rape, becomes strong and alive when she conquers her aversion to guns, commits armed robbery, takes on various phallic trappings (including the cap of a male tormentor) and blows up one of Scott's thumpingly obvious symbols of male power, a big truck. This brings us to many wide-eyed exclamations of spiritual liberation on the run such as: "Something crossed over in me," "I feel awake," and "Everything is different—I have something to look forward to." With this repeated paean to transformative violence, found in none of the male-buddy movies, we have left Dworkin and entered a Mussolini speech. This connection between violence and spiritual rebirth is an explicit fascist theme, wedded to the bleakest form of feminism and buried (shallowly) in a genuinely funny buddy movie. Whew. No wonder the critics worked so hard to avoid confronting what is really going on in this film.

Movie criticism being what it is in America, most of the reviewers seem to have exercised their critical faculties by simply throwing their hats in the air. "Pleasingly subversive," said Kenneth Turan of the *Los Angeles Times*. "A big-hearted movie," wrote Jack Kroll of *Newsweek*. Actually, no. This is a quite small-hearted, extremely toxic film, about as morally and intellectually screwed up as a Hollywood movie can get.

Over twenty years ago, Pauline Kael wrote a shrewd essay about a handful of sixties movies that touched a nerve and "entered the nation's bloodstream" by accidentally catching (as in *Bonnie and Clyde*) or consciously manipulating (as in the now forgotten movie *Joe*) the spreading mood of powerlessness and despair among the young. The mood is the same today. And so is the problem of distinguishing between disturbing art and cynical propaganda. Sometimes, however, it's an easy job.

A BODICE-RIPPER GOES MAINSTREAM

Here is the outline for a romantic novel:

A photographer from Washington state, something of a loner-cowboy type, arrives in Iowa to photograph covered bridges. He has a torrid four-day affair with a bored housewife. Though their love will last a lifetime, they separate because the housewife has "this damned sense of responsibility" to her children and her good-hearted but very boring husband. Years later, the lovers die, still pining for each other. Their ashes are scattered at one of the covered bridges.

What are the prospects for such a book?

Near zero, most publishers would likely say. But at 171 pages, with little main plot, no subplot and only one real character (the woman is a cipher), *The Bridges of Madison County* by first-time author Robert James Waller is an astonishing cash machine for Warner Books.

It has been at the top of the best-seller list for a year. By the end of this year, three million hard-cover copies will be in print and the book is projected to be the best-selling novel of all time in hard-cover. Now the author has a lucrative recording deal. One song on his first album is a four-minute musical synopsis of the novel.

Critics of popular culture have been notably slow to take a whack at explaining the book's success. Frank Rich of *The New York Times* suggests that it's something of a backlash book, celebrating narcissistic hit-and-run flings for men and "pointless marital misery" for women. He may be right. There's also the obvious theme of an empty, ill-defined woman waiting around for a godlike man to give her life and meaning.

Pauli Carnes, a freelancer writing in the *Los Angeles Times,* called the book "pornography for middle-aged women," the story of a wasted life carrying the dubious message that "affairs are not devastating to a marriage, to children." "Ladies" she wrote, "a little reality-check here: no one is going to drive up to your door and rescue your life from dreariness. You made the ruts of your life—take a little responsibility for yourself."

In retrospect, the book was shaped and marketed brilliantly. The lovers are middle-aged—she is forty-five and he is fifty-two—and thus pitched to a segment of the population that still reads books and that can afford to buy them. (The hero finds younger women unattractive because they lack "intelligence and passion born of living.")

If you want to market extramarital flings to the middle-aged, it is best to drench the story in traditional values. This was done too. A conservative state, a covered bridge, old songs, concern for the children, a narrator (the author) lamenting "a world where personal commitment in all of its forms seems to be shattering."

All this lets readers have everything both ways—the thrill of a fantasy fling and the safety of marriage; the simultaneous commitment to rule-breaking and rule-keeping. "It never took away from anything I felt for the two of you or your father," the heroine's letter tells the children.

Now here comes the most triumphant flourish: if it hadn't been for her fling, "I'm not sure I could have stayed on the farm all these years," the letter tells the children. Wow. This was some affair. It's not only a fling that even the kids can admire; it's one that kept her faithful and down on the farm all those years.

Like great advertising campaigns, greatly successful pop novels often work by harnessing all sorts of ambiguity. Take the hero, Robert Kincaid. He's an outdoorsy plain-speaking cowboy type who smokes and drinks a lot and looks like "a wild, magnificent animal" to the heroine.

On the other hand, he's a sensitive new-age vegetarian environmentalist who quotes Yeats and Rachel Carson, who talks as though he thinks he had a lot of past lives. He's "like some star creature who had drafted in on the tail of a comet," the heroine says. We know he is sensitive because he cleans the tub himself after a bath and he closes the screen door quietly, instead of letting it slam like all Iowa males do. In other words, he's just another wild, hard-drinking, tub-cleaning greens-loving Marlboro man from outer space. How can a romance novel go wrong with an all-purpose composite lover like that?

The heroine, on the other hand, has almost no defining character-istics at all. She's Italian, a war bride brought back from Naples after World War II. All we know about her for sure is that she's much too refined for Iowa. Not that Iowa's a bad place, mind you, but the residents seem to know very little about poetry, magic and screen-door closings. The emptiness of the heroine helps marketing too, letting female readers insert their own character into the void.

Presumably this book's galloping success owes something to themes worked out over the years in bodice-ripping romance novels. That mar-ket is extraordinary. Barnes & Noble reported last year that the average romance customer spent twelve hundred dollars in 1991, which works out roughly to 240 paperbacks each year at $4.99 each.

The Bridges of Madison County is an upscale ($14.95), bite-sized, more acceptable reworking of a traditional romance theme. It seems to me a rather cynical, content-free packaging of loss and longing. But it worked and we will see imitators.

SELL THE SIZZLE—SKIP THE STEAK

Ernest Dichter died the other day, more than thirty years past his fifteen minutes of fame. He was so totally forgotten that if my friend Alan Brody hadn't run around to all the newspapers with obit material, we might not have known that a primary villain of the 1950s had passed away.

Fears of communist subversion made it fairly easy to sell conspiracy books during the Eisenhower years. Dichter was the designated con-spirator of one of these works—Vance Packard's *The Hidden Persuaders*, an alarming and therefore vastly successful best-seller about manipulation in advertising and the ominous new field of "motivational research."

Whenever you watch one of those peculiar jeans or perfume commericals, or read a cigarette ad in which no one is smoking, or glance at a billboard on which puritanism is wrestling with hedonism ("Life Is Short. Play Hard."—Reebok), you are being exposed to aftershocks of the remarkable Dr. Dichter.

He arrived here as a refugee from Hitler's Austria, a trained Freudian analyst who moved among the Americans like Margaret Mead among the Samoans, the only difference being that Mead did not become famous by selling her insights to the advertising industry.

Like any anthropologist doing field work among an exotic tribe, Dichter ignored what the natives of America said about their behavior and tried to unearth the hidden meanings and psychological payoffs that actually make the culture go. This made him very valuable to the advertising industry, which was still foolishly trying to sell cars as forms of transportation and soaps as cleansers.

Dichter could see then what even the dullest adman sees now: that the act of buying a car mostly concerns powerful feelings of freedom, sex, nostalgia, status and psychological self-help. When practical considerations intrude, they are mostly of the Jiminy Cricket variety—sensible, nagging ones we'd rather not think much about. Dichter said the satisfying sound of a car door slamming was more important to new-car buyers than anything under the hood.

His advice to advertisers was simple: don't push the product; push the feelings of satisfaction associated with the product. "To women," he said, "don't sell shoes; sell lovely feet." In the 1940s, he showed up at the Compton ad agency and told account executives that their Ivory Soap advertising was woefully behind the times.

On the basis of a hundred interviews with people staying at a YMCA, he concluded that the American trait of instantly forgetting the past and starting over was tied up with the traditional transcultural concept of ritual bathing to remove spiritual dirt. So he suggested the slogan, "Be smart and get a fresh start with Ivory."

There was a great deal of seat-of-the-pants bravado about all this, but it worked. Though primitive by modern standards, his slogan jump-started Ivory sales by artfully plugging in to all sorts of emotional fields. Almost every one of Dichter's ideas about bathing is alive today in various soap ads—the permission to caress yourself, the sense of being reborn and revitalized by daily ablutions, the erotic connection between removing lather and undressing, the bather as child returning to the tub to play, and so forth.

Rather casually, Dichter announced one day that soap would be vastly profitable wherever Protestantism went, a result of all the symbolic spiritual scrubbing unknown in Catholic and Orthodox religious cultures, and in virtually all of the non-Christian world. Ever since Dichter, I have been unable to envision John Calvin without a bar of Lifebuoy soap held aloft.

He devised the "Tiger in Your Tank" campaign for Esso (Exxon), fraught with the now familiar theme of selling fuel as sex and power. He helped switch Marlboro from a feminine to a masculine brand, the most profitable sex change in history. One of his minor missteps was a study for *Playboy* showing that the more insecure the male, the more he wanted a woman with large breasts. *Playboy* understandably rejected it as an article, but *Cosmopolitan* printed it.

His central insight was that you simply cannot sell pleasure to Americans. Our puritan core is too tough for that. You must disguise luxury and overindulgence as puritanism (as in the Reebok campaign) or offer absolution to justify pleasures that puritans normally feel guilty about, as in the recent Miller Time campaign (workers are entitled to a beer because they earned it with a hard day's labor).

Here we are getting close to the bone of what Dichter really did for a living. The country was shifting radically from self-denial to self-indulgence, and he was one of the folks who made the shift seem not only inevitable, but spiritually upscale. A basic problem, he wrote, is to show the consumer that "the hedonistic approach to his life is a moral, not an immoral, one."

Dichter got in deeper with the tobacco industry. His theory of smoking could safely be termed controversial: he thought that smokers are really trying to kill themselves. The obvious flip-side of this is that tobacco companies should lend a little help toward this unconsciously desired end. This is where Dichter comes closest to looking downright sinister. He spent a great deal of his time preparing nonrational themes to push smoking on people who knew very well that it was dangerous.

Last June I drove up to see Dichter in his hilltop home in Peekskill, New York. I just wanted to see what the Great Manipulator of the fifties thought of the hidden Dichteresque themes buried in some cigarette and alcohol ads today. Alas, the interview was disappointing. Dichter was alert, but his observations were straight out of his old books, often word for word. Every question I asked was answered with some reference to the ads and culture of the 1950s. He was still back there, living in his heyday, when ad guys were helping America invent righteous he-donism and high-consumption morality.

The truth is, once he showed people how to do this stuff, a lot of them learned to do it better and left him behind. Still, he was an interesting, ambiguous figure, the Freudian from overseas who con-vinced Madison Avenue to forget about the steak and just sell the sizzle.

NEWPORT'S SEXUAL COMBAT

My survey of feminist attitudes toward Newport cigarette ads was prob-ably not very scientific, and the sample (2) was rather small, but the results are probably worth mentioning: 50 percent of those queried consider the ad campaign outstandingly sick and twisted.

I collected a batch of these peppy and peculiar ads, green-and-yellow-bordered scenes of merrily cavorting yuppies, and I hauled them over to Ms. and showed them to Gloria Steinem. She was very gracious, but when I suggested that certain dark misogynist themes turned up again and again in the ads, she looked totally blank. It seemed like an honest reaction, though Ms., like many magazines, was heavily de-pendent on cigarette ads at the time. Then I sent a set over to Betty Friedan. She called the next day and announced in her wonderful, direct way: "These ads make me sick. They are absolutely perverse. Forget about lung cancer. Any woman who buys Newport is buying sadism."

With Newport ads, either you see it right away or you don't. Yes, maybe the fellow in the winter ad shouldn't have elbowed his girlfriend into the snowbank, and perhaps the fun-loving guy in the barbecue picture shouldn't have jammed the hamburger into the mouth of the wide-eyed woman who was struggling to get past him with a full load of eight burgers, fries, and onion rings—and no tray. And maybe it's not funny that the guy reached around the woman with both hands and clanged a pair of cymbals right in her face. But what the heck.

It's just happy yuppies acting up, right? The women in the ads don't seem to mind, and the ads come out of Lorillard's own agency, so how bad can they be?

Still, all those eerie things pop up. The yuppies often have something bizarre on their faces: two pairs of sunglasses instead of one, ominous masks, a sprinkler, a scarf wound totally around a woman's head.

The Newport campaign, begun in the mid-1970s, is one of the longest running and most successful in the annals of the emphysema industry. The early ads featured amateurish and simpleminded photos of people sitting around smoking and laughing. No coded messages at all. And very low sales. Then some changes showed up: the cigarettes disappeared from almost all photos (after all, they *do* cause cancer), the photography improved dramatically, and the pictures began to show action shots of outdoorsy yuppies horsing around, with the trademark undercurrent of tension and sexual combat. Newport sales began to rise 15 to 25 percent per year. In fact, the campaign helped turn the company around. By fall of 1982, *Marketing & Media Decisions* reported that "Lorillard's bacon was saved by the improved performance of Newport . . . It was the one brand in the Lorillard tobacco patch that showed momentum."

So why are the pictures so powerful? All the jolly horseplay obviously connects the death-dealing product with youth, energy, and upper-middle-class fun. But the male-female conflict built into the campaign reflected and cashed in on some obvious postfeminist resentments. In about half the photos, women seem to be off-blance and menaced, or at least a target for out-of-control male energy. A man stands in the middle of a pool spinning a fully dressed woman around on his shoulders. A woman standing awkwardly on one leg to pull off a stocking is about to be knocked over by her stupidly grinning boyfriend. An apprehensive woman in high heels and elegant coat is being hauled through snowdrifts by some fellow in boots. A woman, dressed like a referee, is about to be slam-dunked in the face by a male basketball player. A woman sits inside a bell, holding her ears. She is smiling, but the implication is that the chortling boyfriend nearby has just rung the bell with her in it.

In Newport's sexual wars, men get pushed around too. A woman's elbow leans against a man's nose. In a miniature golf scene, a giggling woman tees up her ball on the mouth of a supine male. And men get knocked down, pushed into snowbanks, and tapped playfully on the jaw by women wearing boxing gloves. In one Ping-Pong scene, a man's face is totally covered by the swinging paddles of the female players to his left and right. The picture seems to suggest violence and the eclipse of a competitive male by even more competitive females. But the male-as-victim pictures lack menace. Lorillard just can't get around the problem that men aren't menaced by women playing Ping-Pong or pushing them into a pool.

For some reason, the Lorillard people seem intensely interested in fellatio. Newport women tend to suck icicles, drink from hoses whenever they can, and open their mouths a lot as tiny white snowflakes, waterspray, and spermlike feathers from pillow fights drift their way. The women don't mind bondage either. When they are not sucking something, Newport females have a cute little way of getting all tangled up in jump ropes, hoses, streamers, and Chinese fingertraps, smiling all the time. Sometimes they even get themselves symbolically raped and murdered. Three ads point directly at the execution of a female by a male. One by burning, one by suffocation, a third by the sword: a fencer, as faceless as an executioner behind his mask, pins two women against his body with a foil.

How could Lorillard get away with retailing sexual animosity for fifteen years? Part of the trouble is that people no longer have the hang of looking at pictures and finding anything more than obvious surface content. Anyone who does is apt to be lumped with strange people like Frederic Wertham and Wilson Bryant Key. Wertham was the fellow who kept seeing sexual parts turn up in comic books, including triangles of pubic hair slyly hidden in Tarzan's triceps. Key has detected the word *sex* faintly imprinted almost everywhere in the magazine world, from the ice cubes in liquor ads to a *Time* cover on Vietnam. The Newport campaign is nothing that loony or complicated. You just go to any halfway decent photographer and ask him to shoot scenes of sexual hostility disguised as play. The high voltage of the photos comes from the unacknowledged ambiguity—the whole point of the enterprise.

One photographer who did it for Lorillard was Joel Meyerowitz. His work is in many museums, and he has published several collections, including Cape Light and Wild Flowers. When I phoned him, he seemed more embarrassed to be caught doing commercial work than being fingered as the perpetrator of soft-core sex and violence. Like the brand manager and the art director, he stonewalled and said the campaign was simply about fun-loving couples.

► Most women who drink from garden hoses usually do not do so when a man's nose is three inches away and the water is shooting out at one hundred pounds per square inch. The water speed suggests danger. Clearly, the poor woman has some unmet oral needs, or she would have given up Newports and power hoses by now. The hunched, too-close position of the male in an oral-sex photo is the standard soft-core-porn way of suggesting that sex is forced.

◄ In the past year Newport ads have been killing off more males than females. Does research show that female smokers want more symbolically dead males, or is it simply a fair-minded attempt to even the body count? People who ski rapidly into trees tend to be maimed. The sex-and-death theme is carried by the odd phallic demibranch sticking out from the tree.

► This man is emitting a symbolic scream, the only sensible thing to do when a woman symbolically stomps on your private parts while you are unwisely spread-eagled halfway up a tree.

▲ This male is surprising and delighting the female by plunging his hands into her pumpkin. Pumpkin-plunging occurs frequently in the Newport universe. • Suggestions of oral sex are ho-hum in fashion and advertising, but orgasmic fellatio scenes are still puzzlingly rare. Here a devoted girlfriend opens wide, apparently happy to have his machine go off at roughly the level of his crotch and her mouth. Obviously a trouper, she tries to catch as many of his precious bodily gum balls as she can.

▲ The proper way to decode a Newport ad is to ask yourself, What's wrong with this picture? In this case, it's the leaves falling on the man's head. No photographer in America would shoot the picture with a shutter speed so slow that falling leaves would blur. Unless, of course, the red and yellow leaves were meant to suggest the poor fellow's immolation. He's not afraid of leaves: his head is on fire. This might explain why he is wincing. • The male is scrunched down and doing something—we can only guess what—tense enough to make him grimace while the woman is busy being finger-trapped.

▶ Man as penetrator and scorer, woman as receptacle and target. The referee's shirt indicates she is neutral and safe, or would like to be. But the angle of the man's upcoming slam dunk indicates her imminent need for a reconstructed nose and a new set of teeth. As in other Newport scenes where disfigurement seems in store for a woman, the male is wearing the executioner's dark shirt.

◀ A merry seasonal rape scene. A girlfriend tries in vain to defend the victim, but the monstrous male, left over from familiar horror films, carts her off anyway. The smiling pumpkin is having a good time: his victim is wearing Newport's usual half scream—half grin.

▶ This photo has been shot and doctored to eliminate perspective and make the kneeling or sitting woman appear to be directly in the fire. The male's scarf hangs like a priest's amice, suggesting a religious or ritual burning, while his right hand seems to hold her down in the flames—Newport's own Joan of Arc.

◀ Thank goodness the alert art director has made the football jump out of the frame at right. If it didn't, innocents might think this was a rape scene. How often, we might well ask, do men play tackle football with women? When they do, how often do they apply dangerous choke holds to a relaxed female obviously out of the play? If it is a football game, why doesn't the tackler ignore the already choking lineperson and concentrate on the ballcarrier?

▶ Those of you trained by Jesuits know that subjugation is Latin for "under the yoke." Here the male, with taunting leer and vehemently clenched fist, is subjugating his enthralled female. Newport's arbiters of symbolic coding must have been asleep the day this one was approved: the misogyny is so obvious that ten negative letters poured into Lorillard and the ad was pulled. Newport's explanation of the scene: "We thought it was tender."

◀ Newport may be alive with pleasure, but this poor lady is about to be dead without it. The man's dark hair and dark sweater suggest the executioner; his idea of a good time seems borrowed from the Boston Strangler. Do women really like to have their heads mummified like this during their leisure time, and if so, why does she seem to be screaming?

▲ "Ooh," the impressed female seems to be saying, and why not? She is the guest at a private showing of what appears to be the largest condom in America. The proud owner wisely restrains her with an extra-tight handhold.

► Here the woman is doing a painful split, while the lordly and faceless man does nothing to help. Newport forgot the half-smile this time. The woman's face plainly registers alarm.

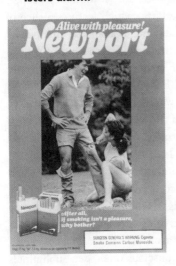

◄ With his left leg positioned between the woman's thighs, the man is having something shortened considerably with a pair of scissors. Hmmm. What can the symbolism be here? And why is he laughing, exactly?

But for some reason, he did acknowledge the half-smile, half-scream on the face of the Newport women. "Garry Winogrand used to talk about that. If a mouth is open, you don't know if it's a smile or a scream. Power comes from ambiguity. Those things are available to all of us in photography." But why bother with a half-scream if the campaign is just about fun? Meyerowitz seemed on the brink of coming clean, but no. I walked him through some of the photos and told him what I thought was really going on. "I must be too much of an innocent," he said. "I'm shocked by what you're saying." A one-beat pause. "Do you think you may be reading too many S & M books?"

HOSTILITY AMONG THE ICE CUBES

Seagram's gin ads have been spoofing the idea that subliminal messages are tucked away in advertising. "Can you find the hidden pleasure in refreshing Seagram's gin?" says one. Not so hidden among the bubbles and ice of a gin drink is a couple dancing or perhaps a woman floating along in an innertube. A helpful arrow points to the image, along with the copy line, "If you think this is just a bubble, look again."

No one knows why, but we appear to be in the midst of a boom of ads mocking subliminals. The spoofers include Toyota, Schweppes, Miller Lite, Absolut and Round Table Pizza, which features a slice of pepperoni that turns into a human face and shouts "Buy this pizza!" The Seagram's campaign looks like a satirical poke at the author Wilson Bryan Key, who has been arguing for years that images of skulls are hidden in ice cubes, and the letters S-E-X are deviously embedded in Ritz crackers. Years ago, when I was working at *Time* magazine, Key phoned to argue that whole bunches of the letters S, E and X had been hidden in a *Time* cover photo on Vietnam. I had to tell him this was impossible: since decision-making at *Time* is modeled on that of the Austro-Hungarian civil service, the authorizations required for each forbidden letter would have instantly converted *Time* into a monthly.

Key's zealotry has deflated what might have been a serious debate about motivational research and advertising. Forget crackers and ice cubes. If you define subliminal print ads as advertising designed to appeal on an unconscious level as well as a conscious one, then subliminals surely exist and are in common use. The best Nike's "Just do it" slogan, and Burger King's "Sometime you've gotta break the rules" are evocative, open-ended statements, likely to be read quite differently by the comfortable middle class and the struggling poor. To the well-off, Nike's advice is to get in shape and Burger King's is to allow yourself a fatty hamburger once in a while. But in harsher neighborhoods, both slogans seem to identify their products with law-breaking and freedom from impulse control. The Hispanic agency employed by Burger King got the point right away, declining to translate "Breaking the rules" directly into Spanish because it implied approval for violating the law or Hispanic traditions. (Merrill Lynch's "To know no boundaries" campaign was a totally upscale variation on the same antisocial theme, playing with the idea of an infinite self, free of all nettlesome restraint and obligation.)

As might be expected, alcohol and tobacco ads seem to resort to subliminal themes most frequently. Most of these are nonverbal and can't easily be analyzed in a column, so let's take one of the more verbal ones. In the Bacardi Black "Taste of the night" campaign ("Some people fear the night because it liberates the other senses"), the overt message is sexual (partially clad woman standing by), but the stronger covert one circles around the theme of night and liquor as liberators of the real you (and your darker side) from the bonds of civilized society. A second ad in this series makes the theme explicit, in fact, too explicit: "Some people embrace the night because the rules of the day do not apply" (possible translation: they can hold you responsible during the day, but not at night, when you're drunk). This dreamy appeal to booze-induced wildness is echoed in the Bacardi white rum ads ("Wild for Bacardi," women in leopard and tiger bathing suits). Bacardi's symbol, by the way, is a bat.

Use of feral animals as a come-on for drinking is an old story. The malt liquors, marketed primarily to poor members of minority groups, use cobra, bull, dragon, tiger, stallion, pit bull. The idea is to sell wildness and power to the powerless (high alcohol content is part of the same strategy). So long as this theme is covert, nobody seems to object, but the G. Heileman Brewing Company has just found out what happens when the fig-leaf is dropped. By naming a strong malt liquor "Power Master," Heileman provoked minority protests and the Bureau of Alcohol, Tobacco and Firearms withdrew approval for the brand name. In a reasonable world, Newport's would have been jumped on years before "Power Master," but then Newport knows how to code things and Heileman doesn't.

THE WELL-HEELED DRUG RUNNER

In the spring of 1990, the athletic-shoe industry came under heavy assault for relentlessly carving out a luxury market in poor inner-city neighborhoods. One of the heaviest assaulters was *New York Post* sportswriter Phil Mushnick. One day he interviewed a Bronx high school coach, who said (as many others have) that the standard way that poor kids come to afford $175 Reebok Pumps is to start selling crack. Kids who can't afford a good meal, the coach said, buy hundred-dollar sneakers once a month because their heroes on TV say they are nothing without that right brand of footwear. "What is the future of our children?" Barbara Jones of West Philadelphia asked Mushnick another day, after her nephew was shot and killed for his Nikes. Mushnick has gone after three of the most highly regarded black men in America—moviemaker Spike Lee, Georgetown coach John Thompson and basketball star Michael Jordan—for shilling for Nike. "As the reports of muggings and murders in the name of procuring this junk rolls in daily," Mushnick wrote, "you'd think Nike's corporate conscience would come to the fore. But no, arrogance and greed win the day."

Spike Lee had his say in an op-ed piece, arguing that Mushnick's crusade was "thinly veiled racism" (no one is ever accused of thickly veiled racism) that targets three black men but not "White Goldenboy Stars" such as Larry Bird and Joe Montana, and implies that black youngsters, but not white ones, are willing to kill for brand-name sneakers. "The deal is this," Lee wrote. "Let's try to deal effectively with the conditions that make a kid put so much importance on a pair of sneakers."

Okay, Spike Lee made some points. Limited options have something to do with sneaker obsession. This debate unfolded as though the word poor is synonymous with black, and as if everyone living in the inner city is totally suggestible and feral. But Lee was more than a bit disingenuous. Bird and Montana are wholly owned subsidiaries of lesser brands (L.A. Gear and Converse) that almost nobody is getting mugged for. Besides, white stars have little hold on the black street culture that has made athletic shoes a crucially important fashion item.

To avoid breaking this down along racial lines, we can fairly say white-dominated corporations, using mostly black stars, are hauling several hundred million dollars a year out of impoverished inner-city neighborhoods for products of little value and no lasting worth. As fashion items, these sneakers retail for $50 to $175 and are generally worn two to five weeks before being replaced with a clean pair, or better yet, a new model. According to Nike figures, black males aged thirteen to twenty-four account for 9.8 percent of the $10.3 billion in annual retail sales of athletic shoes. That's a billion dollars a year. Inner-city religious and political leaders have caught on to the targeting of blacks by liquor and cigarette companies, but so far they have missed the much more obvious predation of the sneaker companies. When black leaders begin to talk about this wasted hundred million dollars a year, we are likely to hear some different thoughts from Spike Lee.

Unsurprisingly, the gym shoe companies depict themselves as innocent entrepreneurs trying, like everyone else, to make a buck by responding to demand. But the bottom line is that these companies are heavily marketing $150 sneakers to people who can't afford them. The knowledge of this obvious fact implicates these giant companies in the wider transactions that enable people without money to buy the product over and over. Paul Palladino, co-owner of a sportswear store in Boston, says the average kid comes in for at least one new pair of sneakers every thirteen days. That would amount to two thousand dollars a year for moderately priced seventy-dollar shoes, bought one pair at a time, and five thousand dollars a year for Reebok Pumps. And many kids buy the whole color line when it comes out, which would send the annual bill over twenty-five thousand dollars for sneakers, plus much more for matching sweats.

We might well ask Nike and Reebok how they think poor kids come by this kind of money. Some work and save, but other inner-city kids acquire it illegally, and the biggest source of illegal money is crack. What Nike and Reebok do not wish to acknowledge is that they are essentially piggybacking on the drug culture. A great chunk of the corporate profits and endorsement money come from drug exploitation and death. Wally Grigo, who owns a sportswear shop in New Haven, Connecticut, has it right. He says, "We're all getting too addicted to drug money. Now a significant part of the population has no incentive to see the drug trade end."

Grigo went cold turkey, putting a sign in his window announcing that drug dealers were not welcome at the store. He says that two shoe companies—one large and famous, one not—had explicitly told him to "hook up" the local drug dealers as fashion trendsetters. When the antidrug sign went up, the sales rep for the smaller company appeared in the store to deliver a predictable reprimand: "The bulk of our business is done with drug dealers. Wake up."

In practice, everybody seems to know that the inner-city sneaker business is a subsidiary of the drug trade. This may be why sneaker companies don't do antidrug ads. "Nike won't even put an anti-drug message on the box," says Grigo. "Spike Lee ought to know better, too. I want to see an ad with Michael Jordan staring right at the camera saying, 'If you do drugs, don't dare buy my shoes.' " Good idea. Over to you, Mike, Spike and Nike.

WHEN THE FEDS TURNED DRUG DEALER

Legal drugs came to America back in June of 1997. Speaking the now historic words, "Okay—let's give it a shot," an obviously reluctant President Quayle bowed to the will of Congress and signed the Prohibition Repeal Bill into law. With the defeat of the Friedmanites, named for their spiritual leader Milton Friedman ("I would distribute drugs the way aspirin is distributed"), control of drug distribution was denied to private industry and placed in the hands of the federal government.

In the first year alone, the government opened forty thousand Re-active Chemical Dispensation Centers, or package stores, all of them frankly modeled on McDonald's hamburger shops: clean and bright, with illuminated color-coded menus up high behind the smiling, non-judgmental sales help. The gold menu (for "golden oldies") featured nostalgia drugs for older buyers—crack, heroin, angel dust, LSD and weak marijuana. Green was for more current and powerful forms of cocaine and marijuana. Red—an active, youthful color—signified designer drugs, most of them concocted by computer in college chemistry labs under government contract.

In year two, the drug program expanded to 120,000 outlets, mostly by taking over the shops of the bankrupt Roy Rogers chain. Despite this enormous capital outlay, and a staff of nearly five hundred thousand workers, government experts predicted that the drug program would be in the black within three years. Violent street crime fell 10 percent. Drug-related prosecutions dropped 80 percent. Since the government was buying most of the cocaine raised in Colombia and Peru, relations with Latin America brightened. Drug Czar Alan Dershowitz said, "Our long national nightmare is ending."

By the end of year two, *The New York Times* expressed editorial concern about the rise in drug use—up about 15 percent since repeal—but Dershowitz called it "a brief statistical spasm." More disconcertingly, the package stores were having trouble holding the line on drug prices. Back in 1989, a rock of crack sold for $3.00 in New York, or four for $10.00. A decade later, in terms of 1989 dollars, the price was $5.79 at a government store, and $4.00 on the street. There were jokes about $600 toilet seats and "normal government efficiency."

Dershowitz told Congress that drug planners had underestimated the costs of the business. Ethan Nadelmann, a prolegalization lobbyist of the 1980s, had predicted a $10-billion-a-year government profit from drug sales, but he hadn't counted on the costs of quality control, product development, insurance, theft and a sprawling civil-service drug bureaucracy. Because of the bombings at package stores, the department had to install foot-thick concrete walls and twenty-four-hour guards. Hijackings were a constant problem. Four tons of cocaine and a shipment of European chemicals disappeared from JFK Airport on a single day. Soon the department was paying the army and navy to escort cocaine shipments from Latin America. Arguing that "economies of scale" would turn the drug business around, Dershowitz hinted that drug advertising should be allowed. Congress said no, but agreed to price supports for a year.

To the amazement of most Americans, the dangerous drug gangs that ruled the streets in the 1980s were still thriving. Violence was down because the gangs had finally come to terms and divided America up into regional monopolies, a standard feature of mature capitalism. Business was booming because the gangs knew that the successors to the yuppies, the affluent TWITS (an acronym for Those With Income To Squander) did not wish to stand on line for drugs at a former Roy Rogers. They wanted a whiff of the romance and danger that come from buying a hot new drug from a slightly ominous contact in a dimly lit club.

When the product liability suits against the Drug Department began to roll in (forty thousand were filed in the month of September 1999 alone), insurance skyrocketed and Congress mandated a six-month testing period for all new drugs. Since most new designer drugs faded from the market in less time than that, this gave the street gangs almost total control of the more fashionable drugs.

But the bulk of the gang business was kids. Since the Prohibition Repeal Law forbade sales to those under twenty-one, the gangs had the high school and college markets as monopolies. When Congress tried to cut into the gang profits by legalizing drugs for eighteen-year-olds, the gangs aggressively preyed upon younger and younger children. Addiction rates for ten- to twelve-year-olds rose tenfold in the decade between 1989 and 1999. A common child-to-parent taunt, made into a bumper sticker, read: "If drugs are legal for you, why are they bad for me?"

With sales slumping, and a 42 percent addiction rate among Drug Department employees, Dershowitz resigned. The new drug czar, Ira Glasser, said confidently that sales would reach the break-even point within six years. With drug victims filling 78 percent of hospital beds, Congress authorized $97 billion to be spent on hospital construction. New forms of brain damage and disease began to show up among users, so Congress mandated weaker doses, thus sending thousands of the more serious users to the black market for their heavier hits. Street crime soared. More addicts meant more muggings to pay for more drugs.

With the cocaine market glutted and a million hectares of Colombian soil under cultivation, the Medellin government started dumping excess coke on American streets at fire-sale prices. No one bought coke legally. That finished off the government stores, which were $4 billion in debt, with only 17 percent of the U.S. drug market.

On December 1, 2002, with 120 million Americans using drugs, with the economy in a shambles and with child abuse at five times the level of 1989, Congress voted unanimously to make drugs illegal once again. Debate began on which civil liberties might be preserved during the cleanup. Former czar Dershowitz said: "So I was wrong. What can I do about it now?" Former czar Glasser said simply, "It was a noble experiment."

THE BRATS AND BRUTES OF PRO SPORTS

Like all dutiful sports fans, I am keeping an eye on the baseball season and the basketball playoffs, but the truth is, my heart isn't in it.

My hometown Knicks are playing at a championship level again, but my enthusiasm is heavily restrained. The Knicks are known as a team that lacks first-class personnel but makes up for it with physicality. This is a euphemism. It means that they beat up their opponents as much as they can. Every so often, when an opponent drives to the basket, the Knicks will just hammer him to the floor. Call it mugger basketball.

The pounding is accompanied by a good deal of "trash talk"— venomous goading of opponents. The Knicks are nowhere near as violent as the Detroit Pistons championship teams featuring Bill Laimbeer and Rick Mahorn. And they have a real coach, Pat Riley, who forces them to play together. But the goon level is distressingly high.

It didn't used to be this way. Many years ago, during a Knicks–Bullets playoff game, one of the Bullets came up from behind the great Walt Frazier and punched him in the face. Strangely, the referee called a foul on Frazier. Frazier didn't complain. His expression never changed. He simply called for the ball and put in seven straight shots to win the game, an amazing display of productive anger. If you want to get huffy about it, it was a great moral lesson as well.

Nowadays, I suppose, Frazier would be expected to hit his opponent with a chair, or at least wait until the man is up in the air under the basket and then deliver some sort of crippling blow. One of the lesser publicized skills in the league is how to hit an opponent so he falls in an awkward way, causing an injury.

The whole culture of the game has changed. The players are bigger, faster, rougher, touchier. In one of his TV ads, Charles Barkley of the Phoenix Suns derides the idea that he is any kind of role model, and says that his job is to "wreak havoc." The ad can be taken satirically, but in fact havoc-wreaking is very big in the game. Pulling down rims and breaking glass backboards is regarded as some kind of in-your-face achievement.

As the game gets more explosive, it is starting to change the responses of the press and fans. During the Knicks–Bulls playoff series last year, New York tabloids referred to Chicago as "Hell," and fans heaped a great deal of abuse on Michael Jordan. What is this all about? Jordan is the greatest athlete ever to play the game. If we are expected to abuse him because he happens to play for the team from Hell, count me out. I don't remember fans abusing Bird or Magic or Oscar Robertson or Bill Russell. They were great opponents, not enemies. But that was when pro basketball was still a game, not a war.

Baseball hasn't evolved into a war game yet, but it too makes me cringe when I open the sports pages. The tone of the game is increasingly set by rich brats. Ken Griffey Jr., a big star with the Seattle Mariners, grabbed his crotch and shouted an obscenity at an opposing manager while running around the bases after a home run. (Thanks for sharing, Ken.) Bobby Bonilla, who signed for $29 million with the Mets, threatened to beat up a sportswriter. For some reason, he thought it was a good idea to make this threat on camera. And the biggest star in baseball, Barry Bonds, who signed with the Giants for $43 million, is also the game's biggest jerk. While watching a videotape of a Giants game, he said he was surprised to learn that he had run around the bases after a home run, hoisting a particular finger to the crowd.

Baseball has always had its jerks, of course, but the big money now sloshing through baseball has made a difference. Stars are hard to restrain when they make ten times as much money as their managers, the sportswriters who cover them, and most of the fans who watch them. Arrogant stars and greedy owners are starting to squeeze the life out of baseball. Fay Vincent, the former commissioner, warned that the public may come to see the game as a clash between cheap billionaires and whiny millionaires.

Many players don't stay put long enough to develop any kind of relationship with their city or its fans. Pitcher Jack Morris played with three different teams—and two World Series winners—in three years. Toronto won two straight World Series, basically with two different teams. It is beginning to dawn on the baseball industry that fans do not wish to root for teams made up of out-of-town hired guns on short-term contracts. When Barry Bonds returned to Pittsburgh, after signing with San Francisco for big bucks, Pittsburgh fans showered him with fake dollar bills. Jim Murray, sports columnist for the *Los Angeles Times*, says these players aren't heroes, "They're just migratory workers."

Fan loyalty is hardly the only problem. Games are much too slow, partly because they're overly packed with between-innings TV commercials. Expansion has once again diluted the quality of the game. And I expect that the new playoff system will dump every halfway decent team into postseason play, making pennant races a joke and pushing the World Series into snow season.

Something about baseball isn't working anymore. The vast commercialization of the game and the cold attitudes that come with it are turning people off. Who will explain this to the owners?

Why Jokes Have No Story Line

Before he was famous for fifteen minutes as a pop oracle, Marshall McLuhan was one of my teachers at college, and those of us who suspected that he might be on to something were known as McLuhanatics. He was an intellectual waterbug, skimming rapidly over every conceivable subject, once wedging Babe Ruth, Marsilius of Padua and Felix the Cat into a single head-spinning sentence. Marshall seemed to know everything, and get some of it slightly askew. When challenged, he would sometimes say he disagreed with many of his own ideas, and therefore was in no position to complain about other people disagreeing as well.

Marshall taught that literacy and the invention of the printing press destroyed the old oral, tribal traditions, shaping a new culture of sequence, privacy, individualism and alienation, and leading up to the modern nation-state. (Marshall always thought big.) Now, he said, the electronic media are reversing the process, undermining print culture and sequence, creating a global village—sort of a giant, throbbing "now generation."

One need not subscribe to cosmic theories to notice that sequence— moving from point a to points b and c as print does across a page, and logical thought is supposed to do in argument—is in trouble these days, very likely a casualty of the electronic media, just as Marshall said. For instance, McLuhan predicted thirty years ago that jokes with story lines would fade and be replaced by one-liners or jokes with fractured story lines (What's orange and wears a mask? Answer: The Lone Tangerine.) That has certainly happened. Traveling salesmen jokes and comic raconteurs like Garrison Keillor are now endangered species. Older and very minor one-line comics like Henny Youngman and Jackie Mason have been recycled as major stars.

Sequence is dropping out of comic strips as well. Not one strip with a continuing story line has been successfully introduced into newspapers in ten years (since *Spiderman*, if you care). Music video is a McLuhanesque mosaic of disconnected images. Make a leap, and notice that story line is disappearing from many fields, including psychotherapy. Older, longer therapies dealing with the whole life story are giving way to quick-fix treatments dealing solely in the here and now.

Even Hollywood, which is in the storytelling business, is relying less and less on story line. (What is the plot of *Bull Durham*, or *Good Morning Vietnam*?). A well-known screenwriter says that dealmakers once went to studios with scripts or at least extended treatments, but "now they go in with a one-sentence pitch for a high-concept movie: What if Arnold Schwarzenegger and Danny Devito were twins?" Toss in a few comic incidents, end the movie somehow, and voilà—another stitched-together storyless story.

The collapse of political argument into sound bites looks like part of the same process. (George Bush's wisecrack that Dukakis has opposed every new weapon since the slingshot is like Henny Youngman boiling down an old joke into a polished one-liner.) As sequence fades, arguments give way to gibes, traditions to fads and convictions to attitudes (free-floating matters of taste).

In politics, as elsewhere, the loss of sequence leads to an ever-shortening attention span. After the appalling revelations about Dan Quayle, Jim Baker told Republicans not to worry—it would blow over in a few days because there was nothing left to say on the subject (no story line to keep it alive, no smoking gun to look for). This sort of discontinuity means that amnesia afflicts our collective memory, and there is no longer any such thing as a permanently impaired reputation. John Dean covered politics for *Rolling Stone*, Claus von Bulow appeared on the cover of *Vanity Fair* and Michael Milken taught at U.C.L.A.

The ever-shortening attention span means that the older print media are under constant pressure to imitate the electronic media, chiefly television: more color, more drama, better graphics, more easily digested little McNuggets of news. But it also means that TV itself is under similar pressure to deliver more jolts, more jeopardy, jazzier pacing and effects. Barney Rozensweig, producer of *Cagney and Lacey*, fears pressure for "fourteen car chases per reel" and recalls the warnings of Marshall McLuhan.

Remote control switches (zappers) reveal the short attention span and shorten it even further by introducing the habit of constantly shifting from one channel to another. Many viewers now check out ten or twelve channels during a commercial. A survey conducted by *Channels* magazine found that more than half of younger viewers (eighteen to thirty-four) say they regularly watch two shows at the same time, with 20 percent keeping an eye on a ballgame or some other third show as well. Some spend entire evenings switching around, watching as many as fifty channels over and over in a series of five-second bursts.

It is always possible that clicking away like this is a sensible response to the low quality of TV offerings, or the triumph of optimism over experience. But the *Channels* survey turned up a great deal of antigrazing sentiment among the grazers. Many hate it but do it anyway because they are bored. It is the viewing pattern of the future.

Erase all sequence and you get millions of unconscious McLuhanatics endlessly seeking smaller and smaller McNuggets of discontinuous stimulation, like drug hits. If he were alive today, McLuhan would say, of course. He always did.

OUR SQUEAMISH PRESS

"Criminal assault" was the old journalistic euphemism for "rape." Everybody used it, and it led to some strange effects: "The victim was beaten, slapped, stabbed, clubbed, and thrown down a stairwell; however, police said she was not criminally assaulted." A Texas newspaper once changed one victim's quote from "Help! I'm being raped!" to "Help! I'm being criminally assaulted!" Perhaps she was lucky that her quote didn't come out as "Help! I'm being forcibly euphemized!"

Nowadays, we shake our heads at the runaway propriety of journalism like that. But the same instinct to report and muffle the news, all in the same article, is very much with us today. Someone could do a Ph.D. thesis on it, focusing perhaps on the immense tonnage of information-free journalism about Andrew Dice Clay and 2 Live Crew. The marvel is that we somehow managed to conduct a national uproar over these lowlife entertainers, while the press labored mightily to ensure that few of us knew what the lowlifes were actually saying.

I read eight newspapers a day and have followed both controversies since early spring. Still, I would very likely have no idea what the fuss is about if I hadn't thought to acquire a set of 2 Live Crew lyrics and a tape of Dice Clay. What does it say about the state of our journalism if a moderately alert reader can doggedly consume reams of America's finest reporting and still have to send away privately for the news?

Consider the de facto media blackout on the content of 2 Live Crew lyrics. A computer search of 108 American newspapers turn up only eleven mentions nationwide of the startling lyric that recommends tearing or damaging girls' vaginas. The coverage of work by the late photographer Robert Mapplethorpe has been almost as bad. The *Washington Post*, with the censorship squabble breaking in its own backyard, gave readers only the mistiest account of the spreading controversy. The general tone of coverage was: Censorship is stupid, but we can't show or tell you what it is that we think shouldn't be censored. Then the paper's ombudsman could take no more. "The euphemisms used in the columns of the *Post* in no sense conveyed the essence of the Mapplethorpe exhibit," he wrote, and went on to reveal what the reporters and editors would not: That the pictures show "a gentleman urinating into the mouth of a companion [and] a man baring his backside, a bullwhip, handle inserted, dangles from his anus."

Apparently exhausted by this lurch toward journalism, the paper made no further comprehensible references to these pictures for ten months, although Washington and the whole country were going bonkers on the issue during most of that time. *The New York Times* did basically the same thing. Finally, as the paper went to press with its umpteenth discreetly uninformative article on Mapplethorpe, the deputy national editor of the *Times* boldly called for a brief insert describing the urine and bullwhip pictures in clear and precise language. The editor was embarrassed about how the paper had botched the 2 Live Crew story and didn't want to make the same mistake with Mapplethorpe. Good move, but a bit late. This was fourteen months into the story. And the *Times* has still not come anywhere close to telling its readers about the 2 Live Crew lyrics. A spokesman told me it won't and can't.

Why do our best newspapers behave this way? Propriety, of course. Spokesmen at both papers talk about a contract with readers not to bring shocking material into their homes. Well, yes. Nobody wants to lose his breakfast over hair-raising press coverage of advanced sexual disturbance. But the press must not protect readers from crucial news out of niceness. The most sensible comment so far came from Wesley Pruden, managing editor of the *Washington Times*, who said his paper's policy "is to describe this as accurately and as tastefully as we can, often clinically. We know this occasionally makes the readers wince, but you can't play games." Exactly. If something important is outrageous, don't walk around the story, or sit around dreaming up gauzy euphemisms. Just tell the readers what it is.

By repeatedly describing the Mapplethorpe photos as "homoerotic" (which is like describing the Marquis de Sade's works as "heteroerotic"), the press left the erroneous impression that homosexual sex was the issue. Similarly, by implying that 2 Live Crew was merely dealing in "party record" and "locker room" language, the press left the impression that the rappers may have been singled out by race, not for recommending physical damage to women. Most irritatingly, most papers managed to hide behind the claims of propriety in their news columns while mocking the claims of propriety in their editorials.

I think the bad reporting broke the tension between legitimate concerns about censorship and artisitic freedom, and equally legitimate concerns about shocking images of sexual degradation casually being accepted into the cultural mainstream. With that tension gone, the stories were flattened out into conventional ones about angry philistines afraid of sex, gays, blacks, art, and social change. A textbook lesson in the distortions wrought by overdeveloped journalistic delicacy.

I am against censorship myself. I think we should deplore all of those who want to impose it, especially at newspapers.

THE GULF WAR'S TASTEFUL CARNAGE

"There's the first evidence of suffering," Peter Jennings said as two wounded Iraqi soldiers flashed on screen during the Gulf War. This was the driest of reminders that we were getting a highly sanitized version of what war is all about. The most horrific televised image of the war showed the legs of a dead Iraqi soldier sticking out from under a truck outside Kuwait. If you were paying attention (the image understandably whizzed by in a third of second), you could see that the legs were unconnected to any torso. I noticed no dead or dismembered Americans, only the bodies of Iraqis and Kuwaitis. In fact the only U.S. casualty seemed to be the soldier with the minor arm wound being brought into surgery. Before his capture, Bob Simon of CBS said: "There's a rule now that we cannot show a soldier who is in severe agony or shock." In fact, only the good emotions of U.S. forces were photographed: happiness or weeping for their dead companions.

This image control was true of pre-TV wars too. In his book *Wartime*, Paul Fussell says that not a single image of a dismembered American soldier was published during World War II, or afterward in the many photo anthologies such as *Life Goes to War*, even though the loss of arms, legs and digits was a common fact of life in every battle, and flying body parts themselves caused injuries, deaths and madness among those untouched by enemy fire. Fussell argues that the source of much of the bitterness and trauma of returning veterans was the fact that the sanitized and largely imaginary war in the minds of relatives and friends at home had nothing to do with the gruesome horror that the soldiers actually saw.

I was reminded of those passages from Fussell's book when the print journalists, finally free of their military handlers, reported some of the shocked statements of American troops who inspected the dismembered and incinerated bodies of the trapped and panicked Iraqi soldiers fleeing Kuwait. In press reports, the words of the traumatized intermingled with jaunty descriptions of the slaughter in the thousand-vehicle convoy as "a great turkey shoot" of "like shooting fish in a barrel." Apparently the scene was as garish as anything Fussell describes in *Wartime*. I imagine that whoever decided to air that fleeting glimpse of dismembered legs was driven by the impulse to give viewers at home some idea of what really happened as the fish expired in this particular barrel.

Before this incident, Rick DuBrow, the television writer for the *Los Angeles Times*, wrote that it had "become clear that attempts to withhold the ugliness from home viewers were part and parcel of policy." In opting to present viewers with only tasteful horror, the networks and military probaly reflected public opinion. Few of us want to be grossed out or have our children traumatized by real images of war. Still, prettifying war is likely worse. By shielding us from the real consequences of deciding to go to war, it makes great violence easier to choose. Before the next TV war, we ought to debate the amount of image control we really want.

HAUTE PORN COUTURE

Naomi Wolf's book *The Beauty Myth* argued that men are imposing a cruel "cult of female beauty" as a political weapon to impede women's progress. Though the book had the strong odor of the overwrought feminist tract, circa 1980, Wolf was sharp on a number of side issues. Here she is on the connection between fashion and pornography:

> Midway through the 70's, the punk-rock scene began to glorify S and M: High school girls put safety pins through their ears, painted their lips bruise-blue and ripped their clothing to suggest sexual battle. By the end of the decade, S and M had ascended from street fashion to high fashion in the form of studded black leather, wrist-cuffs, and spikes. Fashion models adopted from violent pornography the furious pouting glare of the violated woman.

I first noticed the porn-fashion connection in 1975, when *Vogue* magazine ran a seven-photo fashion spread featuring a man in a bathrobe battering a screaming model in a lovely peach jumpsuit ($140 from Saks, pictures by Avedon). Though I was shocked, the model apparently was not, since on the next page, apparently refreshed by being slapped around in a fashionable manner, she and the perpetrator were nuzzling happily next to the headline "Together Again!" Though peace had broken out, the busy perp did seem to be choking her with both hands in a tiny photo on the bottom of the page, possibly because he just hated her plaided silk crepe de chine separates (about $1,050, from Geoffrey Beene).

As Wolf notes, the conventions of hard-core porn, including the violent ones, began to take hold in the fashion world in the 1970s. Some photographers rode to glory on pictures debasing to women, including the late Chris von Wangenheim, with his dogs-and-women shots, and Helmut Newton, who injected the leather-and-bondage themes of male porn directly into the high-fashion world. Images of sexual violence and murder sprouted in fashion magazines and window displays of Fifth Avenue stores.

While poking around in the fashion industry for an article on "S & M Chic," I found that most of my sources played down the porn-fashion connection, calling it a brief foray into titillation that would soon end. In a way, it did. The battered-women fashion spreads and gun-toting Fifth Avenue manikins disappeared. But the images and conventions of porn came to stay. The Guess jeans ads, for instance, are reworkings of familiar male porn, from the image of the docile young woman on her knees, gazing submissively up toward the dominant older male, to the current ad of a man seizing a woman from behind on a motorcycle, which certainly looks like a rape.

In her book *Female Perversions*, the psychologist Louise Kaplan argues that pornographers once groped for style among the fashion magazines and in the Bloomingdale's catalogue, but now the fashion world and the porn world use each other quite openly as resource materials. Kaplan writes: "Nobody knew quite how it happened, but there came a day when nobody could tell who was emulating whom."

The bodysuits and bathing suits cut high up on the thigh, for example, come from the world of porn and were introduced into the fashion world via the bunny costumes designed by Hugh Hefner. Women like them because they make the legs look longer and sleeker. Men tend to like them because of the fetishistic look of a high-riding thigh-baring style that makes the suit look like an arrow aimed at the female genitals.

Against all predictions, the garter belt—very likely the most fetishized garment in the imagination of the American male—has made an amazing comeback. Madonna has helped import many porn styles— pointy bras, tight bustiers, and in general, the underwear-as-outerwear look that plays to female defiance and male voyeurism. In the fifties, Maidenform ads played with the male and female fantasy of a woman confidently walking around town in bra and panties. Now the fantasy has more or less come true.

The current fetishization of fashion extends to body parts too. Plastic surgeons report that women showing up for breast enlargement operations commonly bring along pictures torn out of *Penthouse* and *Playboy* to indicate the size they want. Following the big-breast obsession of

American man, the size is much larger than that sought in similar operations in Europe. In fact, one source tells me that many American women are enlarging their breasts to the exact point where French women come in and ask for breast reduction.

Well, now that bullet bras, garter belts, spiked chokers, wrist cuffs, slave bracelets, gigantic breasts, and outdoor underwear are all in fashion, what else can porn contribute to high style? Would you believe the piercing of the body in strange places? Yes, indeed, there's a trend to wearing rings in the nipples and genitals. This is the clear imagery of sexual slavery, springing from the hardest-core, most hostile porn, but it is presented here as a natural and harmless extension of earrings and nose jewelry. One California business reports five thousand piercings a year, including the nipples of a bank president and the genitals of many Orange County housewives. "It has become cool; it became fashion," a part-time Manhattan piercer told *The New York Times*. Yet another quiet fashion triumph of the pornographic imagination.

THE RISE OF FELONY CHIC

One of the newsmagazines thought it was a cute idea to get Sydney Biddle Barrows to give some advice to Heidi Fleiss. You could tell it was meant to be a lighthearted item, because it ran with a photo of Barrows, grinning from ear to ear, pointing to a blackboard with the word "men" chalked on it. You know, one famous veteran madam giving some lessons to a famous alleged madam from the upcoming generation.

Question: how did we get to the point where selling women's bodies entitles people to do celebrity appearances like this? Barrows, "the Mayflower Madam," has done an advice column in a weekly New York newspaper. *The New York Times Book Review* asked her to review a book on beds. Wink. Nudge.

"Fame forgives all," lamented columnist Richard Cohen about Barrows's transition from ordinary, grubby sex criminal to celebrity madam. Call it felon chic. We just can't seem to resist making celebs out of convicts and indictees. And as Cohen says, once they are transformed into stars, we are not supposed to care or even remember how they got there.

The August issue of *Lear's* magazine features an article on clothing by Jean Harris, the convicted murderer recently released from prison (" . . . the former headmistress—an educator still—muses on the meaning of what we wear," says the subheadline of the piece). And why is Harris writing about fashion? Probably for the same reason Barrows wrote about beds. Some editor thought that turning a convict into a guest writer would grab readers' attention.

The culture is now totally geared to close the gap between notoriety and celebrity. Anyone involved in a scandal is apt to turn up in a jeans ad, on a talk show or (if female) in a pictorial in a skin magazine. In some cases, like G. Gordon Liddy after Watergate, they end up with their own radio show. Or like Claus von Bulow, indicted for attempted murder of his wife (the conviction was overturned), they look out at us from the cover of *Vanity Fair* and later are portrayed by a major star in a motion picture.

In part, the banality of the modern talk show is to blame. The host, overcome with fairness and empathy, washes away all normal revulsion toward the sins of the accused. All that remains is celebrity.

Garrison Keillor caught this aspect of the talk show culture with a fantasy of Bryant Gumbel interviewing Hitler. "A lot of people still have hard feelings toward you because of that whole Auschwitz thing, you know," Bryant says to Hitler. "How do you deal with animosity on that level? I mean, personally, you and Eva. Is it rough on your marriage? How do you explain it to the kids?" Hitler earnestly says he feels sorry for people who live in the past, still spouting threadbare stories about genocide. He is positive and understanding. Soon he would be in demand on TV. Perhaps he would get his own show, opposite Bryant, or maybe Jack Nicholson would play him in *Love Among the Ruins: The Story of Adolf and Eva*.

The stupefying decision by Geffen Records and Guns 'n' Roses to issue a recording by mass murderer Charles Manson shows that Keillor's fantasy is not that far from current reality. Manson has been converted into a pop-culture personality, whose menacing face appears on T-shirts worn by middle-class teenagers.

Increasingly, the media covers the most violent murderers in the same way it covers TV stars or baseball players. The August issue of *Mirabella* features a piece on the female groupies who visit Richard Ramirez, the Night Stalker, currently on death row for a grisly series of rapes and murders in the L.A. area. Ramirez asks the writer why so many woman are interested in him: "Is it just because I'm famous?"

Back in the seventies the editors of a newsmagazine put Squeaky Fromme on the cover and then regretted it. Fromme tried to shoot President Ford, and the regret was that giving the fame of a cover photo to an anonymous shooter would only encourage more shooting. But we are way past that now. John Lennon's assassin, for instance, got star treatment on 20/20 and Larry King Live. "Do you have fans?" King asks. The killer says he feels good and wants to tell people why he did what he did. "Mark, thank you. This has been terrific," King says at the end. Another successful celebrity killer interview.

The same celeb treatment is now commonplace in docudramas. In May ABC offered Murder in the Heartland, a two-part TV movie on Charles Starkweather, who killed eleven people, including a baby, in Nebraska and Wyoming in 1958. In real life, nobody seemed to have a good word for the loathsome Starkweather, but on TV he emerged as a romanticized teen rebel. Tom Shales, the Washington Post TV critic, wrote: "The treatment amounts to glorification; the film might as well have been called Charlie Starkweather, Superstar.

Everyone knows there's too much violence on television, but few people talk about the escalating tendency to portray murderers in a favorable light. By telling stories from the point of view of the killer, rather than that of the victim or cops, a good deal of sympathy is built into the project in advance. A major star will usually play the killer, adding more luster. "Every Ted Bundy, Gary Gilmore, Richard Speck, John Wayne Gacy and Hillside Strangler sicko gets his own TV movie or mini-series," writes Marvin Kitman, Newsday's TV critic.

Kitman wants a voluntary code of ethics to evolve in the TV business. But that won't happen until the public shows more distaste for the process of turning every passing felon into a celeb.

MERRY C-------S TO ALL

The Yuletide work of the American Civil Liberties Union is never done.

While others frolic, the grinches of the ACLU tirelessly trudge out each year on yet another creche patrol, snatching Nativity scenes from public parks and rubbing out religious symbols. Sometimes, on school property, they catch a rabbi or a minister mentioning God or carolers singing "Silent Night" instead of just songs about snowmen. Then they have to turn everybody in to a judge. Otherwise our liberties would be threatened.

In 1992, for instance, the creche squad hit Vienna, Virginia, arguing that a Nativity scene on town property violated the Supreme Court's so-called "plastic reindeer rule." In a 1984 decision, the Court said that a publicly sponsored creche on private land in Pawtucket, Rhode Island, was permissible because it was part of a predominantly secular display including candy canes and plastic reindeer. In an attempt to ward off the creche gestapo, the creche in Vienna was surrounded with two plastic Santas, one reindeer and one snowperson. No good. The ACLU found a judge who struck it down. Presumably a future Supreme Court decison will determine the precise number of reindeer needed to excuse the presence of one baby Jesus in a Christmas display.

Last year, mindful of the legal fees it would have to pay if the ACLU struck again, the town ordered the Vienna Choral Society to ban all religious carols (including a Chanukah song) from its performance at the annual Christmas pageant and stick to songs like "Jingle Bells." To its credit, the choral society was unwilling to accept the town's pre-emptive censorship, and refused to perform. Now the town has a Christmas pageant that contains no hint of Christmas, at least as traditionally understood to refer to Jesus. But an ACLU grinch in Richmond, Stephen Pershing, is apparently still not satisfied. According to *The Washington Post*, he thinks Vienna may be violating the constitution by having any kind of Christmas program at all.

How did we reach the point where running off to judges to get every trace of religion extinguished from public life seems normal? The Founding Fathers would certainly be aghast at the ACLU's fundamentalist version of what separation of church and state requires. America's long history of privatizing religion has an equally long history of allowing it some public functions.

Many Americans say they don't understand the fuss over creches and carols. After all, creches can be moved to privately owned sites and the carols can be sung under private auspices. True enough, but there are two Christmases now, and many Christians feel that the state is taking an increasingly active role in erasing the religious Christmas and in inflating the secular one starring Frosty, Santa and Scrooge.

Justice Kennedy made essentially this argument in his dissent in *Allegheny County v. ACLU*, which banned a large Nativity scene from a Pittsburgh courthouse. Government's enforced recognition of only the secular version of Christmas, he said, "would signify the callous indifference toward religious faith that our cases and traditions do not require. . . . Judicial invalidation of government's attempts to recognize the religous underpinnings of the holiday would signal not neutrality but a pervasive intent to insulate government from all things religious."

Referring to the majority decision, Kennedy wrote: "Taken to its logical extreme, some of the language quoted above would require a relentless extirpation of all contact between government and religion. But that is not the history or the purpose of the Establishment Clause."

No, it isn't. Our history and traditions fit what is now called "the accommodationist model": allow some mild expressions of religion in the public arena, but forbid others that seem coercive or proselytizing. As Justice Kennedy says, a large Latin cross standing permanently atop the municipal building is one thing; a two-week Nativity scene in the park is quite another. This is particularly so when menorahs and other religious symbols are welcome. Most of us presumably can distinguish between a steady diet of Christian hymns at city hall and an annual Christmas concert that includes traditional religious carols. As Justice Kennedy argues, giving the whole program over to Frosty and Rudolph is a powerful secularizing message, not neutral at all.

There is also the troublesome fact that the Christian feast of Christmas is a national public holiday. Having granted it that status, the state logically should either allow minimal public acknowledgment of what it has wrought, or cancel the holiday and invent a new midwinter festival.

The suppression of the Christmas holiday is not going to happen, of course. Instead we get a series of evasive arguments and reindeer-ridden Supreme Court decisions. But the plain truth, in Justice Kennedy's words, is that a government-displayed creche "presents no realistic danger of moving government down the forbidden road toward an establishment of religion," whether or not the creche is "surrounded by poinsettias, talking wishing wells or carolers." There is no real problem here. Isn't it time for anticreche zealots to drop their tedious crusade?

BOXING IN BELIEVERS

Is the American elite routinely disdainful or hostile to religion? Stephen Carter, professor of law at Yale, says yes in his new book, *The Culture of Disbelief.*

Originally Carter wanted to call the book *God as a Hobby.* That acid phrase, which survives as a chapter heading, means this: the intellectual class thinks religion is fine if conducted in private as a personal pursuit, like woodworking or chess. But if religions bring their moral concerns into the public arena, the elite is always ready to stamp its collective feet and howl about dangerous zealots and a crumbling wall between church and state.

It's a solid, well-argued work, but the truth is, the circumstances surrounding the book may outweigh the text itself. First, President Clinton read *The Culture of Disbelief* while on vacation and explicitly endorsed its theme, suggesting that American liberalism is in danger of automatically mistrusting people who take public positions based on religious convictions.

This means that the chattering classes—academics, journalists, activists and arts people—who generally keep religion out of the national conversation; will probably have to chatter a bit about the book and its subject.

Second, the author is an Episcopalian, a liberal, a black man and a Yale law professor, none of which fits the conventional profile of people who complain about elite efforts to marginalize religion. Catholics and fundamentalist Christians have been saying this for years. In 1992 the U.S. Catholic bishops talked of the dominant secular culture's "strong tendency to privatize faith, to push it to the margins of society." Now that message is coming out of Yale Law School, a good thing.

How has the elite culture done this to religion? Simply by acting on unspoken shared assumptions that religion is backward, medieval, embarrassing or irrelevant. Carter points to "rhetoric that refuses to accept the notion that rational, public-spirited people can take religion seriously."

Those assumptions show up regularly in the media culture. It isn't a matter of bias. It's ignorance and the elite-culture conviction that religion should be conducted only inside churches, synagogues and mosques. The Freedom Forum's study on religion and the news media reported that "astonishingly" some TV reporters and producers interviewed for the project assumed that church-state separation "means that religious dealings in moral-political issues are inappropriate subjects in the news." On the ignorance frontier, Garry Wills once said, "Media people are ignorant of religion, afraid of it and try to stay away from it."

One problem is that the elite culture is so wedded to individualism, choice, secularity, and freedom from restraint that it cannot accept the fact that religions are communities that operate in and out of the political arena on shared moral beliefs.

As Carter writes, the churches are intermediate institutions (situated between the individual and the state) "to which citizens owe a separate allegiance." Religion is a form of organized resistance to the state and culture. Its social and political function is to resist conventional wisdom on grounds of clear principle: "A religion is, at its heart, a way of denying the authority of the rest of the world."

In law, the courts have progressively chopped away at the functions of religions as communities. Mary Ann Glendon, professor of law at Harvard, points out that the Supreme Court, largely indifferent to religion, has framed it in individualistic terms: religion is "inviolably private," an "individualistic experience," and a religion "worthy of the name" is the product of "choice."

These are the mental categories of the secular elite, the footprints of what Glendon calls "the dogmas of knowledge-class culture." That culture basically thinks it's illegitimate for religions to do what they are set up to do: act communally and forcefully on moral issues.

In the last two generations, the courts have seriously impinged on traditonal conceptions of the role of religion in America. The Founding Fathers thought that the First Amendment's establishment clause meant that the state should be friendly to all religions, but play no favorites. Now it is taken to mean that the state is neutral between belief and non-belief—that is, it vigorously promotes secularity in all public functions.

In law, the elite culture has vastly inflated the establishment clause (even moments of silence in public schools now seem to establish religions), while progressively constricting free exercise. Carter runs through a series of cases where the regulatory state tells believers what religous principles they can and cannot act upon. As Glendon writes, free exercise "seems to have been left on the sidelines of the rights revolution."

This is why religious groups often seem to be playing defense, and are increasingly depicted as out-of-step backward-looking zealots. But when these groups are undercut, all of society pays a price. Me-first individualism and "choice" are no substitutes for moral traditions.

PART NINE

"WHO KILLED FEMINISM?"

Sex, Harassment, Rape, and Ideology

Is gossip sexual harassment?

The best story in the newspapers of July 20, 1990 was not the sentencing of Pete Rose, the opening of the Nixon Library or the salvaging of the civil rights bill. It was Michelle Locke's wonderful AP story on the new sexual harassment code at Amherst-Pelham Regional High School in Massachusetts.

Here's how Ms. Locke began: "High schoolers who beam sexually charged stares at their classmates or exchange snippets of gossip in the halls, could run afoul of new guidelines designed to curb sexual harassment among students." By the time the last line rolled by ("We're not Puritans," a school official said), I was convinced that Ms. Locke's piece and the Amherst code itself should go directly into a time capsule. This would give our baffled decendants an outside chance to comprehend some of the strange social obsessions of the 1990s.

I phoned the superintendent of schools, Gus Sayer. Is there a serious harassment problem at the school? No, he said, we just thought these rules were a good idea. How much gazing or leering would it take to be brought up on sexual harassment charges? There is no time limit, he said, a single stare might do it. And what if a student told a friend, "I think Marcie and Allen have something going?" "That would qualify as sexual harassment," he replied.

This expansive view of harassment is in the air these days. Driven by feminist ideology, we have constantly extended the definition of what constitutes illicit male behavior. Very ambiguous incidents are now routinely flattened out into male predation and firmly listed under date rape. In a Swarthmore College's rape prevention pamphlet, "inappropate innuendo" was actually listed as an example of acquaintance rape. At the University of Michigan, charges were filed against a male student who slipped the following joke under the door of a female student: "Q. How many men does it take to mop a floor? A. None, it's a woman's job."

Now this stern new femino-puritanism seems to be reaching down into the high schools. Looking and talking can apparently be as career-threatening at Amherst-Pelham as mopping jokes at Michigan. The high school lists all the possible consequences of harassment: parent conference, apology to victim, detention, suspension, recommendation for expulsion, referral to police.

If I were in charge of a national program to ruin sex for the next generation, I would certainly want to include Amherst-Pelham's new rules. The code is a rich compost of antisex messages: males are predatory; sex is so dangerous that chit-chat about it can get you brought up on charges; hormone-driven gazing at girls will bring the adult world down on your neck; women are victims—incapable of dismissing creeps by simply quipping "Buzz off, Bozo," they must be encouraged to run to the administration and say "Someone was looking at me"—and since hallway sex gossip is likely to get to authorities through the services of snitches, friends should probably not be trusted. Better to talk about the weather.

A small irony here is that gossip is the primary means by which an informal social group, such as a class or a student body, creates and maintains norms. Beneath the titillation of gossip, approval and disapproval are constantly being doled out, and behavior is being modified. A male who treats females badly is far more likely to be brought into line by peer-group gossip than by a huffy administration imposing rules from above.

There is another ominous aspect of the Amherst rules. In listing "the spreading of sex gossip" as a school offense, they impose, rather casually, what is apparently the first speech code at an American high school. At least I know of no other high school that censors or punishes private conversation. This too is smuggled in from the college level, where the new speech police have successfully imposed codes to defend the sensibilities of sexual, racial and ethnic groups. The mopping joke was a violation of the University of Michigan code, since found unconstitutional. But many other colleges have installed these dubious programs, including the University of Wisconsin, the whole University of California system and (inevitably) Stanford. Now, I suppose, the yearning to solve problems by curbing speech will begin to hit the high schools.

The *Economist* featured an interesting lead editorial entitled "America's Decadent Puritans." Despite the tough headline, it was a friendly but very sober view of America's problems from "an unashamedly Americanophile" British publication. As it happens, most of the hallmarks of social decline mentioned in the piece are illustrated or strongly implied in the foolish Amherst harassment rules: the itch to censor; litigiousness and endless hearings over the problems of everyday life; the obsession with self-esteem and victimization; the constant truckling to pressure groups; the gradual assertion of a conformist and politically correct way of thinking; the expectation that the courts, the politicians, or somebody will supply us with a stress-free life ("I guess the people in our school, they're trying to make it a perfect world," an Amherst-Pelham student said to Ms. Locke).

That's why these rules are ideal for a time capsule. Let's just stuff them there and skip the whole idea of imposing them on the unsuspecting young of Amherst-Pelham.

HARASSMENT'S MURKY EDGES

As a result of the Hill-Thomas hearings, we all understand that obvious power plays against women—sexual demands from supervisors and "hostile environments" designed to make women feel inferior and off balance—are clearly understood, and clearly illegal. Beyond that there is a good deal of confusion, and no one has been able to define sexual harassment very well. Judith Lichtman of the Women's Legal Defense Fund is impatient with this view, saying that "People may prefer to believe it's a murky subject, but that's baloney. . . . You don't have to be a genius to figure out that you're being hassled." Three inches away from this quotation in last Friday's *Washington Post*, staff writer Kim Masters tells us that while working as a reporter she was genially propositioned by a bureaucrat several times. As Masters tells it—"He never hinted that he would try to hurt me professionally," and in fact he continued to be a good source, giving her "all kinds of leads for stories"—this was a case of sexual harassment, though it is hard to figure out why she thinks so.

Let us try to make the case for murk.

It is now accepted in the social sciences that males and females perceive verbal and nonverbal cues in different ways and therefore are exceptionally good at misunderstanding one another. This regularly produces *Rashomon*-like encounters, with each party aghast at the other's interpretation of what went on. Deborah Tannen's best-seller, *You*

Just Don't Understand, demonstrates that the complaint of the week ("They just don't get it") works both ways in male-female conversations.

Another source of confusion is that our conception of sexual harassment keeps expanding. The "hostile environment" ruling is a just one, but it means that all apparently innocent actions and comments might now be viewed as part of a pattern that injures women. Professors are now being found guilty of the freshly minted offense of improper or unwelcome gazing. Consciousness-raising films indicate that a copy of *Playboy* lying about on a man's desk might come under the heading of harassment. Last month, a female worker in California was ordered to take down a photo calendar of men in bathing suits, lest some quibbling male make a harassment issue of it.

Some arguments against harassment sound as though the goal is to desexualize the workplace, but dating and courtship take place there. There is some evidence that young people are more dependent than ever on the workplace as a pool of potential mates. Is this wrong? If a woman says no to a request for a date, is a second request likely to bring charges of harassment? No one knows. The use of the terms "unwanted" or "unwelcomed" sexual attention creates a Catch-22 for males, who rarely know whether a pitch will be "welcomed" until it's been made. It is almost impossible to read the literature on sexual harassment without noticing its pinched view of sex as eroticized male power. As long as this view is buried in our policies, we will have trouble sorting out harassment issues.

Another strong tendency in the literature is the insistence that the law allow plaintiffs/victims to determine whether an offense has taken place. The courts have accepted this—the point of view of the victim is the point of view of the law. As one attorney for employers said: "If one woman's interpretation sets the legal standard, then it is virtually up to every woman in the workplace to define if she's been sexually harassed."

This puts sexual harassment in the same category as violations of college speech and behavior codes, which often turn on the feelings of the aggrieved rather than on any objective and definable offense. But if feelings are trumps, how do we know when sexism and harassment end and hypersensitivity begins?

The radical subjectivity that this places at the heart of harassment procedures makes for some curious arguments. At the University of Toronto, the suggestion that a third party be allowed to report incidents of harassment led to protests that only the plaintiff/victim, and not any corroborating witnesses, should have the prerogative of reporting and defining offenses.

Perhaps this decisive turn toward subjective determination of offenses was inevitable. It is certainly true that under the old objective, where's-the-evidence standard, few harassers were being punished. But it opens an era in which many males, guilty and innocent, are likely to be tainted by unsubstantiated charges.

Deconstructing Anita Hill

With great dignity and gravity, Anita Hill gave a very peculiar speech marking the first anniversary of the Hill-Thomas hearings.

She gave it at a Georgetown University Law Center conference on "Race, Gender and Power in America." As the title implies, this was one of those hothouse campus meetings where no male Caucasian is on the program, and if one is even spotted in the audience, he could fairly be accused of masochism.

Amid all the talk about "marginalization" and "abnormalization," white males took the customary drubbing. "Most of white men's lives are predicated on ignoring injuries done to women," intoned law professor Judith Resnik in one of the minor indignant sallies against the low-pigment, high-testosterone set.

An awkward moment occurred when someone from the audience suggested that the panelists might be stereotyping white males. This is like a seminarian telling the pope he might be wrong about the Virgin Birth. But no punitive action was taken against the zany questioner and the crisis quickly passed. After some brief mumbling about the variety of opinion among white males, panelists were back on firm ground once again, talking about "structures of subordination" and the need for a "gender-focused political movement."

Given the fiery tone of the conference, Anita Hill's speech must have come as a disappointment. She threw no red meat to the audience. She did not mention Clarence Thomas's name. Even a reference in her printed text to "the press, Thomas supporters and Thomas witnesses" was shortened to "the press and others" when she spoke.

Instead, she delivered a dry speech, based on an abstract and heavily footnoted paper, mentioning Sigmund Freud and Simone de Beauvoir. Her central argument was that much of the public failed to believe her accusations against Clarence Thomas because she was unmarried and had no protector or patron among the "fourteen white male" members of the Senate Judiciary Committee. She called this her "failure and unwillingness" to tap into the "institutions" of patronage and marriage. At oppression conferences, everything is an "institution," but little applause is heaped upon speakers who lament the lack of white male protectors.

Hill was apparently complaining, as indirectly as possible, that she had nothing resembling the hometown support that Clarence Thomas got from Senator Danforth. She says her "sin" was not acquiring patronage before the Senate hearings began. She said: "I thus wandered into Washington, D.C., without a patron or even a proper letter of introduction and with no good explanation of how I came to be there."

This is a puzzling passage. Hill's testimony was backed and praised by powerful Washington lobbying groups. Allies and witnesses rallied to her side. She says the presence of her family during the hearings had telling effect. Yet a year later, she presents herself as a lonely wanderer in Washington.

Whatever one thinks of Hill's testimony, this is a odd way of casting the story. The Hill-Thomas hearings were a momentous political and social event, with repercussions in gender relations, race relations and partisan politics we still can't measure. Among other things, it was the first national teach-in on the charge of sexual harassment, and the first time (outside a sports arena) that large masses of white Americans fully identified themselves with the personal struggle of black Americans.

But at a conference built around her, Hill reduced the political to the narrowly personal, going on at some length about how the committee failed to understand her as a person. Here she is talking about her status as a single woman:

"The attention to my marital status caused people to ponder in an uninformed way as to why I, a thirty-five-year-old black professional woman, was single. . . . Yet to consider the question of my marital status in an informed way, the public would have had to consider the institution of marriage in the context of a number of factors, modern and historical, as they relate to the lives of African-Americans." Say what? Couldn't she just have said plainly that 1) her marital or nonmarital status is nobody's business, and 2) Senator Alan Simpson acted sleazily in talking about her sexual "proclivities"?

Hill spoke moderately, but she adopted the intellectual apparatus of those who view all world events through the race-and-gender prism. She ignored the partisan political hardball at the hearings and shifted the focus away from the black alleged perpetrator to what the white patriarchal superstructure did to her. And she did this using the language of conventional campus deconstruction theory ("Because I and my reality did not comport with what they accepted as their reality, I and my reality had to be reconstructed.")

The reality is that Hill could become a major voice on harassment issues. She is on leave from her law school to study sexual harassment, and she may be given the world's first endowed professorship in sexual harassment, at the University of Oklahoma. Since she will have a lot to say, her apparent embrace of the race-and-gender ideologues is not a good sign.

REASONABLE WOMAN OR REASONABLE PERSON?

In all the tonnage of newsprint devoted to sexual harassment, very little has been said about the "reasonable woman" standard. This is, in fact, a tentative and controversial legal construct, given its most full-throated court approval in the case of a moonstruck IRS worker in California accused of besieging a female colleague with protestations of love and awe. He asked her out several times and wrote a long strange letter basically making the point that he worshiped her from afar. (Her desk was twenty feet away.) The woman sued, charging sexual harassment. Was it "reasonable" for the woman to be afraid of the overly ardent office Cyrano, especially since he offered in the letter to leave her alone if she asked him to?

A U.S. district court threw the case out, dismissing the incidents as "isolated and genuinely trivial," but the Ninth Circuit Court of Appeals, in a two-to-one decision, perceived an "underlying threat" and sent the case back for trial. Though merely remanding the case and not deciding it, the appeals court thought this was the time for a sweeping decison and made one. It bought the argument that reasonable men and women would reliably react differently to the case, thus requiring a "reasonable woman" standard.

The dissenting judge called for a gender-neutral standard. The two-man majority argued that the "stereotyped notions of society," operating in harassment cases, keep women from participating in the workplace on an equal footing with men. True enough. But attitudes are changing and not all healthy ones are guaranteed to be found in the minds of women. Why not a sex-blind "reasonable-person" standard that incorporates the fair-minded views of all? After all, if the stereotypes of society (those of males and females alike) are the problem, why not exclude stereotyped views instead of sensible male views? No good, Judge Robert Beezer said: a reasonable-person test "tends to be male-biased and tends to systematically ignore the experiences of women."

Let us look at what is implied in this decision. One idea is obvious: women need the kind of special tribal protection under the law that feminists have spent the last twenty-five years opposing as patronizing and enfeebling. In effect, the court erected a separate standard of sensitivity for women in the labor force. A more ominous implication is this: we must brush aside the reasonable views and standards of one group—in this case, half the human race—in order to guarantee the rights of another group. A third notion, more than just an implication, is that members of each group (sex, tribe, race) are inevitably frozen in their own biases; groups cannot agree on common objective standards fair to all; in practice, the law is the subjectivity of entrenched groups posing as objectivity.

These last two strains of thought are by now very familiar: they are the views of the radical multiculturalists, now casually drifting into the law. In their balkanized and very pessimistic perspective, there is no such thing as American society or an American mainstream, just a gaggle of clashing cultures trying to wrest some private advantage from one another. Several schools of thought within the law more or less agree with this view, and many are watching the development of harassment law with more on their minds than just protection of female workers.

The two appeals judges are dipping their judicial toes into some deep waters here. What is the next step? Well, if special standards are carved out for one American tribe, why not for others? Attorneys on both sides of the IRS harassment case say it is just a short hop to expanding the principle to ethnic, racial or other forms of job harassment and discrimination. "For blacks who are harassed on the job, you'd use a reasonable black's standard," one attorney said, as if elaborating the obvious. Or perhaps we will have the separate standards of reasonable senior citizens, or Vietnamese-Americans, or Catholics or rednecks.

I cannot imagine that the Supreme Court, as now constituted, will allow the "reasonable-woman" decision to stand. The purposes of law are to subvert subjectivity, to create a public reality all can accept, not to invent or proliferate new realities because the balkanizers are watching and grumbling. Among other things, the "reasonable-woman standard" is insulting to women because it shrinks what ought to be a universal standard of fairness into a mere tribal one. Harassment isn't wrong just because reasonable women think so, but because reasonable people think so and are therefore capable of coming to terms on common standards. Very few reasonable parents, I would think, intend to raise sons by reasonable male ethics and daughters by reasonable female ones.

So far I have noticed two more sproutings of the "reasonable-woman" standard, a bill introduced into the Illinois legislature and a Michigan state court acceptance of the standard. Therefore it is time to announce the "reasonable-columnist standard" in reply: like many muzzy attempts at reform, this is the path of fragmentation and folly. It is unreasonable and should be opposed.

THE TROUBLE WITH FEMINISM

"Who Killed Feminism?" asked the headline. Readers of the Sunday Outlook section of *The Washington Post* did not have to search far for an answer: it was a quarter-inch away in the subhead, "Hypocritical Movement Leaders Betrayed Their Own Cause," just above the byline of Sally Quinn, Washington insider, successful novelist (*Happy Endings*) and one of the best-read reporters the *Post* has ever had.

Quinn's argument was a muscular one. She wrote that the established feminist leaders, and the National Organization for Women, are the domestic equivalents of Communist party apparatchiks in the Soviet Union: ideological dinosaurs, remote from the needs of their constituency, who should step down and let other people take over. "The truth is," she wrote, "that many women have come to see the feminist movement as anti-male, anti-child, anti-family, anti-feminine. And therefore it has nothing to do with us."

These are hardly new criticisms. In fact, they are very close to the ones made by allies of Betty Friedan, cofounder of NOW, when she broke from the group in 1975 to form a "network" of feminist dissidents. The dissidents argued that NOW was rapidly moving away from its core constituency, that instead of focusing primarily on the problems of mainstream women and jobs and family, it was becoming mesmerized by lesbian rights, radical chic and what we would today call the politics of victimization.

The difference today is that successful mainstream women such as Quinn are saying that this wrong turn taken by NOW sixteen years ago has led to a dead end. What kind of shape is American feminism in, when its leading journal (Ms.) is edited by a woman who thinks that "most of the decently married bedrooms across America are settings for nightly rape," and its leading organization (NOW) is headed by a woman with a husband in Miami and a female "companion" in Washington? Is this out of touch, or is NOW quietly banking on a sudden surge of bisexual adultery chic among its membership? Quinn writes: "Can you imagine George Bush telling the world that he was having a homosexual relationship with another man and it was just swell with Barbara?"

Here is the voice of another successful mainstream woman trying to come to grips with the out-of-touchness of feminism: "I am skeptical about the woman's movement. I find myself increasingly saying YES . . . BUT—yes, there may be a war between the sexes, but I am doubtful it is one the women's movement is currently fighting." The speaker is Margaret O'Brien Steinfels, editor of *Commonweal*, the liberal Catholic magazine. Steinfels's analysis is this: mass movements tend to generate a story, or mythic recounting of group experience. These myths are healthy, but they are always in danger of hardening into an ideology that no longer fits the real-life experience of members." Something like this happened to the women's movement," Steinfels said in a recent speech. "Its claim to legitimacy, its declaration that it represents all women is based on an all-encompassing explanation for the plight of women. In other words, men."

Since she does not feel oppressed by "the patriarchy," since her experiences with males, good and bad, do not fit the victim-oppressor model, she feels the movement has little to do with her life. "By definition then," she said, "positive experiences of the kind I have described about my own life, and many other women could describe about theirs, are excluded from the current discourse of the women's movement, and thus from the public conversation about men and women."

The woman's movement has come to depend almost wholly on real-life and fictional stories that fit the myth and reinforce it: tales of abandonment, rape and vast cruelty, what Steinfels calls "an ideology of victimhood—stories that focus on destruction and humiliation" of females by males.

This is nowhere clearer than in academic feminism. On the campus, in feminist studies programs, rape is now the paradigm and central metaphor of male-female relations. What to most of us is a brutal and ugly crime is to conventional feminist academics just male business as usual, the image of what men do to women all the time, sexually and nonsexually. ("The major distinction between intercourse [normal] and rape [abnormal] is that the normal happens so often that one cannot see anything wrong with it"—Catharine MacKinnon, media hero of sexual harassment.) In the secular convents of feminist studies departments, abstruse man-hating and galloping heterophobia are absolutely routine. These attitudes are not much help to real-world women, who have brothers and fathers they love, and who might want to get married sometime.

The trick, as Steinfels says, is to get the excluded voices of women back into the debate without falling into the counter-myth of "anti-feminism," which simply wants women to shut up and go home. Instead of harping full-time on male perfidy, those voices want to talk about intimacy, trust, equality, sharing, child care and a peaceful settlement in the battle of the sexes. As Quinn says, feminists screwed up "by dismissing what really goes on in the hearts and minds of women." Time for change.

THE POLITICS OF DATE RAPE

Is male sexuality inherently aggressive, the result of evolutionary pressures? Or is aggressive sex just something that men decide, coldly and politically, to unleash on women?

This is one argument you won't hear argued much these days. But the two views have different implications for policy and lead to very different assessments of the current debate over date rape.

Here is the traditional view: Evolution has left human males with a dubious gift—a high sex drive directly linked to aggression. This link was once adaptive, or it would not have evolved, but now it is spectacularly maladaptive, which means that it is society's job to break or weaken this link in each new crop of males.

Camille Paglia made this point in an op-ed piece in *Newsday*: "Aggression and eroticism, in fact, are deeply intertwined. Hunt, pursuit, and capture are biologically programmed into male sexuality. Generation after generation, men must be educated, refined, and ethically persuaded away from their tendency toward anarchy and brutishness."

The feminist view of rape is basically political: Men run the world through patriarchal power, and rape is an expression of this power and a useful form of control. If you think this is an exaggeration, take a look at the most influential book yet written on rape, Susan Brownmiller's *Against Our Will*. Brownmiller studied under Herbert Aptheker, the historian who argued that the lynching of blacks in the South was a systematic way that all whites kept all blacks under control. She quite literally adapted this view of lynching to the rape issue: rape, she wrote, is "nothing more or less than a conscious process of intimidation by which all men keep all women in a state of fear."

Among other things, this preposterous view of rape is one with all the sex drained out of it. ("Rape is not an act of sex; it's an act of aggression.") Rape is not viewed as a problem rooted in male sexuality, but as a political problem of males deciding to oppress women. In one form or another, this theme is taken for granted in feminist writing on the subject, with woeful effect. Jane O'Reilly wrote that date rape "is not a mere misunderstanding of sexual signals but an act of aggression by a man against a woman . . . part of pervasive patterns of intimidation and denigration of women by men." No hormones in this sentence either. You and I might think that some "date rapes" involve confusion, fumbling, mixed signals, misperception of male persistence as coercion, and perhaps the retroactive labeling of an unhappy sexual encounter as rape, but O'Reilly knows differently. No gray areas, please. Date rape, like all rape, is always, by definition, an expression of male denigration of women.

I think this is a rigidly ideological view that bypasses not only biology but complexity. On the date rape issue, it leads to an unworldy rationalism. ("No means no," the feminists insist, and men will nod in public if they have to, but privately they know that depending on context and nonverbal signals, "No" can mean "maybe," "convince me," "back off awhile" or "get lost.") The mating game does not proceed by words alone.

It also leads to an eerie demonization of males, as some of the current campus antirape literature shows. (One brochure literally depicts the male in devil's horns and tail.) In both the traditional and feminist views, young males are viewed as needing some sort of tutoring in restraint. But the politicized feminist view positions rape as a hate crime and divides the world into male oppressors and female victims. In its most virulent form (on the campuses of elite universities) this is often part of a broad philosophy that depicts much or all male behavior in terms of rape and violation.

With this as background it is hard to judge the dramatic rise of the date rape issue on campus. How much is genuinely criminal behavior by males and how much is politicized anger or misunderstanding between the sexes? The clearest evidence for predatory male behavior comes from some fraternities. Here the reports of group attempts to denigrate and sexually humiliate women are so strong and consistent that many universities are mounting campaigns to abolish or decisively change the character of frats. Away from some fraternities and athletic houses, the evidence is far more ambiguous. John Taylor, writing in _New York_ magazine, was the first to include date rape as a "politically correct" issue used against the same target every other PC group on campus aims at: heterosexual white males.

Then, too, we have a devastating analysis of the date rape issue done by Stephanie Gutman for _Reason_ magazine. This is a portrait of feminist academics, committed to the idea that date-rape stats are too low, producing deeply flawed studies complete with such ludicrously broad definitions of date rape that the numbers would have to rise. In one study, 43 percent of women "had not realized they had been raped" and redefined past sexual incidents as criminal. Gutman said: "The real story about campus date rape is not that there's been any increase of rape on college campuses, at least of the acquaintance type, but that the word rape is being stretched to encompass any type of sexual interaction." More evidence and less politics, please.

ACQUITTAL AND INJUSTICE IN QUEENS

No one knows whether the brief flurry of sexual banter counted for much with the jury, but everyone agrees that it started when Michael Calandrillo held up a copy of *Sports Illustrated*'s annual swimsuit issue. "Have you ever had sex with a white man?" he asked at one point. The young woman, an immigrant from Jamaica, shot back: "No, have you ever had sex with a black woman?"

This little exchange occurred on March 1, 1990, at a late-afternoon meeting of the rifle club of St. John's University in Queens. The woman wanted to get home quickly to study for an economics test the next morning. Calandrillo offered her a ride but said he had to stop first and get gas money at his house—a fraternitylike, off-campus residence known as "Trump Plaza," shared by several members of the St. John's lacrosse team. Calandrillo let her cool her heels in the car for a few minutes, then came out and waved her into the house, saying, "Come and meet my friends." Inside, she was led upstairs and introduced to two other jocks, Walter Gabrinowitz and Andrew Draghi, and then another male came by. They started to talk about sex.

The woman, then twenty-one, was an open and trusting person, a devout Catholic from a successful family who seemed to assume she would be safe at a Catholic university. Friends said she neither drank nor smoked and strongly disapproved of sex before marriage.

The woman announced that she wanted to go home, but Calandrillo said he had to wait for a phone call and gave her a drink, orange soda in a coffee mug. When she complained about the taste, she said, Calandrillo told her there was vodka in it. She testified: "I told him I never drink, that I had a rum and Coke once and I got sick," but Calandrillo pressed her to drink one more cupful, perhaps two. She recalled protesting again but said he told her angrily, "What . . . are you going to make me waste it? What am I supposed to do with it if you don't drink it?"

She remembers Calandrillo massaging her shoulders and undressing her; she was nauseated and drunk. She says she told him, "Michael, I feel real sick." She passed out and says that when she woke, Calandrillo was sodomizing her. In her account, Calandrillo then left and other men attacked her sexually. When she screamed, she said, Gabrinowitz replied, "You can't scream in here. It's a residential neighborhood." One prosecution eyewitness said he saw her screaming and clawing at one of the alleged attackers. The woman said she floated in and out of consciousness during five hours of sexual abuse and degradation. At one point, she said, two men were slapping her face with their penises. Later she was carried, defenseless and limp, to a second residence, either as a joke or for more sexual use. Then one student, apparently the first decent male in our story, jumped to her defense and got her cleaned up and taken home.

In the first of two or three trials that the woman must endure, the three men facing the most serious charges have all been acquitted. The jury, which included six women, two blacks and a Hispanic, did not buy her story even though the prosecution produced four eyewitnesses, male students at the scene, who corroborated much of what she said.

One jury member said: "Hell hath no fury like a woman scorned," implying that the charges were the result of a soured romantic yearning for Calandrillo. Another juror called her testimony "flaky." In fact, everyone agrees she was a poor witness: almost inaudible, sometimes frenzied, sometimes smiling nervously at the defendants. Twice she ran off the stand, and once she could not pull herself together to mark a chart of the house. There were many inconsistencies, and she never seemed quite sure whether she had one drink or two or three. But then, abused people reliving their traumas rarely make ideal witnesses. Her story rang true for most of the press corps covering the trial and it seems true to me. How likely is it that a conservative, middle-class woman, virtually allergic to alcohol, disdainful of premarital sex and facing an important exam the next morning, would voluntarily get drunk and enjoy several hours of oral sex with five or six strangers?

The defense admitted the sex acts but claimed they were consensual.

Consent? She was upstairs, reeling from what she described as a sneak drink she didn't want. She was isolated in the room, a small person (five feet two, one hundred pounds) surrounded by beefy jocks who she said were using booze and an angry remark or two to push her along. If this is consent, it is the same kind offered by a citizen who says yes when a bunch of cops burst into his bedroom at midnight asking if they can look around. Even if the jury thought she consented to Calandrillo, who is yet to be tried, what shape was she in to consent to all the others?

I remember a rape case I covered as a young reporter. The guy had guilt oozing from every pore, and the woman was still hideously black and blue from the beating he had given her. But the jury somehow acquitted. The guy smirked at his lawyer, the woman slumped in her chair, and the judge, in an admirable display of cold fury, explained to the jury that they had just perpetrated a total miscarriage of justice. Different jury. Same injustice.

FAR-OUT FEMINISM IN THE SENATE

In the spring of 1992 I was invited to join a late-night TV talkathon on rape hosted by Peter Jennings. Before we went on, participants had to watch an ABC special on the subject that seemed to buy into the radical feminist analysis. Sitting nearby was Catharine MacKinnon, the current North American champion in the category of grim feminist ideologue. When she caught the drift of the ABC show, MacKinnon couldn't control her jubilation. "They got it!" she cried out. "It's systemic!"

I took that to mean what it usually means in radical feminist theory: that rape is not a horrible crime perpetrated by individual criminals— it is an integral part of a patriarchal system, either tolerated or tacitly approved as an expression of male domination. In other words, it's a political crime.

The "systemic" argument is a casual group libel implicating all men— and presumably all courts, prosecutors and legislatures—in the crimes of individual rapists. But the gender feminists now dominate American feminism, so the "systemic" argument is now entering the mainstream.

In fact it would be written into federal law if Congress passes the Violence Against Women Act, sponsored primarily by Senator Joseph Biden.

This Senate bill would make many rapes and much domestic violence into federal civil rights violations. But jurisdiction over almost all violent crime belongs to the states. Why federalize these cases? The main rationale is the feminist theory that rape is an expression of group oppression. "One of the advantages of the bill is that it codifies the true nature of rape," Sally Goldfarb of the National Organization for Women's Legal Defense Fund told *The New Republic.*

To bring rape and wife-beating under the umbrella of civil rights protection, it is necessary to argue that these are acts of prejudice and discrimination, like denying someone a job on the basis of race or sex. But they clearly aren't, which is why all the verbal and logical gymnastics are required.

Heterosexual rapists usually rape women. Homosexual rapists usually rape men. The acts are despicable, but the targets are set by sexual orientation, not bias. This odd bill is a perfect example of the now reflexive American habit of reducing almost all social problems to bias. The usual price to pay for this is the shearing away of all bothersome complexity, a spreading politics of group grievance and the sharpening of division between groups (in this case, males and females). It also sets up false battle lines. It's not all females versus all males, but rather all females and most males versus a small number of violent, mostly young male offenders.

Specifically, the bill classifies "gender-motivated" acts of sexual violence as civil rights violations if they are "due at least in part to an animus based on a victim's gender." So civil rights are violated when a rapist rapes because of hostility toward women in general. This approach would bog courts down in analysis of biased attitudes. Instead of just prosecuting rape, thoughts would be sifted, comments would be judged. It's a form of federal hate-crime legislation based on gender.

How is this useful? Answer: it isn't. Like medieval theologians trying to classify angels, authorities would have to spend a lot of time classifying animuses, deciding which rapist's animus was particular and which was generalized and aimed at all women. Then different punishments would be doled out in different courts on the basis of elaborate guesswork.

Why not skip all this and just try to put every rapist away for as long as possible? There's only one clear advantage of stretching rape into a civil rights violation: it props up the group-oppression model of rape, using law to strengthen the weak analogy between random rape and racial subjugation.

There's much more tucked away in the bill. It allows victims of gender-bias violence to sue in federal courts for compensatory and punitive damages. The additional filings would increase the total civil rights caseload of federal courts by 57 percent, according to a judicial impact statement filed by the Administrative Office of the United States Courts.

The bill further burdens an already bloated judicial system. An alleged victim could bring a civil rights suit in federal court, press criminal charges in state court, or both.

This would be a bonanza for lawyers. It would provide a big financial incentive to expand the definiton of rape, a constant goal of radical feminists. It also opens the door to shakedowns based on a threat to sue for rape. A weak allegation that would be dismissed quickly by a criminal prosecutor might suffice in civil court. (Many falsely accused men would presumably pay off to avoid the publicity.) And it could invite publicity-oriented trials in which the desire is not so much to win as to call attention to the supposed injustice of American society.

The bill creates new model programs and encourages sensitivity training for everyone from judges to schoolchildren. There would be a task force, studies, grants to examine sexual stereotyping, plans to deal with runaways and national parks and subway lighting.

The money that would be sprayed out can only be called the first big helping of feminist pork. Rape-crisis centers would share in an annual pool of $100 million in grants. "It would be a great boon to the rape-crisis movement," said Christina Sommers, a professor at Clark University. She does not mean that the money would be well spent on victims of rape. She means it would be used to fund the radical feminism currently organized around rape as a paradigm of male-female relations.

Radical feminists realize what's at stake. The Senate, clogged with recovering harassers and other guilty males, does not. Andrea Dworkin, perhaps America's most extreme feminist, told Ruth Shalit of *The New Republic* that the only possible explanation of the bill's popularity in the Senate "is that senators don't understand the meaning of the legislation they pass." She seems to be right. Shalit told me she interviewed seven or eight Senate sponsors of the bill and none had a clue about what was in it. It's time to read up.

ONLY YOU, CATHARINE

Catharine MacKinnon's new book, *Only Words*, is very short—107 pages of text. It is also very angry. Much of it is one long scream about sex and men.

The book's second sentence is "You grow up with your father holding you down and covering your mouth so another man can make a horrible searing pain between your legs." After that, it gets worse. On page 19, she says some doctors may "enjoy watching and inflicting pain during childbirth," quite a novel idea, it seems to me. By page 60, she is explaining that sexual harassment "begins in your family." Apparently this refers to families of all her readers.

MacKinnon, the University of Michigan law professor who wants to suppress pornography, repeatedly lashes out at horrible sex crimes against women. Good. But, as always in her work, pornography, sex, sex crimes and heterosexual masculinity all fuse into one giant evil.

Follow her argument. Women constitute an oppressed class. Heterosexuality is a social system for the domination and subordination of women. Pornography creates, reflects and sustains this system. All of it—not just violent porn, but mild nudie pictures too—is really violence against women that must be banned.

In MacKinnon's new book, the possibility that sex may involve pleasure and closeness between a man and woman who actually like each other doesn't arise. Instead she talks about "the social coding of sexuality as intimate and pleasurable." (Translation: the oppressive system has led us to believe that sex can be used that way, but it really can't, because sex is about power, which men have and women don't. Since women are so oppressed, there's no real difference between rape and consensual sex. As MacKinnon's sidekick, Andrea Dworkin, writes, "Romance . . . is rape embellished with meaningful looks.")

Does it matter what MacKinnon thinks? Alas, it does. In the mid-1980s, she and Dworkin were way out on the feminist fringe. But she has very rapidly been mainstreamed (a gushing profile in *The New York Times Magazine*, a seat as network commentator at the Clarence Thomas hearings).

Now she has respectability and clout. The stranger parts of her doctrine are rarely mentioned. Her arguments seem to be at the core of current legal attempts to reposition rape and opposition to abortion as sex discrimination. And it is probably safe to say that no champion of censorship has ever been so revered at American law schools.

MacKinnon's thought closely parallels that of campus censors who want hate-speech codes: what appears to be merely distasteful speech (porn, racial and sexual slurs) is really violent action against an oppressed group. This makes her antiporn message easier to take at elite law schools and creates a powerful procensorship alliance on the left.

Nadine Strossen, president of the American Civil Liberties Union, is worried about this. (Me too.) She says the procensorship forces now dominate legal academic meetings and law journals. Strossen thinks appointments and promotions at law schools and certain courses, like those on "feminist jurisprudence," are largely under the sway of procensorship forces. One straw in the wind was a conference last March at the University of Chicago Law School on "Speech Equality & Harm: Feminist Legal Perspectives on Pornography and Hate Propaganda." Strossen noticed that no anticensorship feminist was invited to attend.

Some law professors believe it's only a matter of time before the MacKinnonites put a dent in the First Amendment big enough to allow the banning of some sexual expression. It's already happened in Canada. Last year the Canadian Supreme Court accepted the arguments of Canadian feminists and MacKinnon (she filed a brief), banning degrading sexual materials deemed harmful to women and children.

No proof of harm is required to ban a book or video, merely an assessment of what the Canadian public believes is harmful. In 1992, Canadian customs officials seized 8,118 publications. The 1993 total will include two of Andrea Dworkin's books, confiscated in January. Lesbian bookstores have complained that they have unfairly been singled out for attention. Maybe so, but that's what tends to happen when police or customs agents make censorship decisions according to a vague standard.

The vast expansion of the porn industry is very troubling, but censorship won't stop it, any more than prohibition stopped alcohol (or any more than official punishment for racial jokes helps whites and blacks get along better). And if MacKinnon thinks all women are oppressed by men, why does it make sense to have the male-dominated government decide what sexual materials women get to see? Instead of calling in the cops, a free society ought to try discrediting and stigmatizing people who deal in violent pornography.

I am bound to think that MacKinnonism is a wrong turn for feminism and the left. So many disastrous notions are buried in her work: sex is something done to women; porn is at the root of all women's woes; all sexual imagery involving females amounts to antiwoman violence; men are an implacable and probably unchangeable group foe.

These are really dumb ideas. Is this where feminism wants to go?

Pedophiles in the Schools

New York's Channel 4 news showed some footage of a pedophile group having a quiet chat in the busy atrium of the Citicorp building in midtown Manhattan.

The pedophiles were all members of NAMBLA, the thousand-member North American Man/Boy Love Association, which wants the law to allow adults to have sex with children.

Unaware he was being taped, one member of the group, a public school teacher, urged another, a public school librarian, to keep his membership secret until he had tenure. A third NAMBLA member interviewed by Channel 4 turned out to be a former public school psychologist who had worked with emotionally and physically handicapped children at a Queens elementary school.

John Miller, the WNBC-TV correspondent who broke the story, said last week: "We thought these guys were people who lurk around outside schools. What we found was, they lurk around *inside* the schools."

Lurking may not be the right word. There's no evidence yet of NAMBLA members preying on children in city schools, though at least two local NAMBLA men have been convicted of sex offenses. But Miller has a point. Child molesters don't just hang around playgrounds. They apply for jobs at schools, camps, the Boy Scouts, Big Brothers, YMCAs. "Boy lovers" love to work where the boys are.

So far the effort to haul the pedophiles out of the youth system isn't going all that well, as the current NAMBLA story in New York shows. For six months there was almost no newspaper coverage. The press also ignored the spreading story of parental protests about Peter Melzer, fifty-three, the teacher on the WNBC-TV tape who advised the librarian to lie low. Melzer teaches physics and science at one of the city's elite schools, the Bronx High School of Science. He is on NAMBLA's steering committee and the editorial board of the NAMBLA *Bulletin*, which offers advice on how to entice children into sex ("Leave a pornographic magazine someplace where he's sure to find it").

The City Board of Education has known since 1984 that Melzer was a pedophile. "It seemed to me that nobody wanted to take responsibility for making a decison," said Edward Stancik, a special investigator for the city school system. Stancik released a long report on Peter Melzer recommending he be fired. The former school psychologist and the school librarian are both under investigation too.

So far gay and civil liberties groups have been fairly quiet about the Melzer case, now headed for state disciplinary hearings. Melzer is accused of no crime and NAMBLA says he is being persecuted for speech and political beliefs. But even in the absence of a crime, says Stancik's report, "His misconduct in aiding the *Bulletin* in publishing the advisories for pedophiles . . . makes him unfit to teach children." Yes, that's exactly the point. Leaving a known pedophile in the classroom would be quite a statement about the values of public education.

Melzer, by the way, is a regular delegate to an annual international conference of pedophiles and pederasts. Call it a sexual version of the Predators' Ball. To the folks at NAMBLA, it's important to make sex with children look legitimate. David Finkelhor, a sex researcher on the faculty of the University of New Hampshire, calls NAMBLA "the intellectual elite of child molesting." Most people who prey on children don't bother much about theory, but NAMBLA types feel driven to rationalize what they do. So they have cobbled together a credo out of the gassier rhetoric of victim groups and the children's rights movement.

We are told that man-boy lovers are yet another oppressed group, that NAMBLA is seeking "the empowerment of youth" and sexual self-determination for children, who are being exploited by parents who treat them as property.

This is a corruption of language as well as morals, but it is taken very seriously in some quarters. Since the seventies, at least, one strain of thought in journals of sex research has upheld some of the principles of what might be called child molester's lib: all children are sexual beings from birth, some children do not suffer from adult-child sex, it's sometimes better to have sex from adults than no love at all, and every sexual taboo must be analyzed pro and con including incest and adult-child sex.

Pedophiles have made some headway in politics as well as the world of sexology. NAMBLA is a member of the International Lesbian and Gay Association, which has called on members "to treat all sexual minorities with respect," including pedophiles. Though a great many lesbians and gays detest NAMBLA, the group has been allowed to march in gay parades in New York and San Francisco under its own banners.

Is there a creeping tolerance? I notice that John DeCecco of San Francisco State University, editor of the *Journal of Homosexuality*, is also on the board of *Paidika*, a Dutch pedophile journal. When I asked him why, he said, "They needed a psychologist." No. They "need" respectability, and DeCecco is providing some. The culture is now so soft-minded that many will listen to any self-styled victim group, even one made up of degenerates. That's why it's crucial to keep them out of the schools.

THE GAY TIDE OF CATHOLIC-BASHING

Some rather important unpleasantness occurred at the 1991 St. Patrick's Day parade in New York. In brief, a small group of Irish gays applied to join the march. After various pressures, including a threat to trash the parade if excluded, the Irish gays were let in, joined by an assortment of non-Irish gay militants. The gay group's marshal "had a long string of pearls over a black motorcycle jacket, and his T-shirt read QUEER BOY. He had a purple pansy in his ear." David Dinkins, the city's first black mayor, pointedly marched with the gay contingent. The mayor and the gays were treated boorishly by many in the crowd, and many finger symbols were flipped. One lout threw a full can of beer in the mayor's direction. The obviously angry mayor said the event reminded him of racist treatment of blacks in Birmingham.

This was greeted in the New York press as a victory for inclusion and enlightenment over bigotry. Fair enough. There was bigotry. But the analysis was wildly out of sync with what has been happening between gays and Catholics. Not one columnist or editorial writer showed any awareness of the intense gay campaign against the Catholic Church. Referring to Cardinal O'Connor's pre-parade caution to Catholics ("Show no disrespect back to those who disrespect us") *Newsday* columnist Sydney Schanberg had no idea what the cardinal was talking about. What disrespect?

Let us try to fill him in on this.

In the eighteen months or so leading up to the parade, many churches across the country were vandalized and broken into (six in Los Angeles alone), with gay activists claiming responsibility. Masses and other religious ceremonies were repeatedly disrupted, parishioners harassed and showered with condoms and venomous demonstrations conducted regularly outside churches.

I am not talking here about normal political opposition to church policy on condoms, AIDS or abortion. The bishops have entered the political arena here, and they can take their shots like anyone else. I am talking about a straight-out hate campaign. A catalogue to an AIDS art show, partly funded by the NEA, reflects the general tone: Cardinal O'Connor is a "fat cannibal in skirts" and his cathedral is "a house of walking swastikas." Typical posters outside St. Patrick's ("Get over it, Mary," "Cardinal O'Killer" and "F—— the church") leave no doubt that the purpose is not simply to protest, but to degrade, enrage and vilify.

After the famous gay invasion of St. Patrick's, the press tut-tutted the desecration of the host, but praised the "peaceful demonstration" outside. Having interviewed people on the scene and acquired some of the leaflets handed out, I can tell you that this was no benign protest. It was a classic hate rally, very likely the most bitter anti-Catholic one conducted since the heyday of the Know-Nothings. A similar tone has infected subsequent protests at the cathedral, including one last December, when, in defiance of a court order, another consecrated host was taken from the church and gleefully held up as booty.

Savage mockery of Christianity is now a conventional part of the public gay culture. A ridiculous-looking Jesus figure carrying a cross is always featured in the gay Halloween parade in New York, along with the usual throng of hairy guys dressed as nuns. Some gay clubs and at least one gay movie feature a tableaux of Jesus being sodomized. Gays who disrupt masses in L.A. have dressed as angels with coathanger halos, and in Boston as silly-looking bishops in lavender mitres. Producers of "The Cardinal Detoxes," a poisonously anti-Catholic monologue posing as an off-Broadway play, invited nightly mockery of the church by offering free admission to patrons dressed as nuns or priests. This "Rocky Horror" side of gay culture is ever more virulently anti-Catholic.

Somehow the press has not gotten around to telling this story straight. Given the power of the gay lobby and the stubborn bias of newsrooms, it probably won't be able to perform truthfully for the foreseeable future. For instance, an Act-Up attempt to shout down and drown out an ordination ceremony in Boston was described rather carefully in the *Boston Globe* as "colorful, loud and peaceful." Readers were not told of the parody of the Communion rite featuring condoms as hosts, the mocking of Jesus' sermon on the mount as an endorsement of sodomy, the simulated anal and oral sex and the level of harassment outside the church. Some of the Act-Up angries swarmed around one newly ordained young priest and his elderly mother, pelting them with condoms until police intervened and escorted them away.

The media is way out of line here. Famous newspapers and commentators who scour language for the faintest hint of insensitivity toward gays, blacks and women show little interest in confronting foot-stomping bigotry toward Catholics.

"Is there another group in the country, which, if similarly assaulted, would be treated in this fashion?" asked a writer for *Commonweal*, the liberal Catholic weekly. Probably not. John O'Connor, *The New York Times* TV critic, wrote that Andrew Dice Clay had crossed the "revulsion threshhold" in his attacks on gays, women and various ethnics. I agree. So we all trashed young Andrew. But where is the revulsion threshhold for similar attacks on Catholics?

TOLERANCE YES, APPROVAL NO

Is the public firmly on both sides on the issue of gays in the military? Columnist William Raspberry thinks so. Writing about the ambivalence many Americans feel, he said that most of us are fairminded and want to stop excluding gays, but suspect "that something cultural is going on" behind President Clinton's proposal to lift the ban. When the goal moves beyond fairness "to embrace condonation of sexual behavior, a lot of people—not all of them bigots—start bailing out."

The key distinction, Raspberry notes, is between a homosexual saying, "My sexual orientation and behavior are none of your business," and saying, "I demand that you acknowledge my sexual choices as the exact equivalent of yours."

What he is talking about is the traditional line between tolerance and approval. Tolerance is the primary civic virtue of American pluralism. We agree to get along with people regardless of their beliefs and day-to-day behavior. Approval is quite a different matter. American institutions are not set up to approve various worldviews or to promote the values of those who hold them.

That cultural struggle is being played out in schools and legislatures around the country. For example, crossing the line from tolerance to approval is what provoked the notorious "Rainbow curriculum" controversy in New York City. Instead of settling for a message of tolerance (gays are our neighbors and must not be attacked or harassed), gays and their allies inserted a passage saying that first-graders must be taught the "positive aspects" of homosexual families. Another passage instructed teachers to include references to lesbians and gays in all curricular areas.

But the city's major faiths—Catholic, Protestant, Jewish, Muslim—have taught for centuries that homosexuality is wrong. Why should parents have to send their schoolchildren off to hear the state-imposed message that their religious beliefs are invalid?

In Massachusetts, Governor William Weld appointed a commission on gay and lesbian youth that wants to go further than the Rainbow curriculum. The commission's report calls for a broad array of gay themes and issues to be integrated into all subject areas and departments of all public schools.

Why is this necessary? Because "the primary effects of society's hostility and lack of acceptance are feelings of isolation, extreme low self-esteem, and consequent attempts at self-destructive behavior." But again, it is one thing to teach students not to harass gays. It is another to teach everybody that gay is good as a way of improving homosexuals' feelings about themselves.

No social consensus supports programs approving homosexuality.

Gays have kept discussions tightly focused on civil rights and homophobia. Fine. That's what lobbies do. But not much attention has been paid to the phenomenon of homosexuality itself and the strong reservations about it held by people who are not bigots or haters. We are just at the beginning of a national conversation on homosexuality in which all doubts about its origins and meaning are being put on the table. Right now, the fact is that a majority of Americans is simply unwilling to treat homosexuality as if it raises no moral or social questions.

Given this, a policy of tolerance rather than approval is warranted. Take the debate on gays in the military. Tolerance would mean accepting both gays and straights into the armed forces with no sexual questions asked and no discharges for sexual orientation. No gay officers clubs, no gay regiments, no gay housing. Just tolerance.

In law, it would mean no special legislation one way or the other. No antisodomy laws. No measures like Oregon's Ballot Measure 9, which attempted to brand gays abnormal or perverse. But no gay-rights legislation either. Just laws that cover all people, regardless of what they do in bed.

What's wrong with gay-rights laws? Gay activists argue that they are neutral, merely guaranteeing rights already enjoyed by the straight majority. But don't they actually create a special protected class? A lot of bigots voted against gay-rights legislation in Colorado. But as Virginia Postrel, editor of *Reason* magazine, writes, the swing vote was provided by nonbigots who "simply said 'Stop' to the seemingly endless proliferation of protected categories that divide people into favored and disfavored classes."

Creating these categories has consequences. This path, taken for blacks, a truly victimized group, isn't necessarily appropriate for other groups. And we are not sure where it would lead. Could it provide the legal scaffolding for gay affirmative action and quotas, or attempts to establish same-sex marriages? No one knows.

So here we are back to William Raspberry's dilemma. Few of us want gays, or anybody else, to be second-class citizens. But when gay-rights bills come up, there's that nagging feeling that "something cultural is going on" and that something more than neutrality is being set in motion. The answer is to promote decency and oppose people who demonize gays. Let's continue the national conversation on homosexuality. But avoid special programs or laws at all costs.

THE PUSH FOR GAY MARRIAGE

The next big gay controversy is here, touched off by the state supreme court of Hawaii. The court opened the door to legal gay marriage. It ruled that Hawaii's ban on same-sex marriages "is presumed to be unconstitutional" unless the state can show, in a lower-court trial, that the prohibition is "justified by compelling state interests."

The issue has been bubbling toward the surface for years, mostly in the churches, partly in campaigns around the country for city "domestic partners" legislation that offers gays some spousal benefits of married couples.

During the week of the gay march on Washington, gay marriage was the centerpiece of a long article in *The New Republic* by its editor, Andrew Sullivan, a gay, conservative Catholic. He called it "the critical measure necessary for full gay equality."

There's a traditionalist argument in favor: society ought to sanction almost any arrangement that promotes personal commitment and social stability. But the most common argument, like most advanced by interest groups these days, is a charge of bias, inequality and "privileging." If gays are the social equals of straights, why can't they marry too?

This is a potent argument. Egalitarian arguments seem strong; "privileging" seems unfair. But all societies privilege certain activities and practices and discourage others. Because of family disintegration, we are finally trying to privilege two-parent families and discourage one-parent families.

We privilege parents over nonparents in some ways because we know that parenting is difficult and expensive and essential to society. Marriage is privileged for the same reason. Society has a crucial stake in protecting the connection between sex, procreation and a commitment to raise children. If it didn't, why would the state be involved with marriage at all? All couplings, gay or straight, would be merely private matters, settled by contract or handshake, not licenses.

Are gays entitled to some benefits that married couples get? I think so. Committed couples should have the same health-plan coverage as straights, for instance. When a lover dies, a gay or lesbian shouldn't lose an apartment, or the right to control the funeral.

But this can come about through domestic-partner legislation or registered bonding ceremonies. The insistence on calling these arrangements marriages is quite another matter. It's an attempt to overhaul tradition, language and common sense for perhaps one-tenth of one percent of the population interested in appropriating heterosexual practice and ceremony.

Many gays, like Andrew Sullivan, favor marriage because they honor it, but another motive is at work too. Some gay activists are frankly interested in diluting or breaking heterosexual norms and downgrading the nuclear family to one lifestyle choice among many.

But marriage isn't just about lifestyle or personal fulfillment. It's also about children and the continuation of the human project. Popping loose the connection between marriage and procreation (or at least the possibility of procreation) seems like an extraordinary step, profoundly altering a conception of marriage that goes back thousands of years.

We don't even know what the immediate effects would be. Would it effectively convert the emerging policy of tolerance for gays into one of de facto approval? For instance, at some public schools, eight-and nine-year-olds are currently being instructed in gay sex techniques. Parents are protesting, but if the state says gay and straight marriages are equal, apart from "age appropriateness," what grounds for protest would be left?

Polls show that large majorities of Americans approve some spousal rights for gays, but reject the idea of gay marriage. That seems to point to a compromise based on domestic-partner laws. But large majorities do not always count for much in the age of litigation.

It's worth noting that the apparent victory for gay marriage in Hawaii turned on the word "sex" in the state's equal protection law forbidding discrimination "because of race, religion, sex or ancestry." (The state law doesn't protect sexual orientation.)

This seems to mean that prohibitions against sex discrimination, which most states have, can be contorted into justifications for gay marriage. Julian Eule, a constitutional law expert at UCLA, said the court's reasoning "converts all homosexuality issues into gender issues." Quite a trick.

The court itself found that a right to same-sex marriage "is not so rooted in the traditions and collective conscience of Hawaii's people that failure to recognize it would violate the fundamental principles of liberty and justice." But it managed to conjure up the right anyway by stretching the meaning of sex discrimination.

This is yet another example of our growing judicial problem: we vote for one thing; relentless litigation and imaginative judges turn it into something wildly different. In this case it may amount to a fundamental reordering of society, all done without any input from the people.

PART TEN

"THIS ORGY OF NON-KILLING"

Abortion, Ethics, and Law

WISHING AWAY QUALMS OVER ABORTION

An old friend of mine, very prominent in his field, was the subject of some scandal here in Manhattan. At an otherwise fashionable dinner party, he ventured two objectionable opinions: (1) that there are too many abortions in America, and (2) that abortion is a serious moral issue that is too often treated in a frivolous way. As it happens, my friend is prochoice, but this was not enough to save him from his reputation-wrecking gaffe. Tongues wagged and gossip flew along phone lines. His own wife didn't speak to him for three days.

What accounts for this astonishing and touchy orthodoxy? Two factors. First, any urban gathering is bound to have one or two guests who have had abortions. When a male brings up qualms about abortion, these women are apt to think their abortion decisions are being second-guessed by someone who will never face the dilemma. They may even think they are about to be accused of murder. Or the buried anguish they may feel about their abortions may well up and spill over as bitter argument. Men like my friend think they can keep the discussion safely abstract, but it never works. Beneath the orthodoxy there is too much unfocused conflict.

A second factor, related to the first, figures into the sensitivity about abortion: the rise of feminism and the reticence it tends to impose. Take journalism, for example. Why, apart from those on the right, are there only a handful of nationally known journalists who have published any doubts or qualms about abortion? (Four come to mind: Colman McCarthy in *The Washington Post*, Nat Hentoff in *The Village Voice*, Christopher Hitchens in *The Nation* and Jason DeParle in the *Washington Monthly*.) The reason, I think, is respect for feminism, and reluctance to be seen as siding with its enemies. Because journalists tend to accept liberal values, and because they generally agree with feminists, as I do, that male-dominated society has distorted women's lives, they tend to go along with feminist arguments, even in the highly debatable area of abortion. They tend to dispense with their objections.

You can see this dynamic at work in one of our most thoughtful public men, New York governor Mario Cuomo. Several years ago,

Cuomo went to Notre Dame and gave a magisterial speech on abortion as a complex moral issue. Now, apparently, all the theological, philosophical and moral nuances are beside the point. But in 1989, Cuomo was quoted as saying he felt embarrassed, as a male, to be saying anything about abortion at all.

The result is that a great gap appears in the otherwise consistent opinions of the left about preserving life. These opinions are anti–nuclear war, anti–capital punishment, anti–environmental degradation. You can't kill murderers for their crimes, elephants for their tusks, minks for their fur, sequoias for lumber or snail darters for dam building. The only exception to this orgy of nonkilling is the human fetus. This is surely an odd departure from the evolving principle that we do not kill to solve our problems. The Roman Catholic bishops are committed to a "seamless garment" of stances: no nuclear weapons, no death penalty, no abortion. The left has a garment with a big hole in the middle.

For me, the problem is not feminists' prochoice stance but that the stance has no moral context. All the emphasis is on rights. None is on the morality of using those rights. It is as if we were back in the 1850s: no one is talking about whether slavery is wrong; instead, the whole discussion revolves around the question of whether each slaveholder has a basic right to decide the issue for himself.

There is an obvious tactical reason why no moral discussion has taken place under feminist auspices: any such debate could split the prochoice constituency, a large portion of which thinks abortion is wrong. But it goes beyond that. For years, feminist leaders have treated moral discussion of abortion within the movement as a betrayal or, at best, a distraction. "To even raise the question of when it's immoral," argues Kate Michelman, head of the National Abortion Rights Action League, "is to say that women can't make moral decisions."

People who talk this way, in Jason DeParle's phrase, are attempting "to wish away a very real collision" between female autonomy and our moral obligations toward developing life. Morally serious people may assess these competing claims differently under varying conditions, but they will not bury their heads by calling the fetus a bit of tissue and likening abortion to a tonsillectomy. One famous feminist compared abortion to removing a hangnail.

Fetuses may not be persons yet, and it is hard for me to believe that destroying them in the first few weeks is murder, but they are alive and human, with their own unique identities and genetic plans. What respect and attention are they due? Too many of us are dealing with this issue with a huge amount of denial. Sociologist Barbara Rothman, for instance, says that pregnancy "takes its meaning from the woman in whose body the pregnancy is unfolding." In other words, it's a baby if you want it, a clump of tissue if you don't. That is a bit of self-deception very common in feminist literature.

"There is no question about the emotional grief and mourning following an abortion," says Dr. Julius Fogel, an obstetrician-gynecologist who has performed twenty thousand abortions. "There is no question in my mind that we are disturbing a life process." One researcher says that "only" 1 percent of women who abort, or about sixteen thousand women a year in America, are "so severely scarred by postabortion trauma that they become unable to function normally." Findings such as these do not constitute an argument against abortion. But they certainly tell us we are not in the realm of tonsillectomies.

THE QUAGMIRE OF ABORTION RIGHTS

In 1973, Yale law professor Alexander Bickel, one of the eminent constitutional scholars of his day, had an immediate objection to *Roe* v. *Wade*. Since "moral philosophy, logic, reason or other materials of law" can give no answer to the dilemma of what to do about abortion, he wrote, "Should not the question then have been left to the political process, which in state after state can achieve not one but many accommodations, adjusting them from time to time as attitudes change?"

Obvious answer: yes. If politics had been allowed to operate, we wouldn't be in such a fix today. Lacking an imperial judiciary, other democracies have reached tolerable accommodations and moved on. The court has prevented that here. By foreclosing normal democratic outlets, *Roe* v. *Wade* distorted abortion politics, setting the stage for extreme street politics and frank attempts to pack the courts. If judges are going to impose social policy, then politicians will try to impose judges.

In the 1989 *Webster* decision, four justices seemed poised to overturn *Roe*. And the decision suggested that the right to decide about abortion belongs to the people, through their legislatures, and not to the courts. But in *Planned Parenthood* v. *Casey*, the Court veered away from the expected next step—junking *Roe* altogether—and produced a patched-up head-scratching decision that accomplishes nothing. *Casey* maintains the status quo. *Roe* is reaffirmed. The plurality's argument that the Court can't back down because it has staked its authority and reputation on *Roe* is truly pathetic. It sounds like late 1960s White House rhetoric on why America couldn't afford to leave Vietnam. The adventure had been a giant mistake. It had torn the country apart, but we couldn't do anything about it or we'd lose face.

A comment in *The Wall Street Journal* by Harvard law professor Mary Ann Glendon echoes Bickel: the *Casey* decision "disappoints those who hoped that the Court would adhere to the principle that, in the absence of clear guidelines from constitutional text or tradition, controversial social issues are to be worked out through the ordinary processes of bargaining, education and persuasion, rather than resolved by judicial fiat."

Glendon's book, *Abortion and Divorce in Western Law*, shows how this process worked in other western democracies. France, bitterly divided on the issue in the early 1970s, worked out a compromise and turmoil has ended. Up to the tenth week, abortion is offered to any woman in a state of "distress" over her pregnancy. "Distress" is self-defined, no questions asked. Later abortions are somewhat harder to get.

But ease of access is balanced by emphasis, mostly rhetorical, on the duty to protect developing human life. The French statute names the underlying problem as one involving developing life, not as a conflict between a woman's freedom and a nonperson. "Distress" makes the point that abortion is a serious matter. Regulations call for a one-week waiting period, which can sometimes be waived, and counseling, preferably with the male partner present, on alternatives to abortion and the benefits guaranteed to all mothers. The law states that abortion is not a form of birth control, and backs that up with government promotion of birth control information. To avoid bringing abortion mills into existence, and thus making abortion look routine, the operations are government funded and must be performed by doctors in approved facilities. ("Only in America has a vast profit-making industry grown up around abortion," Glendon writes.)

Could such a compromise take hold in the United States? Not in that form, surely. France has a long tradition of paternalistic government. America has its fierce individualism. But if the Supreme Court can get hold of itself and return abortion to the political process, Glendon thinks legislators would do well to study foreign models.

The French solution can be viewed cynically—easy abortion in exchange for accepting a few platitudes on the value of human life. But Glendon considers it a "humane, democratic compromise" built around compassion and concern for pregnant woman, married and unmarried, as well as concern for fetal life.

The key to the compromise is that abortion is socially positioned as a regrettable exception to the principle that developing life is to be protected. French law embodies the idea that abortions should be kept to a minimum. The idea is backed by social programs, including grants and day care, that help women avoid abortion. The mandatory counseling, a simple discussion of options, does not have the punitive or anxiety-producing tone that arouses such resentment here. Glendon reports that it is "clearly meant to be helpful to the woman while trying to preserve the life of the fetus."

This sort of compromise will not appeal to those who think early abortion is murder, or to those devoted to the hysterical argument that a one-day waiting period is an intolerable act of oppression. But it would appeal to the vast majority of Americans who want the turmoil to end. Polls consistently show that a decisive majority opposes abortion, wants it discouraged and regulated, but is unwilling to use law to forbid abortions. So an Americanized version of the French accommodation may be the future of the issue here. But not until the Supreme Court extricates itself from its nineteen-year Vietnam.

HERE COME THE WILD CREATURES

In nominating Bill Clinton, Mario Cuomo said the Democratic party stands for the "politics of inclusion," but inclusion had its limits, so one of the party's most successful governors was not allowed to speak at the convention. That was Robert Casey of Pennsylvania, who opposes abortion and was therefore excludable.

As Nat Hentoff pointed out in *The Village Voice*, Casey was not just banned. He was rather graphically humiliated by the abortion lobby. One of his political enemies, a woman who had fought many of his programs in Pennsylvania, was brought onstage at the convention and pointedly honored as a Republican for Choice.

Now Casey has been silenced again, this time by a coalition of abortion advocates and street crazies who drowned out his attempt to speak in New York on the subject "Can a liberal be prolife?" Ironically, the lecture was sponsored by Cooper Union and *The Village Voice* as an exercise in free speech. Proabortion views seem to be mandatory on the *Voice* staff ("I'm the only antiabortion person here since the beginning of time," Nat Hentoff said), and since everybody already agrees, the issue is not considered debatable. But *Voice* publisher David Schneiderman suggested the lecture because he was "annoyed" by the Democrats' position on Casey and thought "it was great for a newspaper that doesn't agree with him . . . to let him give the speech."

About a hundred shrieking protesters stopped the speech. According to a *Voice* report, half were from Act-Up and WHAM and WAC (two feminist groups) and half were assorted radicals, some protesting the pending execution in Pennsylvania of a former Black Panther who was convicted of killing a cop.

Hentoff was there to introduce Casey. During his remarks, the chant started: "Racist, sexist, antigay, Governor Casey go away." (This is a ritual chant, long since drained of content. Casey has been unusually strong in appointing minorities and women to high office, and state contracts awarded to minority-owned and women-owned firms rose 1,500 percent during his first five years in office. The prominent pediatrician T. Berry Brazelton says Casey's health programs for women and children are "a model for the rest of the country." Under Casey, the state's AIDS funding rose from $656,000 a year to $21 million. But none of this matters if you dissent on abortion.)

The screaming, chanting and whistling lasted thirty-five minutes, until Casey gave up and quit the platform. Along the way, this exchange occurred: Heckler: "Murderers have no right to speak!" Hentoff: "This is just like the fascists in the beer halls! It's censorship!" Hentoff called it the ugliest crowd he ever saw. Casey has witnessed this sort of thing before. Act-Up, whose motto is "Silence = Death," did its best to silence the governor at his second inaugural, "shouting obscenities through the whole thing," he said. Last week he said that "these wild creatures" who shouted him down at Cooper Union shouldn't be allowed to dictate who speaks and who doesn't. An understatement.

The crowd's primitive understanding of free speech showed up in an exchange between An Act-Upper and freelance reporter David De-Cosse. The Act-Upper, B. C. Craig, said she was happy that Casey wasn't able to give a solo speech, with no prochoice debater to challenge him. If so, DeCosse said, then you should have supported Casey's request to challenge the abortion-rights lineup at the Democratic convention. The Act-Upper replied, "Whoever said that conventions are open forums?"

Waffling about free speech, or open hostility to it, is now a regular feature of the left, ranging from speech codes to censorship of campus speakers, such as Camille Paglia, who deliver insensitive and incorrect messages, unfit for tender ears. A prominent liberal commentator (name withheld, to protect the innocent) says that more and more people on the left are "locked into a narrow orthodoxy, with no connection to genuine openness or ordinary decency." A handy horrible example of this attitude is Donna Minkowitz of the *Voice* staff. She wrote that allowing Casey to speak at the convention would have been like letting Jerry Falwell speak there, and that the *Voice* shouldn't sponsor a prolife speech, because it's like sponsoring one by a Nazi.

It's worth noting that the more egregious activities of the "wild creatures" do not get criticized very often in the press. Sometimes they are not even reported. Outside of the understandable coverage by *The Village Voice*, the suppression of Governor Casey's speech was a nonevent in media-saturated New York City. I noticed no coverage in three of the four city dailies. *The New York Times* ran a four-inch story, buried way inside, only because an unassigned religion reporter happened to be there and phoned it in. Four days later columnist Anna Quindlen mildly criticized the demonstrators way down in one of her many columns deploring the "gag rule." That was it. No other mention in the *Times*. Casey told me, "If it had been a right-wing group shutting down a prochoice speech by the governor of a major state it would have been splashed across page one in the *Times* the next day." So true.

NOT THE WAY TO STOP ABORTIONS

The murder of Dr. David Gunn at a Pensacola abortion clinic was a horrible, indefensible crime. It was also an opportunity for America's columnists to once again depict abortion protestors as disgusting primitives.

Anthony Lewis, the *New York Times* columnist, wrote that "most anti-abortion activists" are "religious fanatics" who think "the end justifies any means." And that was at the beginning of his column, before he was fully warmed up. Look for future Lewis columns revealing that most Arabs are terrorists and most Catholics are plotting to kidnap President Clinton and replace him with the pope.

The words "terrorists," "cultists" and "fanatics" rained down on all sides. These are words that the prochoice lobby pushes journalists to use, and they do. One neat trick was to blur the lines between all antiabortion groups, so that all could share the blame of the shooter. Syndicated columnist Ellen Goodman lumped together Operation Rescue (which professes a pledge to nonviolence) and the more extreme group Rescue America, which organized the demonstration that was going on when Dr. Gunn was murdered. She wrote that prolife groups like Operation Rescue and Rescue America must be dealt with as domestic terrorists as deadly as the ones who blew up the World Trade Center and as fanatic as the cultists in Waco. Wow. Don't hold back, Ellen. Tell us what you really think.

Part of the problem here is the tight alliance between newsroom and prochoice lobby. The campaign to diversify newsrooms has not yet reached the critical turning point where most managing editors can truthfully say they have hired a journalist who actually knows someone who opposes abortion. So reporters write about Operation Rescue people as if they were covering Martian invaders.

Operation Rescue illegally invades and occupies private space. This is an obnoxious tactic, the same one used by antiwar demonstrators, suffragettes and the heroes of Op-R: Gandhi and Martin Luther King, Jr. Personally, I disapprove of much they do, but I admire the courage and moral witness. In putting their bodies on the line for their beliefs,

Op-R "rescuers" have endured savage treatment from police, in West Hartford, for instance, without complaint, retaliation, self-pity or much notice from the press and the ACLU. And their ranks include some of the finest graduates of the civil rights movement.

On the other hand, it is possible to doubt their wisdom. I hate the hectoring of pregnant women at clinics. I think it's wrong to carry the fight to the homes of abortionists, putting pressure on children and spouses. And I think there's a contradiction between commitment to nonviolent moral witness and the growing use of intimidation, stalking and harassment as tactics. Op-R's "No Place to Hide" campaign against doctors doesn't look much like King and Gandhi. It looks like Act-Up.

It's certainly legitimate to publicize the names of abortionists, as Op-R does. Shame is one reason the number of doctors performing abortions has declined, but intimidation and harassment are factors too. Holding up a leaflet or poster containing a doctor's name and the word "Wanted" on it, as Op-R people do, seems like incitement in the current climate. Someone is apt to mentally fill in the familiar words "Dead or Alive."

The current climate includes such things as butyric acid attacks on clinics, bombings, gunfire sprayed at a Michigan Planned Parenthood office, arson at clinics in Texas and Florida, death threats to doctors and stalking of clinic personnel.

Against this background, Operation Rescue really ought to reassess its tactics. If its goal is to shut down clinics at all costs, it will be pulled in the direction of terrorism. If it is more interested in moral witness, it will start treating women and doctors as potential converts rather than enemies.

Mostly, I don't think Operation Rescue is helping to create conditions under which abortion will begin to recede. The sheer practical fact is that abortion will become rarer only when more women come to see it as wrong. Instead of shrieking at women entering clinics, abortion protestors ought to take them seriously as moral decisionmakers.

There are other practical considerations. The press is totally bored by abortion demonstrations (the same boredom problem has affected Act-Up too). So if vast publicity is the goal, it will come only if violence occurs—a no-win situation. More important, the increased pressure on clinics and pregnant women could invite the Supreme Court to cite it as an undue burden on women seeking abortions. If so, the modest abortion regulations now in effect would be struck down.

I happen to think the antiabortion position is a long-term winner. Jacques Maritain, the French philosopher, argued that natural law evolves in the mind of mankind: practices that were once regarded as natural and moral, such as infanticide, torture and slavery, gradually come to be seen by the whole world as barbaric. Abortion, too, I think. But to get there, the appeal has to be to conscience, not to menace at the clinics.

HOLLAND'S COZY LITTLE HOMICIDES

Many dying people exhibit the symptom of "half-knowledge": though aware that death is near, they suppress the thought and talk with perfect sincerity about plans for the future.

If you read *Regulating Death*, the very sobering book about euthanasia in the Netherlands, you may think the Dutch people are suffering from a tribal case of half-knowledge on the subject. As the author, Carlos Gomez, tells it, the Dutch seem to know that something is wrong with their euthanasia regulations, or nonregulations, but they also seem content with what they regard as a humane and rational system.

Mercy killing is technically illegal in the Netherlands, but for almost two decades Dutch doctors have been allowed to kill patients, on the understanding that the cases will be reported to a district prosecutor, who will permit the doctors to plead mitigating circumstances. Thus euthanasia is positioned as a socially approved crime that requires some sort of vague pro forma public airing.

Gomez shows that this airing is usually nonexistent. Most such killings go unreported and uninvestigated. Almost everyone admits that the two hundred cases reported in 1987 represented only a tiny fraction of the actual number of cases. A great deal of blurring and fudging takes place. The Dutch public blurs the crucial distinction between pulling the plug (withdrawing life-sustaining medical intervention) and killing the patient outright. Doctors blur details and lie on death certificates, so no one really knows how many are being killed or whether the killings are confined to terminal patients of sound mind who ask to die. Gomez reports that of a sample of twenty-six killings, there were four cases in which the patient was in no position to give consent, or in which "it was doubtful that consent could have been obtained properly."

This means that in all likelihood, at least every sixth or seventh case of euthanasia in the Netherlands is not "physician-assisted suicide" but homicide, approved by no one, reported to no one.

It also means that the alleged model program in the Netherlands is, in effect, shot through with dishonesty, totally unregulated and wide open to the worst-case scenario of euthanasia—the dispatching of the troublesome or the vulnerable or the medically expensive elderly on the whim of anyone with a medical degree.

Here is the kicker: Gomez warns that Initiative 119, the euthanasia proposition on the ballot in the state of Washington, "is *very* like the current Dutch arrangement." It gives doctors permission to perform what has been an illegal act, but it sets up no system of oversight. As in the Netherlands, the fudgers and blurrers are hard at work. The wording of the bill, apparently inserted to protect doctors from any kind of criminal prosecution, invites fudging on the cause of death—writing "respiratory arrest," for example, and not mentioning the drugs injected to induce that arrest. This means statistics and studies will be unreliable, and as Gomez argues, "Cases of euthanasia would blend imperceptibly into the larger background of deaths resulting from natural causes." As in the Netherlands, the incidence of mercy killing, presented as little more than a statistical blip, could increase to a substantial number with little or no public awareness.

The worst feature of 119 is the lack of strong guarantees that all deaths will be truly voluntary. There are no safeguards to make sure the patient is fully informed and that the death decision is not affected by clinical depression or outside pressure. Subtle and not-so-subtle coercion by hospital staff and family of the vulnerable elderly can be substantial, particularly when care is an obvious economic burden on relatives. A letter from handicapped residents of a Dutch nursing home, quoted in anti-119 campaign literature, says, "We realize that we cost the community a good deal of money. . . . Many times we notice that we are talked into wishing death."

Once doctors are legally positioned as agents of death, the temptation to cut corners on voluntariness will grow. Compassion can push doctors along this path. So can a doctor's well-meaning conclusion that a patient's life is no longer worth living. The first results of the Dutch government's study of euthanasia, appearing in the September 14 issue of The Lancet, blithely mentions that patients were "hardly ever" coerced into requesting death, then drops the subject. The study estimates that 0.8 percent of all deaths in the Netherlands are "life-terminating acts without explicit and persistent request." That's just less than a third of all death-related medical decisions. Many of these involve patients "near to death and suffering grievously," and many apparently don't. Carlos Gomez, who has looked at the raw data behind the Lancet article, charges that the study misleads the public by excluding from the totals two thousand to three thousand additional deaths with improper consent or no consent at all.

The Dutch system is a mess, and Initiative 119 is an attempt to copy it here. If it passes, it is likely that our most vulnerable citizens—the infirm, the handicapped, the outsiders—will pay the price.

MTV'S SEVEN VIDEO SINS

Most summers you can go from Memorial Day right through to Labor Day without hearing much about the seven deadly sins. Not this year, however.

Both the high culture (famous authors writing in The New York Times Book Review) and the pop culture (entertainers and assorted young people talking on an MTV special) have taken a crack at explaining pride, anger, envy, gluttony, greed, lust and sloth. (The Times added an eighth bonus sin, despair.)

The Times authors seemed gravely embarrassed by the notion of sin, but gamely determined to say something original. Writing about anger, novelist Mary Gordon got all tangled up in food imagery: "Its taste draws from those flavors that appeal to the mature and refined palate: the mix of sour, bitter, sweet and salt." Nothing so fancy overcame the folks at MTV. To one young woman on the MTV special, anger is "Kaboom! That's anger. That's anger."

The Times articles struck me as arcane and precious, but I was looking forward to the televison treatment. MTV is, after all, the Vatican of youth culture. What would a postboomer televison-generation examination of specific sins look like? The press release says the program "digs down deep into the soul of the MTV generation." But if this show can be decribed as reflecting the soul of a generation, the whole generation can sue for libel.

It's basically a collection of brief film clips and off-the-cuff comments from youth-culture stars and mostly twentyish noncelebrities. Ice-T, Ozzy Osbourne, Queen Latifah and Kirstie Alley are interviewed, along with a bouncer, a hairdresser and a veteran beauty-pageant winner.

Most comments were too banal even for prime time. "Greed is figuring out what we can get for ourselves," one participant says helpfully. Another thinks sloth is a workbreak: "Sloth. It's good to be like that sometimes . . . sometimes it's good to sit back and give yourself personal time." Someone defines gluttony as "for me, it's just a problem of release." On the subject of pride, Ice-T says it's "mainly a problem of the inner cities—the kids don't have pride." I waited expectantly, but in vain, for someone to come out and explain that "anger is like, you know, when you're really cheesed off." Maybe in the sequel.

Envy is represented by Sean Young's disappointment that she didn't get the part of Catwoman. A baseball pro, sent down to the minor leagues, envies his father, who played major league ball. A gay-bashing sequence is shoehorned in as an example of pride—"hurting others to make yourself look bigger." Anger is represented by a poet who was abused as a child.

Not everything was out of sync. In the greed discussion, two women from the Seneca nation argue over the gambling casinos going up on tribal lands. Environmental destruction as "global gluttony" is brought up, but not pursued. There's a brief but sensible discussion on the issue of how to control greed in an economic system that largely depends on avarice to make it run.

Most secular discussions of the seven deadly sins seem to focus on a lack of self-discipline, a sense of going too far. That's almost entirely missing here. Instead of the language of moderation and self-control, everybody seems to speak the therapized language of feelings and self-esteem.

"Pride isn't a sin—you're supposed to feel good about yourself." "Envy makes you feel bad about yourself." When you have sex with a woman, one rocker says, "She makes you feel good about yourself, but I don't know if it saves you in the end." Even the repentant gay-basher is totally committed to self-talk: "Forgiving myself has been the challenge of my life."

There's a vague sense that sin, if it exists, is surely a problem of psychology. Kurt Loder, the narrator, tells us at the start of the program that we are dealing with compulsions: "The seven deadly sins are not evil acts but rather universal human compulsions that can be troubling and highly enjoyable." Discussion of gluttony quickly deteriorates into chatter about addictions. That's the way all habits and attachments are discussed in the pop therapies the MTV generation grew up on. "I'm addicted to my girlfriend," one male says about gluttony. Someone else says that the twelve-step self-help program is God's gift to the twenty-first century.

It's heartening that MTV attempted a show like this. Lauren Lazin, the producer of the program, said she liked the topic because it deals with human impulses, not a set of rules like the Ten Commandments. "It seemed that a lot of young people were anxious to talk about moral matters," she said. "What better context than sin?" Talking about sin is difficult, though, in a talk-show pop-culture format. Too many jumpy cuts, cartoon characters and two-sentence word bursts.

But what really did the project in was the absence of a moral vocabulary. The people at MTV basically collected a random set of attitudes and feelings and stuffed them into a music video format. Lacking any vocabulary to talk about impulse-control, selfishness, ethical values and moral conflicts, the show went nowhere. Is this a problem of the MTV generation or just MTV?

LOOK OUT FOR THE WORD *FAIRNESS*

Before joining the Supreme Court, Antonin Scalia wrote that "we live in an age of hair-trigger unconstitutionality." Almost no result of the democratic process, he argued, seems immune from attack as a violation of basic constitutional rights. Constant running to the courts to save us from ordinary democracy is a hallmark of our time. One result has been the vast increase in the power of the judiciary. This can be looked at as a by-product of the decline of politics. But it is teaching a whole generation that litigation is our basic form of governance.

In New York City, for example, almost everything of political consequence is decided by courts: the shape of city government, policies on homelessness, who gets on the ballot, who gets to build new buildings or march in ethnic parades. Reformers hardly bother with political organizing anymore. They litigate, virtually full-time. If anything accidentally gets done through normal politics, they are sure to challenge it in court. In an article in *The City Journal*, Walter Olson, author of *The Litigation Explosion*, noticed a phrase buried in the revised city charter calling for "fair distribution among communities" of facilities, from libraries to incinerators and drug-treatment centers.

This nearly passed without comment. Who is against fairness? But Olson argued, quite convincingly, that the phrasing invited, and practically mandated, court rulings on whether the siting of any facility anywhere was fair, complete with endless argument about what fairness means. In effect, everyday city decisions would pass into the hands of judges. This may not happen. The city backed down on some of the wording, but this was a fascinating case of apparently harmless language being used to override the normal bump-and-grind of NIMBY politics and have the courts take over.

In his book, Olson says this has become routine in American law as "crisp old rules" have been replaced with "fuzzy new standards" that make sure things end up in court. He writes: "Vagueness creeps into the law on the padded feet of words and phrases like fairness, equitableness, good cause, good faith, reasonableness under all the circumstances—pillowy expressions that tend to soften the blow of what is, in fact, a grant of wide judicial discretion over some area."

Congress has become exceptionally skilled at producing such linguistic sinkholes. The fuzzy language is usually intended to duck controversial issues by converting legislative decisions into judicial ones, or into bureaucratic ones that usually end up in court. Who can be against the elimination of "sexual discrimination" (Title IX of the Education Amendments of 1972)? But what does that mean? Does it require that all-boy or all-girl athletic teams be abolished? Does it mean that school tests are illegal if scores differ by gender, or that unisex dorms and unisex toilets are required?

Congress didn't say. The issue was too hot to handle. Better to keep things vague, please constituents on both sides of the issue, and let the courts work it out. Similarly, in setting up the Occupational Safety and Health Administration, Congress achieved full fuzziness by mandating whatever was "reasonably necessary or appropriate to provide safe or healthful employment."

The Americans with Disabilities Act of 1990 set a modern world record for legislative vagueness that will not soon be broken. Barriers to the disabled must be removed "where removal is readily achievable" and the cost not "unduly burdensome." Civil rights protection is extended to all Americans with impairments that "substantially limit" one or more of "the major life activities."

One of our major life activities may be trying to figure out what the act means. "I think Congress's intent was to make this social-forcing legislation," said a Chicago attorney. "They are trying to get people to do much more than they would have done otherwise. For that reason, the language is broad and there may well have to be extensive litigation to determine what it means." Yes, I expect so. That's what happens when legislators emit a cloud of squidlike ink instead of actual legslation.

Congress is not just refusing to write clear laws. It has gotten into the habit of dishing out bills that are frankly intended as a prelude to litigation. Many environmental laws are written as if to invite suits. Senator Mitch McConnell (Republican, Kentucky), sponsor of the dreadful Pornography Victims Compensation Act, says frankly that his goal is "to create an atmosphere of civil litigation that makes the industry very fearful." But legislators are supposed to work at precise laws, not atmosphere creation and fear induction.

"When legislators leave statutory language ambiguous, they abdicate their responsibility of giving the law policy content," Judge Alex Kozinski of the Ninth Circuit Court of Appeals wrote in an op-ed piece in *The Wall Street Journal*. This shifts power to judges, he said, subverting one important aspect of our system of checks and balances. And "judges who get into the habit of playing legislator find it tempting to start treating all laws—including the Constitution—as merely a springboard for implementing their own sense of right and wrong." That is the problem. If legislators don't legislate, guess who will.

LAWMAKERS ON THE BENCH

Celebrating the departure of Justice Byron White from the Supreme Court, *The New York Times* rejoiced that his replacement "could mark the beginning of an energetic new era for the court."

The editorialist seems to assume that any serious display of energy on the Court's part will result in the creation of new rights and new social policies approved of by *The New York Times*. Justice White "turned out to be more a witness than a moving force," the *Times* said. Unlike witnesses, moving forces are presumably busy making policy decisions that stubborn or muddled legislatures refuse to make themselves.

But how much policy do we want the Supremes to make?

At the end of his fine book on the Bork nomination, *Battle for Justice*, Ethan Bronner gives this depressing assessment of the rise of the policy-making judiciary: "Americans have grown accustomed to letting judges and bureaucrats make difficult social policy choices for them. They seem resigned to allowing courts and government agencies to take responsibility on issues that a self-governing people ought to work out in greater detail through the democratic process."

Bronner, a reporter for the *Boston Globe*, has no particular ax to grind. He just sees a decline of democratic politics going hand in hand with the rise of a politicized judiciary.

Many others do too. Cass Sunstein, a University of Chicago law professor, published a tribute to Thurgood Marshall last year in the *Stanford Law Review*. In it he wrote: "Even when courts are effective, there are serious problems in judge-led reform from the standpoint of democratic legitimacy. Reform through the courts may dampen the practice of citizenship, an individual and collective good. And if reform does not have a democratic pedigree, it may run into severe resistance."

Sunstein follows this passage with a discussion of the classic modern example of judge-made law with no democratic pedigree and severe resistance: *Roe v. Wade*. Now that legal access to abortion seems secure, public doubts about the scope and reasoning of the *Roe* opinion seem more and more common.

Before she was named to the Supreme Court, in a far-ranging lecture on legal theory, U.S. Circuit Court Judge Ruth Bader Ginsburg called the *Roe* decision "breathtaking" and said it "halted a political process that was moving in a reform direction" and "deferred stable settlement of the issue." In attempting to impose a quick solution to a complicated social issue, the Supreme Court ushered in two decades of costly civil strife. Instead of moving the issue beyond politics, the Court simply delayed, embittered and distorted the politics of abortion.

Is the country really resigned to an ever more politicized judiciary? Could be, but it's more likely that it's happening without the consent of a public that doesn't know how to stop it. As more and more policies are shaped by judges, it isn't very clear how citizens are supposed to register dissent. It's also no wonder that hearings for Supreme Court nominees take on the drama and trappings of political campaigns.

It's a sign of the times that reformers now routinely skip the legislative process and take their issues directly to court. This lesson was learned in the civil rights movement: since segregationists dominated politics in the South, only the legal system could enfranchise blacks. Later, this strategy, crucial and necessary at the time, hardened into a reflex: majorities are wrongheaded and oppressive, politics are complicated and exhausting, so why not try for a judge-imposed quick fix?

This instinct to circumvent politics, or to flee to the courts when you lose at the polls, is profoundly antidemocratic. As Sunstein argues, judge-led reform can weaken our political system, just as it can perversely undermine the goals sought by judges. Jim Sleeper's book *The Closest of Strangers: Liberalism and the Politics of Race in New York*, convincingly shows how reformers debased and polarized the city's racial politics by heavily emphasizing litigation rather than coalition building.

Court-imposed solutions often turn out that way; lacking the stability of a social consensus, they often just breed more trouble. They also tend to undermine serious legislative efforts. If everything winds up in court anyway, why bother to hammer out political compromises? And the more we look to courts for answers, the more judges get used to playing legislator. Four years ago, U.S. Circuit Court Judge Alex Kozinski wrote: "Judges who get into the habit of playing legislator find it tempting to start treating all laws—including the Constitution—as merely a springboard for implementing their own sense of right and wrong."

In the disastrous wake of *Roe* v. *Wade*, the Republicans moved aggressively to politicize the Court. It may be too much to ask the Democrats, after twenty-six years of waiting, to avoid doing the same thing. But the president has a chance here to start depoliticizing the court. It's simple. All he has to do is name someone of known integrity who is more interested in judging than in legislating.

PART ELEVEN

"If You Feel Comfortable, You're Probably Oppressing Someone"

Dispatches from the Cultural War Zone

THE "US" VERSUS "THEM" INDUSTRY

Donald Kao is a New York City youth worker. By reputation he is good at what he does, working the streets, but now he has a new and loftier identity in a growth industry. He is a "diversity consultant."

This means he goes around to colleges and universities, dealing with racial problems and setting up programs for minority groups.

Here are three of the hallmarks of modern diversity consultation, illustrated by Kao and recorded by Stephen Goode in a memorable article in *Insight,* the Sunday magazine of the *Washington Times*:

1. Wherever he goes, Kao tries to get audiences to reach the conclusion that white people are privileged in America.

2. He says, "If you are feeling comfortable or normal, then you are probably oppressing someone, whether that person is a woman, a gay or whatever."

3. He firmly believes that "we probably won't rid our society of racism until everyone strives to be abnormal."

There's a world of information buried in these three statements.

The most obvious thing to notice is that Kao, like most activists caught up in the diversity movement, has more on his mind than just helping minority group members fit in at mostly white colleges. The language—"privilege," "racism," "oppression"—is the tongue of assault and ideology, not of accommodation or racial peace. Call this diversity-speak. It is not the language of inclusion ("us" meaning all students of all races getting along) but the language of "us" ("People of Color") versus "them" (People of White?). Kao helped Brown University set up an "us" freshman orientation program based solely on pigmentation. Each year, the nonwhites arrive a week early and have a nonwhite orientation.

The "us" and "them" mentality is at the heart of what is currently unfolding on the diversity frontier. I tried to meet Donald Kao to thrash this all out, but he declined to be interviewed, on the grounds that the magazine I work for had published an incredibly racist article in 1966. But he was courteous about it, and we sparred a bit before he hung up.

I asked: why do you feel compelled, wherever you go, to preach that whites, and white males in particular, constitute a privileged class? Because, he said, like fish unaware of water, white males swim along unconscious of the edge they have over everyone else. Maybe so, I said, but why not just stress inclusion and fairness? By hammering away at all white males as a group of privileged overlords, don't you sow the seeds for backlash and long-term division along racial and sexual lines? No, he said, white males must learn to "own" their privilege as a prerequisite for change.

"Owning," in my opinion, comes down to this: the attempt to bewilder and disorient young whites with the startling news that they are oppressors, followed by a concerted attempt to render them guilty enough to seek approved re-education by an anointed diversity consultant. Some consultants use multistep programs, based on Alcoholics Anonymous, to root out unconscious bias. And on some campuses, "ethnic studies programs" have taken on a clearly punitive cast, having less to do with real academic work than with forcing whites to sit still for a highly ideological form of indoctrination presided over by diversity gurus.

Here is the fatal flaw of the diversity people. They are wedded to simpleminded pigmental politics. All white people—villains, reformers, bystanders, victims—are lumped together into a generic mass that is deemed to be woefully in need of mental reform. There was no diversity in America until the day before yesterday, because the gradual inclusion of out-groups such as the Irish, the Jews, the Catholics and the poor in general occurred largely within this generic mass, and therefore doesn't count. Diversity, in this narrow view, is based solely on color and gender.

Thumb through some jargon-ridden literature of the diversity people and you will learn that the goal is not liberal reform, but total ideological makeover. "Multicultural Organization Development," for instance, is one of the working papers of the University of Michigan's Center for Research on Social Organization. It talks of "the multicultural ideology," the need to uproot "the monocultural view that society needs to improve, but is basically ok" and to replace it with "the multicultural view that society is oppressive, alienating and needs radical change."

The irony is that many colleges, which bring in "diversity consult-ants" like Donald Kao, think they are buying social peace, when they are actually more likely to be purchasing additional social conflict. Kao's points 2 and 3 make this very clear: normality and social consensus (which colleges and the whole culture have in mind) are inherently wrong, a form of hidden oppression.

This is not properly a liberal/conservative issue. The vast majority of Americans, left and right, think outsiders should be let in, not that the whole culture and its institutions should be torn apart for ideological reasons. In his article, Stephen Goode concludes that the people who want to transform colleges from top to bottom in the name of diversity have eased off a bit, possibly because of the recession. Maybe so, but they'll be back.

THE SEVENTY-FIVE DEADLY ISMS

As part of a rigorous campaign against political incorrectness, Smith College warns its freshpeople about ten different "isms" that afflict campus life. This is nice, but inadequate. Actually there are seventy-five or more dangerous "isms," many listed here as a public service:

Racism, Sexism and Heterosexism—the big three; common sins of straight, white males; hypothetically possible among minority groups but never actually recorded.

Ableism—bias against the physically challenged and differently abled (formerly the disabled or handicapped) by the temporarily abled. The phrase "blind to the truth" would be an example of ableist language. Stairs would be an example of ableist architecture.

Homeism—oppression of the homeless by the nonvagrant homed, or temporarily homeful. Some antihomeists now favor the term "house-less." A Long Island activist recently instructed some street people: "You are houseless but not homeless because home is wherever you are."

Ageism—bias against seniors by the temporarily young.

Adultism—prejudice against juniors; the oppression of imposing standards and values derived from the adult world upon the culture of subadults. "Adultism is where adults tell you what to do, whether it's right or wrong," activist Ramon Santiago, twenty, said during a rally against environmental racism in Brooklyn.

Environmental racism—the siting of smokestacks in Hispanic or black neighborhoods.

Speciesism—the doctrine or feeling that humans are somehow more valuable than mice or insects. "Speciesists allow the interests of their own species to override the greater interest of members of other species," writes Peter Singer, philosopher of animal rights. A person swatting a mosquito would be speciesist. So would a bird eating a bug, a snake eating a bird, a jackal eating a snake, or a lion eating Peter Singer.

Anthropocentrism—Humanity's hubris. See speciesism.

Eurocentrism—failure to see all the world's cultures as equal in the development of freedom, democracy, science, technology, literature, medicine and the creation of wealth.

Militarism—love of war; having an ROTC on campus.

Sightism—insults toward the visually impaired, for instance, the expression "I see what you mean." Also, the belief that visually impaired people cannot do as well as sighted people at all tasks. The Federal Aviation Administration, for instance, refused to allow blind persons to sit in emergency exit rows on airplanes. This was sightist.

Sizeism—prejudice against the differently sized. The words "dieting" and "overweight" are both inherently sizeistic and fatistic, because they imply that something is wrong with being differently sized. Size acceptance activist Sally E. Smith argues that articles on liposuction are sizeistic examples of "one of the last 'safe' prejudices in America."

Lookism and faceism—construction of a standard for beauty; the belief that some people are easier on the eyes than others, which creates an unacceptable hierarchy based on mere appearances. Making faces, as well as admiring them, is not recommended at elite colleges. The former president of Duke University appointed a committee to search out "disrespectful facial expressions" aimed at disadvantaged students.

Animal lookism—the lookist preference for cute animals, like cats, over noncute ones, like rats.

Colorism—prejudice among light-skinned blacks against dark-skinned blacks.

Laughism—inappropriately directed laughter, banned at the University of Connecticut.

Conversational exclusionism—conspicuous banning of persons from private chats, also against the sensitivity-maintenance rules at the University of Connecticut.

Birthmarkism—refusal to see that it is not birthmarks that are unseemly, but rather the society that frowns upon them. Ted Kennedy, Jr., wrote to the *Boston Globe* to complain about an article on "treatment techniques" for birthmarks, when actually, he pointed out, "our attitude is the problem, and that can never be corrected surgically."

Handism—oppression of left-handed persons by the right-handed majority. Several organizations of left-handers complain that "technological biases" in design of tools for right-handers cause injuries among lefties. Language bias too: gauche, sinister, maladroit, left-handed compliment, all compared with upright, dextrous, righteous for righties.

Verbal sexism—an ancient oppression, tirelessly fought. The Sacramento Public Works Department sponsored a contest for a new word to replace the socially offensive "manhole." The blizzard of suggestions, including "sewer-viewer" and "person-access chamber," so overwhelmed the department that no winner was named. But, "out of heightened awareness," Sacramento now calls its unisex street-level person-apertures "maintenance holes."

Shavism—prejudice against the bearded and generally hirsute. Mickey Kaus of *The New Republic*, perhaps jocularly, writes that while growing a beard, he was disinvited by a cable TV show out of "blatant shavism."

Scentism—the imposition of one's perfume, cologne, deodorant or other scents upon people who may not wish to smell them. A Boston-based women's group, pointing out that some women are especially sensitive to odors, argued that social events "should be advertised as scent-free, and sniffers posted at the entrance to ensure that all who enter are in compliance." Enforcement powers of the new aroma police were not outlined.

Another women's convention banned the handing out of pamphlets on grounds that "you put the woman you're handing something to in a position where she has to say no, and everyone knows how difficult in this culture it is to say no." This might have been codified as coercive pamphletism, but, alas, was not.

A great deal of thought now goes into the development of fresh isms. Like a cell subdividing, lookism was broken down into its important components—faceism, sizeism, weightism, heightism, shapeism and most recently, breastism. (No word yet on legism or thighism.) When you're outvoted, that's majoritarianism. If people expect you to meet some standard or get some credentials, that's credentialism. If you draw a map that puts Europe and North America at the top, and generally darker-skinned peoples below in the southern hemisphere, that's borealcentrism. And thanks to the diligence of campus feminists, we now have genderism, patriarchalism, machoism, masculinism, androcentrism, rapism, phallicism, phallocentrism and phallogocentrism.

Note that the "environmental racism" listing indicates the possibility of multiple offense. For instance, smiling while handing a woman a diet cola could be construed as sizeist, lookist and sexist, and perhaps handist and laughist as well. Splashing on some Old Spice would combine scentism and shavism into aftershavism. And recommending a book by an adultist, speciesist and borealcentric white male would make the whole list light up with grievous offense. Please be careful out there.

ART FOR POLITICS' SAKE

David Bosworth has a good question about the controversial Christ-in-urine photo by Andres Serrano. Bosworth is an associate professor of English at the University of Washington, Seattle, writing in *The Georgia Review*. He is quite critical of the assaults on the National Endowment for the Arts (NEA) over grants to Serrano and other artists. But his question for the art establishment and the academic world is this: "What if the icon dropped into the jar of urine had not been a crucifix but a figure of a leader *you* hold most dear: Nelson Mandela? Cesar Chavez? Golda Meir?"

This is what is known as a rhetorical question. Bosworth knows very well that if Serrano's "Piss Christ" had been labeled "Piss Malcolm X," or "Piss on Act-Up," nine-tenths of the intelligentsia would have roared Ted Kennedy on as he rose in the Senate to demand a review of NEA funding. As Bosworth suggests, beneath all the piety about principle and freedom and censorship, it is all very much a matter of whose ox is being gored.

Like many of us, the author is no fan of Jesse Helms. As director of his university's creative writing program, he identifies with artists and he considers Helms a small-minded, hypocritical and potentially dangerous politician. But, unlike most critics of Helms, he has developed a fine eye for the routine hypocrisies of the art establishment: passionately anticensorship people who support campus speech codes and want Andrew Dice Clay pulled off the air; specialists in ethnic fairness who think black actors should play Macbeth, but remain silent when Actors Equity says a Eurasian role can only be filled by an Asian actor; admirers of Robert Mapplethorpe who could be counted on to demand action if some of his naughty pictures had shown the humiliating sex acts being performed on a woman instead of a gay male. "There's a lot less principle here than meets the eye or assaults the ear," Bosworth writes. Quite so.

The most common howler told in the counterattack on Helms is that the denial of subsidies is somehow a form of censorship. Many can't seem to let go of the idea that being rejected for a government dole is somehow a grave violation of the First Amendment. But as Bosworth says in the sort of plain English that eludes so much of the art world, "The government wasn't restricting free speech; it was restricting *paid* speech."

The most glaring duplicity comes over the question of who is playing politics with NEA money, grant-seeking artists or their critics. Defenders of controversial artists such as Karen Finley and Tim Miller basically say this: the government must not get itself in the philistine position of funding only art that Congress and the taxpayers admire—decisions about art must be above politics, or there will be no avant garde art at all.

That sounds good, but the "above politics" stance is basically fake. "This is where I begin to get confused," Bosworth writes. "Weren't these the same artists who, over beers with me, would tout their own fierce political commitment and proselytize, often eloquently, on the necessity of a politically centered art? Weren't these the same people who, when sitting on panels dispensing prizes, used their own political compass, unabashedly, unashamedly, to select the winners? Was one political in the evening, but 'above politics' in the morning?"

Bosworth is dead right about this. Piously esthetic when applying for grants, many artists and would-be artists are gleefully political when awarding and spending them. Karen Finley, whose "art" is basically a series of political harangues, says her work tries to show "that people are born into victimization, the patriarchal nature of the society." Tim Miller says that the argument over his grant is an attack on cultural freedom, but as the *Los Angeles Times* noted recently, Miller is "part of an emerging vanguard of artist-activists . . . who have been politicized around gay rights, AIDS, racism and reproductive rights issues." Lots of luck, Tim. But please, conduct your political fund raising on your own and leave the Treasury alone.

In retrospect, the NEA flap spent too much time concentrating on Jesse Helms, obscenity and such routinely bizarre aspects of performance art as chocolate-covered breasts. The real issue is politics. Do the taxpayers have some sort of obligation to fund political art of either the left or right? If so, let's hear the argument out in the open, not hidden in rhetoric about esthetes and philistines.

This issue is unlikely to fade. Art and left activism are merging, riding the currents of the multicultural movement. Robert Brustein, former dean of the Yale Drama School and artistic director of the American Repertory Theater, acknowledges that in the art world "the populist assault on 'elitism' . . . has now turned into a full-scale assault on 'Eurocentric' culture" and that multiculturalism is now being widely used "as a device of political consciousness-raising." He's talking about a political agenda. In this rising movement, it is an article of faith that art is not something apart from daily life. It is a political weapon.

In other words, we are in for quite a spell of agitprop art, with taxpayers being asked to help underwrite the overthrow of their own values. How many of us want to say yes to that?

A MARATHON OF PIQUE

A transsexual professor from a Jesuit university is at the podium, comparing herself to Frankenstein's monster and reading a poem about how angry she is. "Rage constitutes me in my primal form . . . my rage is a silent raving."

She has come to the right place. This is an academic conference on "Rage!" complete with a rage-istration desk, much chanting and poetry and one enraged representative from every aggrieved sexual and ethnic group in America. It is sponsored by California State University, San Marcos.

The transsexual, Susan Stryker of San Francisco University, describes herself as a little boy from Oklahoma who turned out to be a transsexual leatherdyke with a Berkeley Ph.D. She is angry with lesbians for not accepting her as a woman. She is also angry with the culture—a common target here—which she believes is suffering from a bad case of "transphobia." She wants to reclaim the word "monster" for transsexuals, just as gays are trying to reclaim the word "queer."

Sheng-mei Ma of James Madison University in Virginia spoke on "The Politics of Teaching Victimhood in Asian-American Literature East of California." He was enraged because teaching victimhood, and getting East Coast white students to see themselves as guilty oppressors of Asian-Americans, is apparently not going well.

Ma said his own classes were so resistant that he felt "rage over students' indifference and the dismissal of my expertise after years of self-denial." Even by the indulgent standards of this conference, Ma's level of self-absorption was high. He complained bitterly that as a new immigrant, he had used the term "a police" instead of "a police officer" and someone had corrected him on the usage.

He also complained that as a grad student he had to take a three-dollars-an-hour library job that "reduced me to a small yellow boy." Now, he said, he was now forced to teach at a second-rate college. During the question period he said this was, of course, an ironic statement, not to be taken literally.

The march of the enraged continued for two and a half days. An Arab-American who resents being thought of as a terrorist read a poem about the Phoenicians discovering America. Two feminists argued that women's violence, however deplorable it may seem, must be viewed as a response to suffocating pressure from the patriarchy.

A gay activist, Jay Chipman of the University of Pittsburgh, urged the conference attendees to "brace yourselves for battle." He said heterosexism is so powerful and privileged that "a multidirectional, multifaceted intercultural war" is under way, though it "has not yet reached the stage of armed conflict." He bared his chest to show simulated scars from gay-bashing, and then donned an army uniform.

He was immediately followed by a speech on the rather startling topic, "F—— Community: or Why I Support Gay-Bashing." As it turned out, the speaker, Ian Bernard of San Diego State University, is a radical gay enraged by nonradical gays who want to join mainstream America.

In the speech, "self-centered white gays and smug white lesbians" took quite a pummeling for endorsing "liberal pluralism, free speech, the American dream and other such BS." Gays who want to marry or join the army "are just the latest version of straights," Bernard said.

The most poignant person at the conference was Sharon O'Dair, a thirtyish Shakespeare specialist at the University of Alabama, who seemed torn between her working-class background and her status as a professor. O'Dair said she is embarrassed by her "intellectual privilege" and deliberately uses the word "ain't" because she has vowed not to abandon her class.

On the one hand, she wants blue-collar culture to share her love of Shakespeare. On the other hand, the race-gender-class ideology now dominant on campus says that "books institutionalize subordination" (her phrase), setting some people above others, thus helping to maintain systems of class and privilege.

So as a bookish professor, she feels stuck in the enemy camp, alienated from her working-class roots and also alienated from middle-class academics who tend to look down on the working class. And perhaps she is also alienated from real intellectual work by her fashionable campus ideology about books as instruments of social control. She is "pissed off" but doesn't seem to know what to do.

An awkward moment occurred when a white male professor made a presentation about rage in movies by black directors. This was a contretemps. Blacks in the audience politely pointed out that whites must not assume the role of expert on black experience. Whites in the audience were quick to praise the black objectors. One said: "When I heard you, I didn't hear a person ranting and raving. I heard a person of warmth, a mellow person."

Much of the conference, however, averted mellowness. There was general agreement that America is inherently oppressive and that the only correct response is to organize around group victimization and rage. Anger is the attention-getter and the fuel that makes the system go. Given the state of campus politics, this was a logical meeting to have—a celebration of group rage.

FEAR AND LOATHING AT HARVARD LAW

Another bitter battle is raging at Harvard Law School, this one touched off by a cruel parody of a murdered feminist professor. Harvard Law is the Beirut of modern legal education, featuring endless strife between traditionalists (a mix of conservatives and liberals) and radicals (gender feminists and critical studies people, who believe that American law is not fair and neutral at all, but an instrument to protect wealthy white males).

Mary Joe Frug, professor at the New England School of Law and wife of Harvard law professor Gerald Frug, was stabbed to death on a Cambridge street by someone wielding a seven-inch knife. Out of sympathy, the *Harvard Law Review* published her last, unfinished piece of writing, "A Postmodern Feminist Legal Manifesto."

This was a controversial decision, and not just because of the article's heavy ideological baggage (Frug argued that "legal rules permit and sometimes *mandate* the terrorization of the female body"). By law review standards, the style and tone of the article were eccentric. Frug chattily discussed Madonna. She used four-letter words for sex and for one particular female body part. Her opening line was, "I am worried about the title of this article," and in one excruciating sentence, she said the initials PM (in postmodern) reminded her of "premenstrual" and "post-menopausal." In short, it was an unusually ripe target for parody—or would have been if the author hadn't just been stabbed to death.

The editors of the annual parody issue of the law review, *The Harvard Law Revue,* ran through that stop sign and published a ghastly and amazingly unfunny takeoff of Frug's piece, identifying her as "Rigor-Mortis Professor of Law" dictating from beyond the grave. After protests, the two writers came forward and apologized. But given the continuing war at Harvard Law, what might have been a one-day story about cruelty, or at least tackiness, blew up into a bitter month-long attack on the writers, the *Review* and the Law School as purveyors of "institutionalized" hatred toward women.

Fifteen of the sixty-four professors at Harvard Law signed a statement calling the parody a symptom of entrenched misogyny at the school.

Then twenty-one other professors signed a letter denouncing that state-ment as inflammatory. Professor Laurence Tribe weighed in with hor-rendous rhetoric—calling the article "hate speech," and part of "a slow-burning holocaust against women." He served up some weasely rhetoric reinforcing the feminist argument that the parody and the stabbing of Frug were somehow connected. "What is the point of teach-ing?" he asked, referring to the parody writers. "I'm sharpening their knives to stab innocent victims." To top it off, he compared the writers to Klansmen and Holocaust revisionists.

Flooding the campus, this hate-stab-holocaust theme virtually begged to be completed by yet another noun: punishment. Sure enough, David Kennedy, a professor from the critical studies group, put out an angry memo pressing the administration to consider bringing charges and sanctions against everyone involved in the parody issue. Watch the sleight of hand here: Kennedy's memo converted satirical speech into sexual harassment, then labored to convert this alleged harassment into assault. (He wrote that the writing and publishing of the article "lie at the point where sexual harassment verges into assault.") Obvious question: how can anyone whose mind works this way be teaching at Harvard Law?

Charles Fried, former solicitor general and another member of the Harvard law faculty, said Kennedy's note was an example of "post-modern criminal procedure—you complain to an administrative body that something so terrible has happened that it must have violated something, though you don't know what it is." Fried says we have arrived at the heart of politically correct doctrine: that the claim of unequal treatment somehow trumps the First Amendment, and "the claim of insensitivity trumps everything." The most flamboyant of Har-vard law professors, Alan Dershowitz, was more blunt: "Kennedy dialed 911 and called the speech cops."

One sobering lesson here is that respect for free speech is under heavy attack, even at elite law schools. What respect remains on campuses these days is highly selective. As Dershowitz points out, a Black Muslim speaker at Harvard accused "Jew doctors" of injecting the AIDS virus into black babies and raised no ruckus at all, but a sophomoric spoof of a dead woman's highly spoofable article tears the campus apart.

There's another form of double standard. Feminist lawyers routinely attack white male privilege, sometimes arguing, as Frug foolishly did, that males intentionally set up laws to demean and terrorize women.

But if opponents return fire in the same tone (or in parody), they can now expect to be accused of creating a climate of misogyny and hatred.

Most of the partisans on the radical-PC side of this debate used "climate" or "environment" or "atmosphere" arguments to avoid a direct assault on free speech, and to depict the small-bore incident as part of an ominous conspiracy, a vast assault on women.

This, I'm afraid, is the way the game will be played on campuses from now on. Unwelcome speech will not be answered with criticism. It will be attacked as dangerous and punishable because of poor climates ("a Stalinist idea," in Dershowitz's words). This is the real lesson of the continual warfare at Harvard Law.

THE PLIGHT OF THE LAST MINORITY

Dear Mr. Leo,

I certainly commend you for your sensitivity in reporting on minority groups. This is particularly important because, as you know, everybody in America is now in one.

Since our group is way behind in developing minority pride, please try to mention us. We are the straight white American males (SWAM). Some people have started to call us the Hetero-Euros, the Anglo-straights or the male Vanillas. Others call us the Leftovers, because once everybody scurried into an official minority group, whoever was stuck behind had to be one of us (either that or drop out of politics entirely).

The good news is that we are starting to find our way. The other day the *Los Angeles Times* gave us credit for achievement in fashion. It said that one prominent rap artist sometimes wears "Eurocentric suits" (created by the famous male Eurocentrist Giorgio Armani).

A sculptor in San Francisco named De Guzman graciously gave our group sole credit for modernist sculpture. What he said is that straight, white males are responsible for repressing and squeezing all funkiness and complexity out of modern sculpture. I'm sure he meant this in the positive sense.

Also, we just got an important plug from Karen Finley, the performance artist who was turned down for an NEA grant, even though she takes off her blouse onstage and artistically covers herself with chocolate and alfalfa sprouts. Personally, I think she should have gotten the money—I like chocolate. Anyhow, Karen said that the denial of her grant was the last gasp of straight white male power in America.

While it's nice to get this sort of recognition, some of us think it is starting to take on negative undertones. Columnist Ellen Goodman made a little joke recently about the rats in laboratory experiments, saying that some people think the term "white male rats" is redundant. We are responding to this in the usual measured way pioneered by established protest groups. Joined by animal rights activists, we have picketed her office, sued her newspaper, defaced her collection of Ms. magazines and threatened to play Barry Manilow records loudly outside her home.

Julian Bond wrote that white males seem to be losing their confidence and may need special help in defending themselves against affirmative action programs. This may have been humor. Researchers are still scouring the text for signs of any possible jocular intention. Pending their decision, I would say that he is right: SWAMees are increasingly suffering from low self-esteem. We are the national punching bag. We have lost too many role models to indictment (Pete Rose, Mike Milken), to general simpering and questionable onscreen cross-dressing (Phil Donahue) or to burial under Giants' Stadium in the Meadowlands (Jimmy Hoffa).

Every emerging culture needs heroes, and the shocking thing is that we have been losing ours, left and right. Plato and Rock Hudson turned out to be gay. Billy Lee Tipton, the old-time jazz musician, turned out to be a female. Some black scholars say that the ancient Egyptians were black, and that ancient Greeks ripped off African culture and pretended it was their own. Next thing you know, modern science will turn out to be the product of a lesbian colony on Guam.

On the campus, this is the worst possible time to be a straight, white male. Many SWAMs simply lie about their color and sexual orientation, just to avoid being provocative. Ashamed of their background, many often make loud and derisive anti-SWAM remarks about typical SWAM pursuits such as croquet, Beach Boys music and white-collar crime. A few have developed such self-loathing that they voluntarily attend SWAM-bashing colleges like Stanford, where they feign delight in the study of Burmese feminism and Biafran political theory. Worst of all, they boo along with the rest of the students if the name of a remaining DWM (that's a Dead White Male in Stanfordese) accidentally comes up in class.

At Harvard, the East Coast capital of SWAM-bashing, Robert Coles apparently thought he had covered himself by including a number of gay, female and black writers in his literature course. But, alas, he has been catching flak from students for not teaching *enough* authors from these groups. SWAM-bashing usually peaks at Harvard in the spring. This year the get-the-SWAM activities were particularly brisk and the president of the university stepped down, possibly because he was a SWAM himself.

As you might imagine, our SWAM Anti-Defamation League (SWAM-ADL) is swamped. Volunteers are working twenty-hour days with only brief dinner breaks for American cheese sandwiches on Wonder Bread. We are trying to cope with all the accusations that SWAMs are solely responsible for such familiar horrors as war, pestilence, hatred, alienation, the greenhouse effect and Neil Bush.

Each day brings a new slur. Did you know that meat eating is our fault too? Yes, indeed. A recent book, *The Sexual Politics of Meat: A Feminist-Vegetarian Theory*, by Carol Adams, says that carnivorousness is one expression of sexist, patriarchal, homophobic Euro society. Nothing in there about the rise of the third world, but otherwise she hit all the usual points. Look for her on the Stanford curriculum.

Thanks for listening. Perhaps we will meet at the SWAM Pride Day parade.

Yours truly,
Anonymous

DEMONIZING WHITE GUYS

Attention, men of the Caucasoid persuasion. Have you made a terrible mistake by being born white males? Consider these recent items from the press:

The *New York Observer*, a weekly newspaper in Manhattan, fired columnist Sidney Zion because a female higher-up decreed that the paper "should begin getting rid of these middle-aged white men" (sexism, ageism, racism). The group Women Men and Media honored a black female columnist for her assaults on "the male and pale" media powers (casual racism, melanistic feminism). The catalogue at the Whitney biennial art show suggests that whiteness is a "notion" or "fallacy" (logically stupefying artistic racism). And *Newsweek* published a strange and jeering cover story on white males (sexism, racism, institutional sophomoricism).

What is going on here? Simple. Like guerrillas moving down from the hills to attack the cities, the race-and-gender people are no longer just sniping from marginal positions on campus and in the art world. With the aid of an ever-credulous press corps, they are now pumping their doctrine into the general culture. That doctrine is that America will increasingly be divided by a truculent tribalism, with nonwhites and white women ganging up in a grand alliance to wrest power from white males.

There are several things to say about this.

It's really indefensible. It's wrong to attack or fire people because of race and gender, even if they happen to be white guys. And no one who is serious about social justice in America thinks it's a good idea to divide up teams by skin color or gender and set them against one another.

It's dangerous. At a time of high racial tensions and high immigration, it is distinctly unwise to keep telling native-born whites that nonwhites and immigrants are a unified bloc that's about to take over. In the nineteenth century, crazies of the right strummed this theme and touched off the atrocities of the anti-immigrant Nativist movement. Why does it make sense for the crazies of the left to strum it now? At the very least, this strategy risks the rise of an angry popular movement to shut down immigration and programs that primarily benefit minorities. Does anybody remember the David Duke scare?

The idea that the white women of America will join an alliance to bring down white men is so hilarious that it could only have been thought up on a university campus. In the academic world, women are viewed as a separate power group abused by a relentlessly rape-minded and harassing masculinist oppressor. In the real world, women marry men. Let's assume that most women want equality, good jobs and families, not front-line action in a war to topple their husbands, brothers and sons.

The race-and-gender people are basically using a Marxist analysis of society, with the role of capitalist oppressor now played by the white male. This is a weird distortion that forces believers to argue that all white males are privileged, even those who clearly aren't. I would hate to be the race-and-gender special agent dispatched to Appalachia to explain how socially powerful white males are, or to explain to Bill Cosby or Colin Powell how oppressed he is. With a grim Marxist analysis that has mutated into an attack on white males, the race-and-gender people are constantly confusing capitalism, corporate culture and white maleness.

There is no grand alliance of nonwhites against white men. Amitai Etzioni, sociologist and author of *The Spirit of Community*, calls this alliance "a construct" created by the academic world and the media. Like whites, nonwhites are divided into many ethnic groups going every which way, with lots of tensions. Some groups are moving rapidly into the mainstream, making them ineligible for alliances based on victim status. Some aren't.

The idea that white guys, or white people, are on their way out in a multicultural America is part of a disinformation campaign. The implied argument is this: since we will soon outnumber you, you had better give us what we want now, or we won't take care of you when you are a minority. But is it true that America is on the verge of becoming a country with a "minority majority"? This seems to be another construct of press and academe. It is partly based on dubious straight-line projections of immigrant fertility similar to those that so frightened the native stock a century ago. More important, it is based on the supposition that Hispanic immigrants will stand apart from the mainstream as a permanent minority. There are strong signs that this won't happen. Hispanics already show high rates of intermarriage. Of American-born males of Puerto Rican ancestry, an astonishing 40 percent are married to Anglos. With Hispanic assimilation and intermarriage with other whites, the year 2050 will probably see a nonwhite minority population of about 25 to 30 percent, sizeable and significant, but nowhere near a "minority majority."

Why is this important? Only because some demographic projections, like the current wave of attacks on white males, are expressions of a hard-edged race-and-gender ideology now seeping into the general media. There's an ugly tone of "we will outbreed you" to some of the projections. And we are getting into the ugly phase of attacks on white guys. The race-and-gender folk will bear watching.

AFROCENTRISM ON THE MARCH

Under the banner of "multiculturalism," the rush is on to install an Africanized or "Afrocentric" curriculum in inner-city public schools. Though many plans are circulating, the most prominent is the one developed for the Portland, Oregon, schools in 1982. This outline, known as the *African-American Baseline Essays,* was used as a basic resource document by the city of Atlanta, and it is the model for Afrocentric programs being developed in Indianapolis, Prince Georges County, Maryland, and Washington, D.C.

Here are some highlights of the *Baseline Essays:*

■ Africa was "the world center of culture and learning in antiquity." Ancient Greece largely derived its culture from blacks.

■ Ramses and King Tut were black. Cleopatra was partly black, partly Greek.

■ Africa has a rich history of mathematical, scientific and literary accomplishment, mostly suppressed or stolen by whites. Study at great African universities was "fairly common" among ancestors of slaves brought to America.

■ The greatness of African science can be realized by deduction ("since Africa is widely believed to be the birthplace of the human race, it follows that Africa was the birthplace of mathematics and science") or by historical observation (the blow-gun, which made possible the pistol and the machine gun, and the African study of electric eels, which may have led to the invention of the battery). If the African scientific tradition seems to be in eclipse, this is because of colonialism, the "uncritical adoption of western scientific methodologies" and the current "continent-wide lack of interest in science."

■ The oral-aural tradition of Africa is lively and liberating, whereas the West's (and presumably the East's) dependence on the written word can be debilitating: in print, "interconnected pulsations of expressive culture are imprisoned or exiled to a perpetual underground."

At the heart of the *Baseline Essays* is an unlikely claim that consumes more than 35 percent of the curriculum's text: ancient Egypt was a black nation. To gloss over black success, Europeans "invented the theory of 'white' Egyptians who were merely browned by the sun." Experts do not seem to support this view. I phoned seven Egyptologists at random around the country, and all seven said it is completely untrue, then asked that their names not be used. "It's politically too hot to say this [in public]," said one. (She added that there is a small germ of truth to the theory: a number of blacks from the south moved freely and easily in ancient Egypt, which was not a race-conscious society.)

The argument that Egyptians were black would seem to position blacks as slaveowners of the ancient Hebrews. This is finessed in the *Essays* by describing the Hebrews as wanderers who entered Egypt to escape famine and stayed on as guest workers.

If anything, the *Baseline Essays* are restrained by the current standards of Afrocentric theory, because militance has ratcheted up several notches since 1982.

Asa G. Hilliard III, an educational psychologist from Georgia State who developed the *Baseline Essays*, now says that the Greek gods, the Ten Commandments and the Olmec civilization in Mexico are all derived from black culture. In Hilliard's view, Moses was an Egyptian priest, and early images indicate to him that Jesus and Buddha were black.

This sort of improbable assertion is common among Afrocentrists. Leonard Jeffries, Jr., chairman of the Black Studies Department at the City University of New York, thinks the Statue of Liberty was supposed to be black. Jeffries, perhaps the major figure in the Afrocentric movement in New York state, is frankly racist: he dismisses whites as "the ice people," whose endless savagery is due to a lack of melanin, the all-important skin chemical that turns blacks into benign "sun people" and gives them intellectual advantages over whites as well. He serves on the state multicultural curriculum development committee along with African Studies professor Ali A. Mazrui of the State University of New York at Binghampton, who writes that "the decline of Western civilization might well be at hand. It is in the interest of humanity that such a decline should take place." Perhaps the most prominent of all the Afrocentrists is Molefi Asante of Temple University, who once severely criticized some black collegians for rejecting Afrocentrism and founding an interracial group instead. ("Such madness is the direct consequence of self-hatred," Asante complained.)

The first thing to be said about all this is that it splits the black community into those who are willing to go along with the systematic propagation of fantastic history and bizarre theories and those who are not. Afrocentric conventions don't seem to attract black scholars of the first rank. But it may reach the point where they will come under increasing pressure to fall in line. Our urban schools are now in danger of adopting a sort of Tawana Brawley theory of history in which facts do not matter, only resentments and group solidarity.

The *Baseline Essays* call for "understanding, respect and appreciation for the history, culture and contributions of other groups," yet the attacks on Europeans and western civilization begin on page one (in an introduction to African art) and continue throughout the text. This tone of smoldering resentment may increase racial group solidarity and vent frustration, but it is hard to see how a curriculum based on it will help black youngsters prepare for jobs or fit into the wider society.

The Afrocentric curriculum is usually presented as an attempt to develop pride in black children by giving them a racial history. Valencia Mohammed, an outspoken proponent of an Afrocentric curriculum in Washington, D.C., says, "Our holocaust continues until we get back what was taken from us, including the history of our contributions." But what kind of pride and self-esteem are likely to grow from the use of packaged untruths? And how much more cynical will black children be when they discover they have been conned once again, this time by Afrocentrists?

The new Afrocentric history is not a collection of random claims to have invented this and that. It is built around a coherent and powerful central myth of stolen black glory and the unjust ascendance of implacably hostile whites. Hilliard makes clear that in the "colonial" western approach to history and academic work, honest science is never permitted. Perhaps many of the critics now studying the issue will veer away from this story line. Let us hope so. It is a surefire formula for separatism and endless racial animosity.

The answer to Ms. Mohammed is that yes, the story of blacks and black achievements has clearly been slighted and must be told in our schools, as part of national and world history. There is no serious opposition to this. The trouble is that California and New York, two large states that have moved decisively to incorporate African and Afro-American history into the curriculum, have come under heavy fire anyway. The real issue is control: will the history taught in our schools be the work of the best and most honest scholarship, or will it be politicized and controlled for uplift and propaganda effect by various ethnic groups, as in the *Baseline Essays?*

In upstate New York, a Native American lobby demonstrated how a curriculum can be altered by adroit special pleading. After a visit by an Iroquois delegation to the State Education Department, the school curriculum was amended to say that the political system of the Iroquois Confederacy influenced the writing of the U.S. Constitution. The idea that the Founding Fathers borrowed from the Iroquois is a century-old myth. No good evidence exists to support it. But it is now official teaching in New York state. To the surprise of very few, this decision shows that some school authorities, eager to avoid minority-group pressure and rage, are now willing to treat the curriculum as a prize in an ethnic spoils system.

This climate helps account for the spread of Afrocentric theories, or at least the lack of a critical public reaction to those theories. No one knows how far this will go. An assistant superintendent of schools in Washington, D.C., was quoted as saying it would take ten years to thoroughly Africanize district schools. What does this mean? (He declined to return phone calls.) *The Washington Post* reports that "school officials want the change incorporated into every grade and every school, from social studies and physical education to math and science." No word yet on what Africanized science would look like, but Africanized math might mean proficiency in the Yoruba numerical system discussed in the *Baseline Essays.* Pride in historical accomplishments is important, but does anyone seriously think that Yoruba math will help these kids rise in the world?

Any explicit teaching along race lines in public schools is very troubling and it is creeping up on us with almost no protest. There is also the problem of setting precedents. What would America look like if each ethnic group won its own curriculum? Backers of multiculturalism usually divide the world, rather arbitrarily, into five ethnic groups: blacks, whites, Hispanics, Asians and Native Americans. But those clumsy groupings are sure to splinter. Leonard Jeffries is already talking about a proposal for a separate Haitian-Creole curriculum. Install one and demands for Cambodiocentric or Italocentric curricula would likely follow. New York City and Los Angeles have public school students who speak in more than a hundred different native tongues. Does this mean we must keep multiplying curricula, or should we try to unify our children with an honest and fair curriculum that celebrates what we have in common as Americans?

Our best analyst of this new and revised ethnic separatism is Diane Ravitch, professor of history at Teachers College, Columbia University. She draws a distinction between "particularists" and "pluralists." Particularists are closed to the idea of a common culture and want sharp lines drawn between ethnic groups. Pluralists are open to the constant transformation of America by peoples drawn from every corner of the earth. Particularists are prone to attacking the mainstream, but the pluralists say, in effect, "American culture belongs to all of us. The United States is us, and we remake it in every generation."

TEMPEST IN THE NEWSROOM

The University of Massachusetts at Amherst has a long history of racial tension and sixties-style takeovers of offices, and the only known student race riot triggered by a World Series, pitting mostly black Mets fans against mostly white Red Sox fans in 1986. Now it has achieved outstanding weirdness in the latest skirmish of a twenty-year battle over its student newspaper, the *Collegian.*

On the day after the Rodney King verdict, the paper declined to publish an editorial condemning the decision. A fiery editorial was on hand, but some editors balked at running it, partly because it seemed sympathetic to the looters. No one seems to have thought of quickly writing a compromise editorial. This made the paper a target for anger over the verdict.

Citing long-term insensitivity to "oppressed communities" a group of one hundred to two hundred protesters overran the *Collegian* offices, breaking a window. Editors say equipment was damaged and the offices trashed. Protesters say this isn't so. The paper's degree of insensitivity is also in dispute. Over the years, each group that considers itself oppressed has been granted its own page or beat in the *Collegian*—blacks, Third World students, women, multicultural students (Native American, Latin American, Asian-American), and lesbians/bisexuals/gays. In response to complaints about a heavy stream of pro-Palestinian rhetoric from the Third World page, a Jewish affairs beat was added. This spring protesters demanded an editor for women of color, and a minority coeditor to share power with a white editor. (The staff of the *Collegian*, like the student body, is 90 percent white. Seven of the last nine editors in chief have been female, but only one nonwhite has held the post.)

David DuBois, a black professor in the Journalism Department, says the main issue at the paper is racism. If so, it is hard to document. The professor gave no examples. Asked to cite or fax examples of racism, protesters mostly mentioned three incidents. One was an anti-immigration opinion article. Another was the charge that the paper had referred to Arabs as "sickening." (Actually, the paper had complained editorially about the U.N.'s "sickeningly pro-Palestinian" stance.) The last was the case of an editor from India who narrowly won re-election over a write-in candidate, Bozo the Clown.

Saying that they feared for the safety of the staff, the editors took the paper underground, putting it out from the apartments of staff members. In response, protesters stole most of the nineteen thousand copies of the paper's May 4 edition from various distribution points. The administration put out a statement saying that it "has no wish to take sides." Instead it framed the dispute as a human relations problem and supplied a mediator, who conducted negotiations in public. Howard Ziff, a white professor of journalism, called these tumultuous proceedings "a cultural revolutionary Red Guard trial," with editors feeling menaced by a hundred or more protesters.

The mediator, Grant Ingle, was quoted as saying: "The practices of the *Collegian*, if they were employers, would be illegal." But when asked to identify these practices, he spoke in general terms about "a hostile environment" and "a poor climate racially." But some of that charged climate is surely due to differences between traditional journalists who want to report news and advocates carving out special pages to push the views of their groups.

After two days of negotiations, with talks suspended for the night, one protester proclaimed, "The people will not allow this," and led a second raid upon the *Collegian* offices. A lot of screaming and scuffling followed. Marc Elliott, the outgoing editor in chief, said someone tried to hit him with a chair. Trying to protect his film, one photographer fled into a darkroom, locked the door and escaped through a vent.

The second storming of the news offices broke the spirit of resistance at the *Collegian*. Elliott and the incoming editor in chief, Dan Wetzel, capitulated to all demands. Wetzel said the chancellor of the university, Richard O'Brien, had pushed them to do so, saying that if they didn't, the campus would have a race riot on its hands. O'Brien says Wetzel "is lying through his teeth."

Regardless of who is telling the truth—the whole dispute is a factual hall of mirrors—it seems clear that the administration acted badly.

By not reacting to the theft of the newspapers, the administration let a serious act of censorship go by without comment. This has become a disturbing pattern, with students' papers being stolen at Dartmouth, Stanford and Georgetown Law, with almost no criticism from authorities who are supposed to stand for freedom of expression and freedom of the press. And by remaining neutral after two invasions of the *Collegian* offices, the administration allowed mob rule to prevail. The plain fact is that the protesters got what they wanted wholly because of the *Collegian* staff's fear of physical assault.

"Occupation is a mode of organizational change" on campus, said Grant Ingle, who didn't sound as if he disapproved. In effect, the university invites students to use intimidation by rewarding these tactics. Chancellor O'Brien says invasions of offices "are part of everyday life around here." But if the administration developed a backbone and took charge, maybe they wouldn't be.

THE MENACE OF QUOTA-THINK

A curious story from a friend who follows New York City politics closely: Three municipal employees, all white males, recently decided not to attend an important committee meeting because their attendance would skew the racial balance in the room. This is the quota mentality, the dominant mind-set these days on racial and sexual matters. Better to skip work than to present an ethnically flawed group profile.

A group of militant female artists, seized by this mentality, is accusing the Metropolitan Museum of Art of being sexist because 95 percent of the paintings in the museum are by males, whereas 85 percent of the nude statues are female. Alas, there is no male-female balance in the history of art, but museums nowadays should presumably fashion one for past eras anyway, a sort of retroactive affirmative action. The best way out would obviously be for the Met to discover several hundred ancient male nude statues, all superbly wrought by hitherto unknown female artists.

By law, all textbooks used in California public schools must apply this sort of retro-quota in history, art and science: contributions of males and females must be presented in equal numbers. For reasons beyond the control of California, perhaps 95 percent of achieving artists and scientists have been male. Most of us regret this exclusion of females. California just erases it and tells its children a high-minded historical whopper.

Another example of the quota mentality in action was the flap over the number of black soldiers in the Persian Gulf War. Blacks account for 12 percent of the American population and over 24 percent of American troops. If you are a quota hard-liner, all you must do to demonstrate unfairness is point out that twenty-four is a distinctly higher number than twelve. By why is it unfair? This is a volunteer army, and the training and benefits the army offers (along with the risk of getting shot) will obviously appeal more strongly to those on the way up economically and those striving to escape mean streets at home. Some of those arguing now that blacks are being exploited in the Gulf action are precisely the people who argued for years that the armed forces should open up more to minorities and become instruments for social equality. Now that this has been done, the objectors have flip-flopped. And if the army announced tomorrow that it would accept a 12 percent quota of blacks, and no more, wouldn't the objectors flip once again and complain about racial exclusion?

Quota-thinking has become reflexive, even outside the normal pa-rameters of the affirmative-action debate. Operation PUSH's campaign against Nike boils down to the argument that since blacks buy so many sneakers they should proportionately share, as a group, in Nike profits. The same argument has surfaced in Hollywood: since blacks buy one-third of theater tickets, they deserve one-third of important industry jobs and control of one-third of all movies. (How would this quota principle apply to the basketball industry, which has predominately white ticket buyers and predominately black jobholders?)

Quota-thinking seems to be invading the criminal-justice system as well. The statistical argument that a disproportionate number of blacks suffer the death penalty is a valid one. Many courts have been guilty of a double standard. But the argument has an unstated corollary: that if arrest and conviction rates for blacks are unusually high, that too must be the result of prejudice. This has slipped into casual conversation among some analysts as "the criminalizing" of young black males, as if the higher crime rate is something society imposes and not an obvious result of something criminals do. The same hidden quota can be unearthed behind many of the plans to prosecute parents for the behavior of their children. They are controversial and perhaps unwise plans, but are usually opposed by the American Civil Liberties Union on the ground that poor people are likely to be disproportionately prosecuted. That apparently means that for every poor mother of a violent gang member you arrest you must in fairness pick up a rich gang mother.

In politics, candidates more frankly promise job quotas by sex and race. Dianne Feinstein, in her campaign for governor of California, promised to hire women and minorities in direct proportion to their population in the state. That is approximately what her successful opponent, Pete Wilson, promised when he was mayor of San Diego, and what former mayor David Dinkins promised in New York. This sounds benign—in a perfect world each job category should have diverse workers—but in effect it sets up a system of group entitlement at the expense of merit. A fraction of Indian blood has become very valuable under quota plans. That may be one of the reasons the number of Americans listing themselves as Native Americans has tripled since 1960. Quotas also mean firing people if their group numbers get too high. By strict quota-thinking, that should happen to blacks now in Compton, California, which is turning from a mostly black to a black and Latino city. Latinos hold fewer than 10 percent of the city jobs and account for 30 percent of the population. Must black job-holders clear out, simply because the town's ethnic mix is changing, or is that something that voting and the give and take of politics can take care of better than quotas?

Enough. Quota-thinking is a social menace. Let's be done with it before it poisons our politics.

RACIAL ARITHMETIC IN CALIFORNIA

A good many Washington commentators are convinced that the quota issue is "Willie Horton II," that is, a basically irrelevant nonstarter, useful for distracting and inflaming impressionable voters. This seems to be yet another curious case of that familiar regional eye ailment known as inside-the-Beltway myopia. In America, the large country just outside the Beltway, quotas are a live issue indeed. Even if the Republicans should somehow manage to exorcise the spirit of Lee At-water and shed all cynicism and manipulation by noon tomorrow, quotas would still be a major issue in the 1992 elections.

On my desk is a minor example of the growing quota mentality, a report to the Forest Service from its Task Force on Work Force Di-versity. Twenty years ago a report like this would simply have said, in effect, it isn't right for the service to be almost all white and male— let's open it up. But this report, infected by current notions of multi-culturalism (there are many cultures or tribes that have to be appeased as groups) says that by 1995, the service "must have percentages in recognized groups equal to the percentages in the Civilian Labor Force in 1990." Quota time. Though momentarily stumped on what would be a proper quota for the disabled, the report says, "We think the appropriate number will be about 5.9 percent." Yeah, that's about right.

The Forest Service says that this report, a wellspring of odd but doctrinally correct multiculturalism, has been accepted "in spirit." This probably means that the leadership, being basically sane, will try to bury it if they can and just try to hire people from both sexes and all races. But here is the problem: to buy some peace, administrators often tell the multiculture believers to go off and make a report. When the report arrives, all thunder and lightning, it sometimes takes on a scary life of its own, raising so much fuss that administrators are tempted to buy peace once again by adopting it, even if it involves quotas, or as in the case of schools, ceding control of the curriculum to various pressure groups. In the worst-case scenario, it enters and then polarizes partisan politics, with the Democrats trapped by angry constituents into defending assorted zaniness and quotas, thus putting the whole future of the party at risk.

This is roughly the dynamic at work in California, where the most serious quota drama is currently being played out. In brief (and, as Dave Barry says, I am not making this up), the Democratic majority in the state legislature is attempting to establish, by law, that California state universities and colleges will grant degrees to ethnic and racial groups in direct proportion to their share of the state's high school graduates. This astonishing plan, pushed by Speaker Willie Brown and ex-Fonda husband Tom Hayden, is an explicit rejection of what used to be called civil rights and affirmative action (openness, giving everyone an equal chance, removing obstacles to individual freedom and advancement). We are way beyond that. Now we are in the arena of group entitlements, bringing the colleges under political control and dividing up university degrees and jobs as part of a spoils system run from Sacramento. Since the Democrats vote as a bloc on this, only the luck of a last-minute veto by a retiring Republican governor saved California from this quota plan last year, just as the likelihood of another veto by the current Republican governor, Pete Wilson, will save it this year or next.

To its great credit, California has been deeply concerned with the low rate of college graduation among some minorities for two decades. The disheartening news is that gradution rates for Hispanics and blacks are still very low. With frustration rising, the ideal of getting as many blacks and Hispanics as possible ready for college changed to the ideal of proportional representation in freshman admissions, then to the ideal of graduating roughly equal numbers of each group and finally to Willie Brown's favorite kind of ideal, one with legislative teeth.

The quota provision is in Willie Brown's bill, Number 2150, which has been temporarily shelved because of the budget crisis. Perhaps wisely, it is shrouded in a fog of euphemisms. Proportional representation in admissions and graduation is "educational equity," described as a central priority that California universities "shall strive to approximate, by 2000." If that sounds like the soothing language of goals, not quotas, don't be lulled: the "shall strive" is backed by tough provisions of reports, impact statements and the reminder that "governing boards shall hold faculty and administrators accountable" for all this legislated equity (that is, their jobs are on the line). Since the bill neglects to provide funding for remedial help that unprepared minority students really need, I assume that if the bill passes, the universities would quickly capitulate and grant as many worthless political degrees as the legislature wants.

Even now, voices are being raised around the system that every student has a "right" to graduate, and that a "privileged elite" (administrators and faculty) is arbitarily witholding a desirable good (automatic diplomas) from "underrepresented minorities." This is the language of pork-barrel politics, not education, and that is what the Brown bill is all about.

MULTICULTURAL FOLLIES

New York state's new and improved report on multicultural social-science education landed with a splash on page one of *The New York Times*, although it was hard to figure out from the news article what the document actually said. Having obtained a copy of the report and read it several times, searching alertly for any stray nuggets of meaning, I can certainly understand the *Times*'s problem. The authors of this paper are not strong in what we like to call communication skills. Things are hinted at, groped toward, retreated from, reraised, buried in meaning-defiant abstractions.

Here, for instance, is an explanation for teaching "multiple perspectives": "This is not to argue that all information is necessarily valid. Rather, we argue that all information deserves to be understood in the context within which it has been developed. This assertion is advanced, in part, because, for much of our knowledge, validity is difficult to establish independent of context." Got that? OK, let's move on.

This grisly prose naturally makes one nostalgic for the unimproved 1989 New York state multicultural report (*A Curriculum of Inclusion*). Here was a report a columnist could sink his teeth into, a flat-out, screaming attack on western culture written in plain English, the way multicultural diatribes are supposed to be. This was the work of State Education Commissioner Thomas Sobol's first totally stacked panel on the subject (only one white person could be squeezed onto the seventeen-person committee in a state that is 75 percent white). His second panel, cleared and pruned by the Board of Regents, was put together more cagily: more white faces, cooler heads, wonderfully elliptical non-writers. Each panel had its flamboyant black Europhobe. The first featured an appendix by Professor Leonard Jeffries, Jr. (white are the "ice people," savage and violent because of a lack of skin melanin); the second had Professor Ali Mazrui, whose qualifications to help shape our social studies include being a citizen of a foreign country (Kenya) who wishes the West would fall into the sea. ("The decline of western civilization might well be at hand. It is in the interest of humanity that such a decline should take place.")

Back to the drab second report. I take it that "multiple perspectives" is one of the big ideas here, because the term pops up mystically about sixty times. In a rare lurch toward clarity, an example is given: Indians and pioneers look differently upon the white settlement of the West. I would expect so, but there is no sense here that history is a discipline oriented toward truth, not a parceling out of racial perspectives. (The fact that most of the Southwest was more or less stolen from Mexico is not a "Latino perspective." It's the truth.) Worse yet, I notice that at one point "multiple perspectives" gives way to the phrase "multiple truths." In context, and again nothing is said plainly, this would seem to say that schools should teach each racial and ethnic group its own private tribal truths.

If rendered into actual English, here's what I think this report would assert (and remember, many of these notions are accompanied by their opposites, thus giving the report built-in deniability):

■ All history and all truths are tribal, and the history now taught in schools is mainly a self-serving story concocted by dominant whites.

■ There is no common culture in America.

■ Race and ethnicity are the primary and permanent realities for most Americans, and provide the basic structure of society. (The image of America that shines through here is not that of a nation but of a mini–United Nations made up of sovereign racial groups.)

■ Being an American or a "resident of America" doesn't count for much with many people. (In notes to a subcommittee, one prominent panel member wrote: "A student's reference group may not be that of the nation in which he or she lives.")

- Schools should be centers for political activism.

- Schools must not overstress textbooks and reading. (Multicultural education will require pictures, posters, videos, magazines, inexpensive artifacts and woven materials. Possible interpretation: let's stress show-and-tell as a hedge against the possibility that our kids won't really be able to read and write.)

These points obviously reflect the views of Sobol's prescreened worshipers at the altar of multiculturalism, but are they the views of most blacks, immigrants or New Yorkers in general? Despite all the racism, most surveys I have seen seem to show high levels of patriotism among black Americans. In my opinion, most blacks do not wish to stand apart from America; they want in, and they want the nation to live up to its principles.

The same is true of immigrants. A great migration is underway, from south to north, from east to west, because people want what America and the West have to offer and they are willing to tear up their lives to move and get it. Not one sentence in this dismal, backward document mentions what this "it" is: freedom, democracy, the promise of tolerance and equality. Whom should we believe about America? Sobol's two dim panels or the immigrants who are voting with their feet to get here?

TAKING TRIBALISM OUT OF HISTORY

Here is the best news in years on the multicultural front: after a year or two of amazing tribal tumult, the state of California has picked a series of fair and accurate social studies textbooks acceptable in urban and suburban schools alike. The K-8 series, Houghton Mifflin's *Social Studies*, was approved by school-board votes of seven to none in Los Angeles had five to one in San Francisco and will be used in nine of the state's ten most heavily populated districts—only Oakland, where Afrocentrism and separatism are strong, has voted to reject. Last week, even Berkeley, on the fence for months, voted three to two to accept. All is not yet peaceful. There is still some ethnic grumbling. But

California has clearly turned a corner and points the way out of the multicultural mess for school systems in other states. Significantly, this has happened in a state where white children are a minority in public schools and five of every twenty-eight pupils currently speak little or no English.

This is all the more remarkable because of the widespread despair only a year ago. Gilbert Sewell, who monitors these matters for the American Textbook Council, complained of "cultural gridlock" at the raucous hearings last July on the Houghton Mifflin series and another contender, Holt, Rhinehart's one-volume *Story of America.* The air was filled with anti-Eurocentric sound bites. Moslems, Jews, fundamentalists and atheists all complained of unfairness. Chinese-Americans said the texts trivialized the brutality inflicted on ancestors who built the transcontinental railroad. Gay activists were officially outraged that the alleged sexual practices of Julius Caesar, Michelangelo, Alexander Hamilton and Eleanor Roosevelt were not mentioned. Afrocentric radicals, as usual, wanted Africa credited for the success of ancient Greece and Rome, and jeered and slurred blacks who testified that the books were fair. A group called Communities United Against Racism complained that a covered wagon should not be on the cover of one text because it is a symbol of anti-Indian oppression. The group says that the line "Much of the history of the United States is the story of how America has met the challenges of pluralism" should be changed to "how America has annihilated other cultures."

The first good sign was that feminists and Hispanics were inconspicuous at the hearings. The usual pro-English anti-Spanish bias of American texts had been eliminated by Houghton Mifflin and women are at last given their due in every area and subject covered. Indians, too, are treated in lavish detail and with great respect. Many changes were made to accommodate legitimate objections. But the key to California's success was not parceling out favorable coverage to interest groups. It did not start with the question, "How do we placate every angry splinter group?" It started with the question, "What will our children have to know to live in a a multicultural world and carry on the American experiment?"

New York state, which foolishly started with the first question, packed its first panel with marginal cranks and polarized the state. California started consensus building with solid citizens of all races, historians and a written "framework" for textbook publishers to fill. The framework stressed strict historical accuracy, civic values and emphasis on the experience of people from all of California's ethnic and religious tribes.

It worked. New York's education commissioner, Thomas Sobol, has made a hash of things and accomplished nothing over four years, while his counterpart in California, Bill Honig, has finished the job and done it well, presiding over the writing and the adoption of a wonderful series of books that touches every base. Honig says: "If you cave in the first time you hear somebody shout 'racist!' you'll never get anything done. If you stand up and say, this is right and we're going to do it, you'll get 95 percent of the people behind you." Though black radicals got most of the ink at hearings, Honig says, "We had black scholars get up and say, 'I've been waiting all my life for this book.' "

So far as I can see, the books are scrupulously fair to everyone from Black Elk to Columbus. The two volumes on America weave together the tales of each group, with anecdotes, biographies and social history, into a credible and highly readable story of America in motion. (*America Will Be* is one title, a line from Langston Hughes.) Religions, ethics, the problems of running a democracy are all taught. At one point, readers are asked to think about the dissent of Roger Williams and Anne Hutchinson in the eighteenth century in terms of Martin Luther King's in the twentieth—a nice touch. The text is filled with little nuggets that Gilbert Sewall calls "stoppers," such as the fact that the Indians were able to convert acorns into a stable and usable starch. There is emphasis on trends, ideas, pastimes, dress and the lives of ordinary folk. The sins and successes of America are all there. The problem of "the one and the many" that poisons discussions of multicultural matters has somehow been solved: individuals, tribes, nation, and civic values are all stressed. There are things in the books I disliked and would toss if I could. But the series is a winner, a better and fairer school text about America and the world than anyone has yet produced, and I hope it does well.